THE NEW RIGHT AND THE CONSTITUTION

THE NEW RIGHT
AND THE CONSTITUTION

TURNING BACK THE
LEGAL CLOCK

───

BERNARD SCHWARTZ

NORTHEASTERN UNIVERSITY PRESS

BOSTON

Northeastern University Press

Library of Congress Cataloging in Publication Data
Schwartz, Bernard, 1923–
The new right and the Constitution : turning back the legal
clock / Bernard Schwartz.
p.   cm.
Includes bibliographical references and index.
ISBN 1-55553-082-6 (alk. paper)
1. United States—Constitutional law—Interpretation and
construction.   2. Conservatism—United States.   I. Title.
KF4550.S335   1990
342.73′02—dc20
[347.3022]   90-39468

Designed by Patricia Dunbar

Composed in Bodoni by The Composing Room of Michigan, Inc.,
Grand Rapids, Michigan. Printed and bound by The Maple Press,
York, Pennsylvania. The paper is Warren's Sebago Antique, an acid-free sheet.

MANUFACTURED IN THE UNITED STATES OF AMERICA
95 94 93 92 91 90   5 4 3 2 1

For
BRIAN
Whose encouragement and help
made this book possible

CONTENTS

PREFACE

OVER the past decade, quietly and with little fanfare, various schools of conservative jurisprudence have come to dominate the legal landscape. Former Attorney General Edwin Meese and Judge Robert H. Bork, whose views achieved such notoriety in 1986 and 1987, belong to the least extreme of these schools. Other, far more radical ideologues are little known outside the legal community. But, with the election of President Bush, all this may change. Now that the Bush court appointments are starting to follow the Reagan pattern, the views of New Right jurists may soon become accepted judicial doctrine.

This book contains a detailed discussion and critique of New Right jurisprudence. It points out how its concepts would turn back the constitutional clock by a century. As the book shows in detail, Jim Crow, child labor, the third degree, and a destructive individualism may once again characterize American society.

Extreme though the views discussed in this book are, they have started to be reflected in the decisions of Reagan-appointed judges. Their influence will continue to grow during the Bush years unless their views are shown for what they are—a radical attempt at constitutional revision wholly inconsistent with the needs of the present-day society.

In addition to the usual published materials, I have made use of the oral and documentary sources made available to me for my books on the Warren and Burger Courts. Much of this material was given me on a confidential basis. I have tried to identify all statements and documents except where it has not been possible to do so while preserving confidentiality. The quotes from conference sessions are from the notes taken by at least one justice who was present.

I have been afforded generous access to the papers of the justices and gratefully acknowledge the help given by the Manuscript Division, Library of Congress. I also wish to acknowledge the efforts of Deborah Kops, Ann Twombly, and the staff at Northeastern University Press, my literary agent, Gerard McCauley, the support of Dean John Sexton and the New York University School of Law, the work of my tireless secretary, Mrs. Barbara Ortiz, and the generous help of the Filomen d'Agostino and Max E. Greenberg Research Fund of New York University School of Law.

B.S.

New York
April 1990

THE NEW RIGHT AND THE CONSTITUTION

INTRODUCTION

W E A R E ," a federal judge tells us, "in the midst of a very important phenomenon in jurisprudence: the emergence of a new school of thought. For the first time in a generation, legal scholars are mounting a serious challenge to the jurisprudential approach that has dominated American legal thinking since the New Deal."[1]

The New Right in legal thinking has altered the American jurisprudential landscape as much as the political New Right has changed our political map. But the legal New Right has done more than shift the focus of legal thinking; it has reset the juristic agenda in accordance with its conservative imperatives. Since the constitutional revolution of the mid-1930s—"the switch in time that saved nine"[2]—the dominant themes in jurisprudence had been set by liberal jurists. The liberals' major premise was the need for effective governmental power to curb economic excesses and to redress the inequalities that resulted from them. They firmly believed, with Justice Louis D. Brandeis, that "[r]egulation . . . is necessary to the preservation and best development of liberty."[3] Their chief aim was thus to ensure that American law mirrored American society in its transition from laissez faire to the welfare state.

During the generation that followed, the liberal legal thinkers had things much their own way. Except for complaints that the "meaning of the Constitution does not change with the ebb and flow of economic events,"[4] conservative jurisprudence virtually retired from the field.

All this has changed in recent years. Outstanding contributions to

3

jurisprudence are being made today by conservative jurists. Indeed, it is the legal New Right that has been at the forefront of recent juristic thinking. Now it is those on the left of the legal spectrum who have been contributing little that is original to contemporary jurisprudence. Except for a supposedly new school that is little more than a pale rehash of the legal realism of a generation ago, liberal jurisprudence has become all but moribund.

The purpose of this book is to examine the implications of New Right jurisprudence for American law. Though ostensibly a conservative approach to public law, it is in reality a most radical one, in the most literal sense of the term; it would make over our law "root and branch" to accord with the sweeping views of its proponents. In support of this conclusion I shall analyze the implications of the different positions espoused by New Right jurists.

The analysis begins with a discussion of the "original intention" approach urged by conservative legal thinkers. I shall then consider their attack on Supreme Court decisions that protect personal rights not specifically guaranteed in the Constitution. Conservative jurists are more or less united in their views on these two subjects: They believe firmly in the preeminence of what they term the "historical Constitution"—one whose text should be interpreted in light of the specific intentions of its framers. They are also critical of those nontextual rights, such as the right of privacy, that the Court has discovered in the Constitution. To the conservatives, the personal rights guaranteed in the Constitution are few and definite. They see the elevation of other rights to the constitutional plane as an instance of judges reading their own moral conceptions into the organic text.

Next I shall turn to jurists whose work is beyond the mainstream of conservative jurisprudence. These thinkers urge views more extreme than those advocated by what may be called the more traditional New Right—represented by Judge Robert H. Bork and former Attorney General Edwin Meese. Indeed, Judge Bork himself terms them advocates of "conservative constitutional revisionism."[5] To the public, the Bork-Meese views represent the paradigm of New Right legal thinking. Certainly, these views have received the most attention, for they stimulated the great constitutional debate that culminated in the Bork hearings before the Senate Judiciary Committee. But the Bork-Meese approach represents only one facet of the new conservative jurisprudence. It is in some ways a less important facet now, for it no longer represents the cutting edge of New Right jurisprudence. Later chapters will be devoted to the more far-reaching approach of those on the edge of the new conservative legal thought—jurists whose theories would completely transform our public law.

These New Right jurists place particular emphasis on property rights, harking back to a time when a federal judge could say that "of the three fundamental principles which underlie government, and for which government exists, the protection of life, liberty, and property, the chief of these is property."[6] The new conservatives have also advocated an expanded interpretation of the Takings Clause of the Fifth Amendment. Under this interpretation, a provision intended only to confirm eminent domain power is metamorphosed into a limitation of public power that could leave government shorn of its most essential authority.

The discussion then turns to the New Right criticisms of Supreme Court decisions on racial discrimination. Though the critics deny that they intend it, the animadversions here would take us back to the law before the *Brown* decision[7] ruled segregation unconstitutional.

A further development in conservative legal thought is the attempt to recast our public law in the mold of economics, extending the use of cost-benefit analysis into the area of personal rights—where, I shall argue, it has particularly harmful consequences. I then include a chapter on the attacks directed by New Right jurists against the modern administrative agency; at issue is the agencies' independence from presidential authority. Last of all, there is a discussion of the work of some of the jurists discussed in this book who have been appointed to the federal bench. Here I examine how the tenets of New Right jurisprudence are starting to be elevated to the level of judicial doctrine.

My overarching theme is illustrated by the subtitle of this book: "Turning Back the Legal Clock." If fully implemented, the New Right approach to law would turn back the constitutional clock to the days when Leviathan had only two swords: war and justice. Such a repeal of the twentieth century may appear quixotic, but it is precisely what would occur if the more extreme New Right views became accepted jurisprudence.

Before dealing with the jurists on the far right, however, I shall dis-

5

cuss the two concepts now in the mainstream of conservative legal thought—the jurisprudence of "original intention" and the rejection of rights not specifically guaranteed in the Constitution. These concepts, I will show, are inconsistent with the essentials of American constitutionalism.

1

ORIGINAL INTENTION
THE IMPOSSIBLE DREAM

L IKE HAMLET'S FATHER, "original intention" is a ghost that re-
fuses to remain in repose. The notion that constitutional construction
should be based solely upon the intention of the framers has, despite its
utter fatuousness, never been laid to rest. For it is one of those delusively
simple concepts that promises a facile solution to the most difficult of our
legal problems—purporting, in the process, to eliminate the uncertainty
that too frequently prevails in constitutional law and to curb the excesses
of judicial activism.

In reality, however, the hope that original intention can become a
juristic vade mecum is destined to fail. What Edwin Meese hailed as a
new "Jurisprudence of Original Intention"[1] is in actual fact both undesirable and unworkable. It would turn back the constitutional clock by two
centuries and fossilize our public law. Its proponents are best answered
with the famous words of Judge Learned Hand: "These are false hopes,
believe me, these are false hopes."[2]

INTENTION AND RELEVANCY

Justice Oliver Wendell Holmes once remarked skeptically about the
influence of jurisprudence on legal practice, "I don't believe most judges
knew or cared a sixpence for any school."[3] Holmes's career, however, was
proof of the importance of legal theory. On the supreme bench, Holmes
was known as the Great Dissenter. His dissenting opinions were based on

7

appeals to a future when the Court would correct the errors into which it had fallen.[4] And it was the Holmes approach that eventually came to be followed by American judges. When Holmes asserted, "The life of the law has not been logic: it has been experience," and that the law finds its philosophy in "consideration of what is expedient for the community concerned,"[5] he was sounding the clarion of twentieth-century jurisprudence. If the law reflected the "felt necessities of the time,"[6] then those needs ought to determine what the law should be.

Though the twentieth century has followed the lead of Justice Holmes, it is precisely this approach that has been rejected by advocates of the jurisprudence of original intention. For Holmes's "felt necessities of the time" they have substituted the black-letter text and "the original intentions of those who framed, proposed, and ratified the Constitution."[7] Where original intent can be determined it should be followed, they assert, however contrary it may be to the judge's conclusions on "what is expedient for the community concerned." According to its leading judicial critic, Justice William J. Brennan, "[T]his view demands that Justices discern exactly what the Framers thought about the question under consideration and simply follow their intention in resolving the case before them."[8]

The Brennan statement may seem an unduly simplistic summary of the original-intention position. But the leading proponents of that position have defined it in similar terms. In a widely reported 1985 speech Attorney General Meese declared, "It has been and will continue to be the policy of this administration to press for a Jurisprudence of Original Intention. In the cases we file and those we join as *amicus*, we will endeavor to resurrect the original meaning of constitutional provisions and statutes as the only reliable guide for judgment."[9]

Judge Bork has asserted the same view, so far as judges deciding constitutional cases are concerned. As Bork put it in a 1985 address, "[O]nly by limiting themselves to the historic intentions underlying each clause of the Constitution can judges avoid becoming legislators, avoid enforcing their own moral predilections, and ensure that the Constitution is law."[10] Indeed, as Bork sees it, "[O]nly the approach of original understanding meets the criteria that any theory of constitutional adjudication must meet in order to possess democratic legitimacy."[11]

Critics at both ends of the legal spectrum have shown that original-intention interpretation is both unsound and unworkable. In the first place, there is the question of how original intent is to be determined. The record we have of the proceedings of the Philadelphia Convention of 1787 is, to one who works in twentieth-century legislative history, strikingly incomplete. Madison's notes,[12] the fullest account we do have, were taken while their author was perhaps the most active participant in the convention's proceedings and, for all their ring of authenticity, are at best a sketchy transcript. We have no way of knowing how completely the statements recorded by Madison reflected the actual intentions of the fifty-five men who sat in Independence Hall during the summer of 1787.

The same is true of amendments to the Constitution. The Bill of Rights was essentially the work of one person, Madison himself. Except for his June 8, 1789, speech introducing his amendments,[13] however, Madison said practically nothing about them. His June 8 speech itself really tells us very little, being made up mostly of general statements. The remaining legislative history of the Bill of Rights is all but unknown. The report in the *Annals of Congress* contains only a small part of what must have gone on in the old City Hall on Wall Street in New York, where the First Congress met.

Then, too, there is the question of whose intent is to govern. "Who were 'the Framers' and how are we to make sense of the idea that this large and disparate group had a unified 'intent'?"[14] Should the statements of all the framers be considered equally, or should those who took a leading part be given more weight? Should a statement by Madison in the House Bill of Rights debate count for more than one by Congressman Samuel Livermore? What if it was Livermore who expressed the sentiments of his colleagues on a matter more accurately than anyone else? And why limit intent to the delegates or congressmen who originally voted the constitutional text? Why isn't the intent of the state ratifying conventions or legislatures equally pertinent? Of course, the materials on ratification are so skimpy[15] that those on the Philadelphia Convention or the First Congress seem a veritable cornucopia by comparison.

More fundamental, however, is the question of whether, even where we can discover an unambiguous original intention, it must necessarily be taken as the final word on constitutional construction. In answering this question, we should start with Chief Justice John Marshall's seminal dictum—that we must never forget that it is a *constitution* we are expounding,[16] a living instrument that must be construed so as to meet the practical necessities of government during each period in the nation's history.

The Constitution partakes not at all of the prolixity of a political code;[17] from its nature, it deals in generals, not details.[18] Solely its great outlines are marked, its important objects designated; the minute particulars left to be deduced.[19] The Constitution states, not rules for the passing hour, but principles for an ever-expanding future.[20]

It is erroneous to assume that the resolution of any constitutional issue involves merely correct application of the canons of legal construction. In this respect, original-intention interpretivism is but another version of the unduly narrow view once stated by the Supreme Court: "When an act of Congress is appropriately challenged in the courts, as not conforming to the constitutional mandate, the judicial branch of the Government has only one duty; to lay the article of the constitution which is invoked beside the statute which is challenged and to decide whether the latter squares with the former."[21]

Such a description of constitutional law as a merely mechanical process, akin to the construction of a contract or a will, is a distortion of reality. With a basic document such as ours, drawn in so many particulars with purposed vagueness,[22] constitutional law must be more than machinelike exegesis of a fundamental text. Original intention may be a useful starting point; but it is only a starting point. Even when it can be unambiguously ascertained, it cannot be the decisive factor in interpretation, when it may mean a decision that fails to meet the "felt necessities of the time." Constitutional law based solely upon original intention would be comparable in worth to a law of real property that relied only upon the language of the Statute of Westminster II.

ORIGINAL INTENTION AND PAPER MONEY

The inadequacy of original-intention interpretivism can best be shown from an example of its application that most commentators do not use— the power given to Congress "to coin Money, [and] regulate the Value thereof."[23] During the early history of the United States, federal paper currency, with notes issued as legal tender, did not exist. Instead, as

John Kenneth Galbraith points out, "[T]he money of the United States was precious metal. . . . The only paper currency was the notes of banks."[24] During the Civil War, however, Congress was forced to make substantial changes in the currency system. In three legal tender acts, it provided for the issuance of $450 million in United States notes not backed in specie (the so-called greenbacks) and provided that those notes were to be legal tender at face value in all transactions.[25] A constitutional controversy soon arose over Congress's power to make its paper money legal tender.

During the Civil War the Supreme Court astutely avoided deciding a case challenging the validity of the greenback laws. After the war, the issue could not be evaded. In *Hepburn v. Griswold*,[26] a bare majority ruled the legal tender acts invalid. One of the main reasons Lincoln appointed Salmon P. Chase as chief justice in 1864 was to ensure a favorable decision on the constitutionality of the legal tender laws, for Chase, as secretary of the Treasury, had been their chief architect. But the new chief justice disappointed the presidential expectation. Writing of Chase's attitude toward legal tender, Henry Adams comments, "As Secretary of the Treasury he had been its author; as Chief Justice he became its enemy."[27] It was Chase who delivered the majority opinion in *Hepburn v. Griswold*.

What in another judge might have been considered high moral courage was in Chase condemned as but another example of political jobbery. His act was interpreted not as an indication of judicial independence but as a bid for the Democratic nomination for president.

The young Holmes pointed out, in a contemporary comment, that *Hepburn v. Griswold* "presented the curious spectacle of the Supreme Court reversing the determination of Congress on a point of political economy."[28] At the same time, it cannot be denied that the *Hepburn* decision was in exact accord with the original intention of the framers of the Constitution. If there was one point on which the men of 1787 were agreed, it was the need to prevent a repetition of the paper money fiasco of the American Revolution, when the expression "not worth a Continental" was born. The framers "had seen in the experience of the Revolutionary period the demoralizing tendency, the cruel injustice, and the intolerable oppression of a paper currency not convertible on demand

11

into money, and forced into circulation by legal tender provisions and penal enactments."[29] They therefore determined to give the government they were establishing the power to issue only a metallic currency.

This can be seen both from the constitutional text and the framers' debates. Their use of the term "to coin Money" clearly indicates "their determination to sanction only a metallic currency."[30] As Chief Justice Chase put it, "The power conferred is the power to coin money, and these words must be understood as they were used at the time the Constitution was adopted. And we have been referred to no authority which at that time defined coining otherwise than as minting or stamping metals for money; or money otherwise than as metal coined for the purposes of commerce."[31]

The accuracy of the Chase statement is confirmed by the only dictionary available to the framers—the one compiled by Samuel Johnson. It defines the verb "coin" as "to mint or stamp metals for money" and the noun "money" as "metal coined for the purposes of commerce."[32]

The available records of the Philadelphia Convention itself also bear out Chase's view of the framers' intent. The original constitutional draft gave Congress power to "emit Bills on the Credit of the United States."[33] Gouverneur Morris moved to strike out these words. Except for one delegate, who said that he "was a friend to paper money," those who spoke on the matter supported the motion. Madison asked whether it would not be "sufficient to prohibit the making them a *tender*." "This will remove," he said, "the temptation to emit them with unjust views." Morris replied that striking out the words was the better approach. "The Monied interest," he declared, "will oppose the plan of Government, if paper emissions be not prohibited."

Among the supporters of the motion were two future members of the Supreme Court. Oliver Ellsworth, according to Madison's notes, "thought it a favorable moment to shut and bar the door against paper money. The mischiefs of the various experiments which had been made, were now fresh in the public mind and had excited the disgust of all the respectable part of America. By withholding the power from the new Government more friends of influence would be gained to it than by almost anything else—Paper money can in no case be necessary."

James Wilson concurred: "It will have a most salutary influence on the credit of the States to remove the possibility of paper money. This expedient can never succeed whilst its mischiefs are remembered. And as long as it can be resorted to, it will be a bar to other resources."

Another delegate pointed out that "paper was a legal tender in no country in Europe." Madison further records, "He was urgent for disarming the Government of such a power." Finally, George Read "thought the words, if not struck out, would be as alarming as the mark of the Beast in Revelations," and John Langdon said that he "had rather reject the whole plan than retain the three words ('and emit bills')."

The Morris motion to strike the words carried, nine to two. Madison appended a note to the debate, explaining his affirmative vote by stating that he "became satisfied that striking out the words . . . would only cut off the pretext for a paper currency and particularly for making the bills a tender either for public or private debts."[34]

The framers' intent with respect to paper money and making it legal tender is as clear as anything that we know about the Philadelphia convention. As Luther Martin, himself a delegate at Philadelphia, explained it in November 1787, a "majority of the convention, being wise beyond every event, and being willing to risk any political evil, rather than admit the idea of a paper emission, in any *possible* event, refused to *trust* this authority to [the federal] government."[35] Nor can it be doubted that the decision in *Hepburn v. Griswold* was completely in accord with the original intention of the framers on the matter. Yet if the *Hepburn* decision was thus categorically correct in terms of original intention, it was plainly wrong so far as the needs of the nation were concerned.

It is all but impossible to conceive of a functioning modern economy without paper money, in which the only currency is specie. Yet that is exactly what would have been required under *Hepburn v. Griswold*. Well might the Supreme Court later say that its decision on the matter would "affect the entire business of the country, and take hold of the possible continued existence of the government. If it be held by this court that Congress has not constitutional power, under any circumstances, or in any emergency, to make Treasury notes a legal tender for the payment of all debts (a power confessedly possessed by every independent sovereignty other than the United States), the government is without those means of self-preservation which, all must admit, may, in certain contingencies, become indispensable."[36] Hence, the *New York Herald* could assert, if *Hepburn v. Griswold* meant what it said, it "involved the whole country in financial chaos and the Government perhaps in bankruptcy and repudiation."[37]

Hepburn v. Griswold itself, however consistent it was with the framers' original intention, was not destined to achieve this disastrous result. When the case was decided, the Supreme Court consisted of only seven members, who divided four to three on the ruling. To deprive President Andrew Johnson of the opportunity of filling expected vacancies, Congress passed a law providing that no vacancy on the Court was to be filled until it was reduced to below seven members.[38] With President Grant's election, the situation was changed, and an 1869 statute raised the number of justices to nine and authorized the president to make the necessary appointments.[39]

On the very day when the decision adverse to the government was announced in *Hepburn v. Griswold*, Grant appointed two new justices (Strong and Bradley) who were known to support the constitutionality of the legal tender acts. After they took their seats, the Court permitted argument again on the validity of the greenback laws. This time, in the *Legal Tender Cases*[40]—decided only a year after *Hepburn v. Griswold*— Justices Strong and Bradley, plus the *Hepburn* dissenters, made up a new majority. Finally putting to rest the controversy over congressional authority, the Court ruled that the nation's fiscal powers included the authority to issue paper money vested with the quality of legal tender. Original intention had been tried and ultimately found wanting, even though this was one case where the framers' intent was as clear as it could possibly be.

BACK TO THE RACK?

There is another obvious example demonstrating that original intention, even where clear and unambiguous, cannot be the determinative factor in constitutional interpretation when it completely fails to meet the "felt necessities of the time."[41] It arises under the Eighth Amendment's prohibition against infliction of "cruel and unusual punishment." If there is one branch of the law that has changed dramatically over the past two centuries, it has been the penal law. At the time the Constitution and Bill of Rights were adopted, punishments that we would find plainly offensive were a settled part of the criminal law. If original intention were "the only reliable guide for judgment,"[42] those punishments would still be unaffected by the Punishment Clause.

During the House debate on what became the Eighth Amendment, Congressman Samuel Livermore observed that "villains often deserve whipping and perhaps having their ears cut off; but are we in future to be prevented from inflicting these punishments because they are cruel?"[43] Whipping, cropping the ears, and the like were common when the Bill of Rights was adopted. They were clearly not thought to violate the constitutional prohibition at that time. Indeed, in the First Judiciary Act, adopted the same year that Congress voted the Bill of Rights, whipping was classified with moderate fines and short imprisonment as a relatively mild punishment[44] and, as such, obviously not within the Eighth Amendment prohibition.

In the states, punishments we now consider barbarous were the rule. In Delaware, for example, hanging, and drawing and quartering for the crime of treason[45] were not abolished until the state's 1829 code was passed. But that law continued to provide for standing in the pillory, cropping of ears, selling into servitude, branding, and whipping as punishments for crime. These punishments were, of course, gradually eliminated. But it was not until 1905 that the punishment of the pillory was done away with in Delaware. And, as recently as 1963, the state's highest court upheld statutes providing for the penalty of whipping.[46]

Or we can take the view on the matter of one of the most humane men of his day, Thomas Jefferson—who, though absent in France at the time of the Constitutional Convention, is virtually considered a framer because of the crucial part he played in establishing the American polity. In his Bill for Proportioning Crimes and Punishments, Jefferson provided the penalty for rape, polygamy, or sodomy: "[I]f a man, by castration, if a woman by cutting thro' the cartilage of her nose a hole of one half inch diameter at the least." For maiming or disfiguring another, Jefferson's punishment was that the perpetrator "shall be maimed or disfigured in like sort."[47]

Today, we would say about most of these punishments what a Pennsylvania court once said about a sentence under which the defendant was to

15

be placed in a ducking stool and plunged three times in the water, for the offense of being a common scold: "[I]t is revolting to humanity, and is of that description that only could have been invented in an age of barbarism."[48]

It should, however, be borne in mind that the very element of degradation, which makes such punishments repulsive to modern penology, was what made them seem so suitable to a community in large part still dominated by the puritan ethic. But the concept of punishment has changed drastically during the past two centuries and with it the reach of the Punishment Clause. Today we would say that punishments such as whipping and the pillory involve such degradation as to violate the Eighth Amendment. As Justice Harold A. Blackmun once put it, use of the strap, "irrespective of any precautionary conditions, offends contemporary concepts of decency and human dignity."[48]

The fundamental theme of Eighth Amendment jurisprudence was set over three decades ago by Chief Justice Warren: "The basic concept underlying the Eighth Amendment is nothing less than the dignity of man. . . . The Amendment must draw its meaning from the evolving standards of decency that mark the progress of a maturing society."[50]

The Warren posture is surely to be preferred to one that relies on original intention. The latter approach would freeze our penology according to concepts that prevailed at the end of the eighteenth century, which would in turn place all punishments common at that time beyond constitutional attack. The Eighth Amendment must, as Warren states, be treated as a constantly evolving provision that reflects changing conceptions of human dignity. The "primary principle" behind the amendment, Justice Brennan tells us, is "that the State, even as it punishes, must treat its citizens in a manner consistent with their intrinsic worth as human beings."[51] What comported with human dignity when penal sanctions were inflicted "by way of disgrace and ludibrium (which is the intent of this kind of punishment)"[52] should hardly be the constitutional standard two centuries later, even if it is consistent with the original intention of Madison and his congressional colleagues. It is hard to take seriously a constitutional jurisprudence that would permit penal law to return to the days when even Blackstone could state, after listing the

penalties then provided by the criminal law, "Disgusting as this cata-
logue may seem. . . ."[53]

DUE PROCESS AND ARBITRARY POWER

The inadequacy of the original-intention approach is particularly apparent whenever we deal with the crucial skeleton clauses in the Constitution. Chief among these have been the prohibitions against deprivation
"of life, liberty, or property, without due process of law" and against
denial of "the equal protection of the law." Such phrases, as Justice
Frankfurter has pointed out, "do not carry contemporaneous fixity. By
their very nature they imply a process of unfolding content."[54] In clothing these wholesale clauses with meaning, the Supreme Court has been
left almost completely at large. Furnished with no guide beyond the very
general language of the text, the high bench has been able to give
meaning to such phrases in accordance with its own policy considerations in specific cases—sometimes, alas, failing to keep the corpus of
the law internally consistent.

Would the problems flowing from the purposed vagueness[55] of a clause
such as the Due Process Clause have been avoided if original intention
had been taken "as the only reliable guide for judgment"?[56]

It cannot be doubted that the original-intention approach would have
made judicial interpretation of the Due Process Clause a relatively simple matter. To the framers of the Fifth Amendment, the meaning of *due
process* was confined to its literal language—that is, "due" means regular or fair, and "process" means procedure. At that time, in other words,
due process meant only what we now term *procedural* due process. The
substantive aspect of due process had not even begun to develop.

There is a Due Process Clause in the Fifth Amendment because the
New York convention that ratified the Constitution used the term "due
process" instead of "law of the land" in its version of section 39 of Magna
Carta in the constitutional amendments that it proposed.[57] Madison had
the New York draft before him, as well as other state-recommended
amendments, when he wrote his draft of the Fifth Amendment.

We do not know what led Madison to use the New York "due process"
language over the more traditional "law of the land" terminology em-

17

ployed, for example, in the Virginia-proposed amendments to the Constitution.[58] Perhaps it was Hamilton, with whom he was in close contact at the time, who influenced him in this respect. Hamilton was one of the few men at that early date who realized that the phrase "due process" might make a difference.

On January 17, 1787, the New York legislature had passed "[a]n Act concerning the Rights of the Citizens of the State."[59] That statute contained a provision that no one shall be deprived of any right except by "due process of law." John Lansing, who introduced the draft of the proposed amendments in the New York Ratifying Convention, undoubtedly took his draft's due process clause from the 1787 New York statute. We do not know who was responsible for the clause there. Both Lansing and Hamilton were members of the New York legislature, so either one of them could have drafted the "due process" language, or it could have been done by the law's sponsor or some other member.

We do know, however, that Hamilton was fully aware of the term from a speech that he delivered in the New York Assembly on February 6, 1787. On that occasion Hamilton indicated that the term "due process" in the 1787 statute was intended to make it plain that "no man shall be disfranchised or deprived of any right he enjoys under the constitution" by a mere act of the legislature. "Some gentlemen hold that the law of the land will include an act of the legislature. But Lord Coke, that great luminary of the law . . . interprets the law of the land to mean presentment and indictment, and process of outlawry, as contradistinguished from trial by jury." But, Hamilton went on, "if there were any doubt upon the constitution, the bill of rights enacted in this session [i.e., the January 17, 1787, Act] removes it. It is there declared that, no man shall be disfranchised or deprived of any right, but by due process of law. . . . The words 'due process' have a precise technical import, and are only applicable to the process and proceedings of the courts of justice; they can never be referred to an act of legislature."[60]

The implication is that the words "due process" were inserted into the 1787 statute to increase the protection given to individual rights—an intent that has clearly been realized by the subsequent development of "due process." We should not, however, assume that the draftsman of the 1787 New York statute used the term "due process" in anything like the

18

broad meaning it has since acquired in our constitutional law. The Hamilton speech quoted above indicates that the contrary was the case. When Hamilton said that "due process" was only "applicable to the process and proceedings of the courts of justice," he clearly was thinking only of procedural due process, not of the broader connotations we are familiar with today.

Without question, Madison, in drafting what became the Fifth Amendment, used "due process" in the same procedural sense. Yet this scarcely affects the crucial significance of what he did. The term "due process" could expand to meet even the substance of legislative power; the same was not true of the "law of the land" phraseology, which probably would have been used in the Fifth Amendment had Madison not followed the New York example and employed the "due process" language.

This is not mere theory. When the Constitution of India was being drafted, the constitutional adviser to the drafting committee consulted Justice Frankfurter, who told him "that the power of review implied in the 'due process' clause was not only undemocratic (because it gave a few judges the power of vetoing legislation enacted by the representatives of the nation) but also threw an unfair burden on the judiciary. This view was communicated . . . to the Drafting Committee which introduced a far-reaching change in the clause by replacing the expression 'without due process of law' with the expression 'except according to procedure established by law.'"[61]

The Indian Supreme Court has interpreted the latter term to include a law enacted by the Indian Parliament. Hence, property taken by a statute is taken "by law" as the term is used in the Indian Constitution.[62] Similar "law of the land" terminology in the American Constitution would, in all probability, have been interpreted the same way.

Yet, if original intention is to control even due process, it would have to be given the same limited connotation. This would mean the elimination of substantive due process from our constitutional law. This would, in turn, remove the great safeguard that our courts have developed against arbitrary governmental action.

Due process may, as we have seen, have had a narrow meaning to those who inserted the term into the Constitution. But it does not follow that that restricted meaning should still be followed. When Madison wrote "due process" into the Constitution, he could scarcely have foreseen the expansive manner in which the guaranty would be construed, just as he could not have foreseen the future society that would adapt the guaranty to its own problems. But his great contribution was to write in words that enabled later generations to mold them to accord with changes in the community's sense of justice.

More important is the need for the broader concept of due process in a system such as ours. This need was well stated by Justice Harlan (usually taken as the paradigm of the responsible conservative judge by original-intention jurists): "Were due process merely a procedural safeguard it would fail to reach those situations where the deprivation of life, liberty or property was accomplished by legislation which . . . could, given even the fairest possible procedure . . . , nevertheless destroy the enjoyment of all three." Hence it is, Harlan goes on, that "the guaranties of due process . . . have in this country also 'become bulwarks against arbitrary legislation.'"[63]

That due process would be interpreted by American judges to impose limitations of substance as well as procedure was well-nigh inevitable if the Constitution was to serve as a substantial safeguard for individual rights. Governmental action restricting those rights that touches no particularized prohibition is not subject to constitutional control, unless it be by the Due Process Clause. If that result is to be avoided, due process must be interpreted as a substantive, as well as a procedural, guaranty. As such, it bars governmental action deemed arbitrary. In the oft-quoted language of the highest Court,

> Arbitrary power, enforcing its edicts to the injury of the persons and property of its subjects, is not law, whether manifested as the decree of a personal monarch or of an impersonal multitude. And the limitations imposed by our constitutional law upon the action of the governments, both State and national, are essential to the preservation of public and private rights, notwithstanding the representative character of our political institutions. The enforcement of these limitations by judicial process is the device of self-governing communities to protect the rights of individuals and minorities, as well against the power of numbers, as against the violence of public agents transcending the limits of lawful authority, even when acting in the name and wielding the force of the government.[64]

To advocates of original intention, all this is irrelevant. Thus Judge Bork tells us that the "text of the due process clause simply will not support judicial efforts to pour substantive rather than procedural meaning into it."[65] Therefore, he urges, the courts should "abandon the whole enterprise of substantive due process as an inherently lawless usurpation by judges."[66]

In the American system, however, law is something more than mere will exerted as an act of power. The guaranty of due process, though having its roots in Magna Carta's "by the law of the land" and always considered an essential procedural safeguard, has in this country also become the basic bulwark against arbitrary governmental action.[67] In this sense, it is the Due Process Clause, more than any other organic provision, that has maintained the balance between authority and liberty. "Due process . . . has represented the balance which our Nation, built upon postulates of respect for the liberty of the individual, has struck between that liberty and the demands of organized society."[68]

If application of the Due Process Clause were to be governed by original intention, the basic restraint on arbitrary power would be all but eviscerated. If due process is interpreted to guarantee only particular forms of procedure, it would remove "the very substance of individual rights to life, liberty, and property"[69] from constitutional control.

Original intention applied to due process would have another undesirable consequence that is overlooked by most commentators on the subject. It may be seen from an analysis of *Bolling v. Sharp*,[70] the companion case to *Brown v. Board of Education*,[71] the landmark 1954 school segregation case. The segregation cases presented to the Court at that time involved schools in four states and the District of Columbia. Chief Justice Warren's original *Brown* draft had dealt with all these cases together, as shown by its opening sentence: "These cases come to us from the States of Delaware, Virginia, Kansas and South Carolina and from the District of Columbia." The Warren draft went on to say that, though they were separate cases, "the basic law involved in their decision is identical to the point that they can on principle properly be considered together in this opinion."[72]

In treating the state and D.C. cases together, the Warren draft was making a legal mistake. The rationale for striking down segregation in the states cannot be used to reach that result in Washington, D.C. The

21

state action in *Brown* was invalidated under the Equal Protection Clause of the Fourteenth Amendment. Yet that amendment is binding only on the states, not the federal government. The latter is bound by the Fifth Amendment, which contains a Due Process Clause but no requirement of equal protection. Obviously, the Court would not decide that the states could not have segregated schools, while the District of Columbia could. But the result had to be reached in terms of due process, rather than equal protection, analysis. Ultimately, the *Bolling* opinion asserted that "discrimination may be so unjustifiable as to be violative of due process."[73] Segregation by a state that violated equal protection would violate due process if it was required by federal law. Hence the D.C. school segregation, like the state segregation struck down in *Brown*, was ruled unconstitutional.

If, under the original-intention approach, due process were to be stripped of its substantive aspect, the *Bolling* rationale would not be possible. Hence to a jurist such as Judge Bork, "*Bolling* . . . was a clear rewriting of the Constitution by the Warren Court."[74] In *Bolling* itself, the Court declared, "In view of our decision, that the Constitution prohibits the states from maintaining racially segregated public schools, it would be unthinkable that the same Constitution would impose a lesser duty on the Federal Government."[75] But that is precisely what would happen if the Due Process Clause of the Fifth Amendment were restricted to the procedural meaning that it had when the amendment became part of the Constitution.

JIM CROW REDIVIVUS?

Perhaps the best answer to the advocates of original intention is that, if their approach had been followed strictly, *Brown*[76] itself would not have been decided the way it was. Those who urge original intention now concede that *Brown* was decided correctly. Thus, according to former Attorney General Meese, the *Brown* decision

> earned all the plaudits it received. But the Supreme Court in that case was not giving new life to old words, or adapting a "living," "flexible" Constitution to new reality. It was restoring the original principle of the Constitution to constitutional law. The *Brown* Court was correcting the

damage done 50 years earlier, when in *Plessy v. Ferguson*,[77] an earlier Supreme Court had disregarded the clear intent of the Framers of the civil war amendments to eliminate the legal degradation of blacks, and had contrived a theory of the Constitution to support the charade of 'separate but equal' discrimination.[78]

The Meese interpretation of the "clear intent" of the Fourteenth Amendment's framers is, to say the least, questionable. The reargument in *Brown* itself had focused on the understanding of "the Congress which submitted and the State legislatures and conventions which ratified the Fourteenth Amendment" with regard to the amendment's effect on school segregation.[79]

Well before the reargument, Justice Frankfurter had also focused on the intent of the Fourteenth Amendment's framers. Early in the previous term, Frankfurter had given Alexander Bickel, then one of his law clerks, the job of doing intensive research on the question of original intent. Bickel's work, based on months of plowing through the musty, near century-old folio volumes of the *Congressional Globe*, was finished late in the summer of 1953. His lengthy memorandum, carefully revised by both Frankfurter and Bickel himself, was printed and sent to the other justices just before the *Brown* reargument in early December. Frankfurter's covering *Memorandum for the Conference* summarized the result of Bickel's labors: "The [Bickel] memorandum indicates that the legislative history of the Amendment is, in a word, inconclusive." According to the memo, the Thirty-ninth Congress, which voted to submit the amendment—with its guaranty of equal protection—to the states for ratification, did not indicate an intent to have it either outlaw or not outlaw segregation in public schools.[80]

The conclusion that the legislative history of the Fourteenth Amendment was "inconclusive" on school segregation was significant enough to be repeated as the first important point in the Court's unanimous *Brown* opinion.[81] In an unpublished draft concurrence, Justice Jackson stated it somewhat differently: "Their exhaustive research to uncover the original will and purpose expressed in the Fourteenth Amendment yields for me only one sure conclusion: it was a passionate, confused and deplorable era." As Jackson saw it in his draft, "It is hard to find an indication that any influential body of the movement that carried the Civil War Amendments had reached the point of thinking about either segregation or education of the Negro as a current problem, and harder still to find that the Amendments were designed to be a solution."

Yet, though the congressional debates on the Fourteenth Amendment do not deal with school segregation, there is a clear indication that the framers did not intend the amendment to eliminate the practice. "If we turn from words to deeds as evidence of purpose," states the Jackson *Brown* draft, "we find nothing to show that the Congress which submitted these Amendments understood or intended to prohibit the practice here in question. The very Congress that proposed the Fourteenth Amendment, and every Congress from that day to this, established or maintained segregated schools in the District of Columbia, where its power over purse and policy was complete. This system was notorious and must have been known to every Congressman who voted for District of Columbia appropriations down to this very day."[82]

In the first *Brown* conference, on December 13, 1952, Chief Justice Vinson also stressed congressional actions in the matter—particularly those of the Congress that voted the Fourteenth Amendment. It was, Vinson told the conference, "hard to get away from that contemporary interpretation of the amendment," since the "men there [were those] who passed [the] amendment."

Vinson also noted at the conference that Congress had never acted to "pass a statute deterring and ordering *no* segregation." On the contrary, soon after the Fourteenth Amendment's adoption, "Congress evidently did not want to pass the Sumner bill against segregation." In summing up on this point, Vinson asserted, "I don't see . . . how we can get away from the long acceptance [of segregation in the District of Columbia]. For 90 years [there have been] segregated schools in the city."[83]

The contemporary actions of the legislators who voted the Fourteenth Amendment clearly indicate that they did not at all intend to abolish segregation: "[T]he fact that in 1862, 1864, 1866 and 1874 Congress . . . enacted legislation which specifically provided for separation of the races in the schools of the District of Columbia, conclusively support[s] our view of the Amendment"—that is, that it was not intended by its framers to do away with school segregation.[84]

In the unpublished draft concurrence that he prepared in *Brown*, Justice Jackson stated the original-intention doctrine as follows: "It is customary to turn to the original will and purpose of those responsible for adoption of a constitutional document as a basis for its subsequent interpretation."[85] Despite the Meese statement at the beginning of this section, the *Brown* decision did not return the law to the original intention of the Fourteenth Amendment's framers. On the contrary we have just seen that they did not intend to eliminate segregation. Indeed, their actions in providing for segregated schools in the District of Columbia show that they did not believe that the amendment had made segregation unconstitutional.

But that is the whole point about application of the original-intention approach to school segregation. Since the Fourteenth Amendment's framers did not intend it to prohibit school segregation, reliance on original intention as the determinative factor could have meant a different decision in the *Brown* case. Such a result demonstrates, better than anything else, the total inadequacy of the original-intention approach.

CHIEF JUSTICE REHNQUIST AND THE ESTABLISHMENT CLAUSE

Chief Justice Rehnquist is an outstanding example of a judge who has used the original-intention approach to reach results inconsistent with those reached under the prevailing jurisprudence. Perhaps the best example of the Rehnquist posture in this respect is to be found in his dissent in *Wallace v. Jaffree*.[86] The Court there struck down an Alabama law that authorized teachers in public schools to "announce that a period of silence not to exceed one minute in duration shall be observed for meditation or voluntary prayer." The statute was ruled violative of the First Amendment's prohibition against any "law respecting an establishment of religion."

In the *Jaffree* case, original intention was used as the decisive element not only by then-Justice Rehnquist, but also by Judge Hand, the district judge who had first decided the case. Hand found that the statute had been enacted "to encourage a religious activity."[87] That made the law unconstitutional under the Supreme Court decisions invalidating school prayers and other religious exercises.[88] But Judge Hand refused to follow the precedents because he had concluded that the original intention of the framers of both the First and Fourteenth Amendments was contrary to the Supreme Court's interpretation of the Establishment Clause.

Judge Hand's conclusion on the matter was: "This Court's review of the relevant legislative history surrounding the adoption of both the first amendment and of the fourteenth amendment, together with the plain language of those amendments, leaves no doubt that those amendments were not intended to forbid religious prayers in the schools which the states and their political subdivisions mandate."[89]

This was true, Judge Hand wrote, because the First Amendment was intended "to prohibit the federal government only from establishing a national religion."[90] Nor was this changed, according to Hand, by the Fourteenth Amendment. "The historical record clearly establishes that when the fourteenth amendment was ratified in 1868 that its ratification did not incorporate the first amendment against the states."[91] The states remained "free to define the meaning of religious establishment under their own constitutions and laws."[92] Since "the establishment clause of the first amendment to the United States Constitution does not prohibit the state from establishing a religion, the prayers offered by the teachers in this case are not unconstitutional."[93]

Not surprisingly, the court of appeals rejected "the District Court's remarkable conclusion that the Federal Constitution imposes no obstacle to Alabama's establishment of a state religion."[94] The Supreme Court's *Jaffree* opinion conceded that, before the Fourteenth Amendment, "the First Amendment's restraints on the exercise of federal power simply did not apply to the States."[95] But this situation was changed by the Fourteenth Amendment. According to the *Jaffree* opinion, that amendment "imposed the same substantive limitations on the States' power to legislate that the First Amendment had always imposed on the Congress' power. This Court has confirmed and endorsed this elementary proposition of law time and time again."[96]

Justice Rehnquist's *Jaffree* dissent did not go as far as the district judge and challenge the settled rule that the Establishment Clause is binding upon the states, since it is incorporated in the due process guaranteed by the Fourteenth Amendment. On the contrary, the Rehnquist dissent states expressly, "Given the 'incorporation' of the Establishment Clause as against the States via the Fourteenth Amendment . . . , States are prohibited as well from establishing a religion."[97]

Rehnquist asserts, however, that the Supreme Court's Establishment

Clause doctrine has been based upon "a mistaken understanding of constitutional history."[98] More specifically, he concludes that the settled jurisprudence on the clause is wholly contrary to the original intention of the framers of the First Amendment—particularly that of James Madison, whose draft served as the basis of the Bill of Rights. However, the Rehnquist original-intention endeavor suffers in this respect from the two great defects of previous efforts in this vein. First, how is original intention to be determined? And even if it can be determined, should it be *the* controlling factor two centuries later?

The Rehnquist determination of original intention on the Establishment Clause is based on the legislative history of the First Amendment. According to Rehnquist, it shows an intent that the clause should have a meaning completely unlike that given to it in Supreme Court jurisprudence: "[W]hen we turn to the record of the proceedings in the First Congress leading up to the adoption of the Establishment Clause of the Constitution, including Madison's significant contributions thereto, we see a far different picture of its purpose than the highly simplified 'wall of separation between church and State.'"[99]

Rehnquist derives the intent behind the Establishment Clause almost entirely from what Madison said and did during the sessions of the First Congress. Rehnquist starts with the language Madison proposed for what ultimately became the Religion Clauses of the First Amendment: "The civil rights of none shall be abridged on account of religious belief or worship, nor shall any national religion be established, nor shall the full and equal rights of conscience be in any manner, or on any pretext, infringed."[100]

Madison's proposed amendments were referred to the Select Committee of Eleven, of which Madison himself was a member.[101] The committee changed Madison's proposal on religion to read, "No religion shall be established by law, nor shall the equal rights of conscience be infringed."[102] Rehnquist characterizes the House debate on the committee draft as "not . . . particularly illuminating."[103] During the debate, Madison replied to a congressman who said that "[h]e feared it might be thought to have a tendency to abolish religion altogether."[104]

The report we have tells us "Mr. Madison said, he apprehended the meaning of the words to be, that Congress should not establish a religion, and enforce the legal observation of it by law, nor compel men to worship God in any manner contrary to their conscience."[105] To prevent Congress from making "laws of such a nature as might infringe the rights of conscience, and establish a national religion . . . he presumed the amendment was intended, and he thought it as well expressed as the nature of the language would admit."[106]

Congressman Benjamin Huntington of Connecticut was afraid the amendment would close the federal courts to actions to collect contributions pledged by church members. Madison replied that he thought "if the word national was inserted before religion, it would satisfy the minds of honorable gentlemen. He believed that the people feared one sect might obtain a pre-eminence, or two combine together, and establish a religion to which they would compel others to conform. He thought if the word national was introduced, it would point the amendment directly to the object it was intended to prevent."[107]

There was opposition to Madison's proposed insertion. Elbridge Gerry objected to the word "national" on the ground that a federal government, not a national one, had been established. Then, the report says, "Mr. Madison withdrew his motion, but observed that the words 'no national religion shall be established by law,' did not imply that the Government was a national one."[108]

Justice Rehnquist relies essentially upon these Madison statements to support his view on the original intention behind the Establishment Clause. "On the basis of the record of these proceedings in the House of Representatives,"[109] Rehnquist asserts, Madison was "obviously not . . . a zealous believer"[110] in a complete separation between church and state.

> His original language "nor shall any national religion be established" obviously does not conform to the "wall of separation" between church and State idea which latter-day commentators have ascribed to him. His explanation on the floor of the meaning of his language—"that Congress should not establish a religion, and enforce the legal observation of it by law" is of the same ilk. When he replied to Huntington in the debate over the proposal which came from the Select Committee of the House, he urged that the language "no religion shall be established by law" should be amended by inserting the word "national" in front of the word "religion."[111]

Rehnquist's conclusion is this: "It seems indisputable from these glimpses of Madison's thinking, as reflected by actions on the floor of the House in 1789, that he saw the Amendment as designed to prohibit the establishment of a national religion, and perhaps to prevent discrimination among sects. He did not see it as requiring neutrality on the part of government between religion and irreligion."[112]

Hence, according to Rehnquist, even if it is correct to bracket Madison with Jefferson in the effort that led to the Virginia Statute of Religious Liberty,[113] it "is totally incorrect" to suggest "that Madison carried these views onto the floor of the United States House of Representatives when he proposed the language which would ultimately become the Bill of Rights."[114] On the contrary, it is clear to Rehnquist that the Madison who introduced the Bill of Rights intended the Establishment Clause to have only a narrow meaning: "[I]t forbade establishment of a national religion, and forbade preference among religious sects or denominations."[115]

Historians have derided the use of history by the Supreme Court as "law-office" history.[116] Their criticisms certainly apply to the Rehnquist effort to uncover the original intention of those who elevated the Establishment Clause to the constitutional plane and to use that intention to repudiate the consistent caselaw on the matter. In effect, Rehnquist the legal historian convinced Rehnquist the justice that all his distinguished predecessors had completely misread the historical intent of the Establishment Clause, and this was enough to persuade the learned judge to reject both the wisdom of prior Courts and the weight of the precedents they had established.

Against the mass of case law interpreting the Establishment Clause, historian Rehnquist has marshaled the sketchy statements made by Madison during the Bill of Rights debates. But those statements were made in connection with Madison's original draft of the Religion Clauses and his proposal to amend the Select Committee draft Establishment Clause so that it would bar only establishment of a *national* religion. Madison may well have intended his draft, as Rehnquist claims, "to prohibit the establishment of a national religion."[117] But the later proposal to add "national" was withdrawn by its sponsor. Can we reasonably suppose that that proposal expressed the intent of the House whose opposition led Madison to withdraw it?

29

In addition, we should bear in mind that the language of the Religion Clauses was substantially changed from the original Madison draft. The change was initiated with the redraft by the Select Committee already quoted.[118] Then, during the discussion of Madison's motion, Representative Livermore commented that he was not satisfied with the proposed amendment's language. "He thought it would be better if it was altered, and made to read in this manner, that Congress shall make no laws touching religion, or infringing the rights of conscience."[119] After Madison withdrew his motion, the House passed the Livermore proposal. Then, a week later, on a motion introduced by Fisher Ames and without any discussion that we know of, the House voted the following substitute provision for the amendment: "Congress shall make no law establishing religion, or to prevent the free exercise thereof, or to infringe the rights of conscience."[120]

The Senate sat behind closed doors until February 1794, when a resolution directing that future sessions be public was passed. No report of the early Senate debates is available. Instead, we have only the skeleton-like account of the legislative history in the Senate *Journal* and the even skimpier account in the *Annals of Congress*. They tell us the exact changes made in the House amendments, as well as what other amendments were rejected, but they tell us nothing of the discussion during the Senate debates. All we know about the Senate proceedings is that various versions were introduced and that the Senate passed the following language: "Congress shall make no law establishing articles of faith or a mode of worship, or prohibiting the free exercise of religion."[121]

The House refused to accept the changes made by the Senate in the proposed Bill of Rights and asked that a conference committee be appointed. That committee drafted the final version of the Religion Clauses, which was agreed to by both Houses and ultimately ratified as part of the First Amendment.[122]

The link between what Madison said and did during the congressional debate and the original intention behind the Establishment Clause is substantially weakened by the fact that Madison's original draft on religion, as introduced by him in the House, underwent the important alterations discussed before they emerged in final form.[123] It is true that Madison was a member of both the House Select Committee and the conference committee that drafted the ultimate version of the clause. But we do not know what role he actually played in those committees, particularly in the drafting process that led to the Establishment Clause versions submitted by them.

Irving Brant, Madison's leading biographer, says of the substitute introduced by Fisher Ames, which for the first time brought the Establishment Clause language close to its final version, "There can be little doubt that this was written by Madison."[124] This assertion is backed, however, by nothing more than its author's intuition and the statement that Ames had not taken part in the debate and had generally not been in favor of the Bill of Rights.[125] Brant concedes, "There is no positive proof that [Madison] wrote the final version which came out of conference."[126] Nevertheless, he goes on, that version "could be ascribed to Madison on the basis of the legislative history, even if its wording did not clearly identify him as the author."[127]

It is hard to see how Brant reaches this conclusion when the final wording was changed so substantially from both the original Madison draft and the narrow interpretation urged by Madison during the House debate, when he proposed to insert "national" into the clause. As finally passed, the Establishment Clause bars not only the establishment of "any national religion" (the prohibition in the original Madison draft) but any "law respecting an establishment of religion." This is broader than both the prohibition in Madison's draft and the one advocated by him in the report we have of the House debate.

The Establishment Clause is not limited to governmental acts creating an "established church as it had been known in England and in most of the Colonies."[128] That would have been the effect of Madison's draft clause, but the language finally chosen is broad enough to ensure that government will not be able to exert its power in the service of any religious end. As the Supreme Court tells us, the First Amendment's "authors did not simply prohibit the establishment of a state church or a state religion. . . . Instead they commanded that there should be 'no law *respecting* an establishment of religion.' A law may be one 'respecting' the forbidden objective while falling short of its total realization. . . . A given law might not *establish* a state religion but nevertheless be one 'respecting' that end."[129]

Madison's original draft may, as he explained it during the House debate, have been intended to mean merely that the federal government

31

was not to set up a state church. [130] But why should the limited purpose expressed by Madison here be taken as the original intention behind the Establishment Clause when the language finally chosen is consistent with a much broader purpose than that expressed by Madison?

After all, as Justice Frankfurter once said about the Fourteenth Amendment, "Remarks of a particular proponent of the Amendment, no matter how influential, are not to be deemed part of the Amendment. What was submitted for ratification was his proposal, not his speech."[131] What was submitted for ratification was the Establishment Clause passed by Congress, not Madison's draft amendment or his speech in the House debate. Yet even if we take Madison's views as *the* expression of the Establishment Clause's original intention, we may still have a "modest doubt" about the selective approach to Madison's intention employed by Justice Rehnquist. His *Jaffree* opinion relies on Madison's statements during the House debate to demonstrate that the purpose behind the clause was far narrower than the interpretation given it by the Supreme Court. But Madison made other statements indicating that the scope of the Establishment Clause in its final version was more far-reaching than in his original draft or the statements relied on by Rehnquist.

In 1790 the same Congress that voted the First Amendment debated the census bill. Madison, who had proposed an enumeration by occupations, was asked why he had not provided for a count of the professional classes. He would do so willingly, he said, but pointed out, "As to those who are employed in teaching and inculcating the duties of religion, there may be some indelicacy in singling them out, as the general government is proscribed from interfering, in any manner whatever, in matters respecting religion; and it may be thought to do this, in ascertaining who [are], and who are not ministers of the gospel."[132]

In 1811 President Madison vetoed two bills because they violated the Establishment Clause. The first was an "act incorporating the Protestant Episcopal Church in . . . the District of Columbia," which vested in the church "authority to provide for the support of the poor, and the education of poor children." Madison's veto asserted that this "would be a precedent for giving to religious societies, as such, a legal agency in carrying into effect a public and civil duty."[133]

The second bill vetoed provided for a land grant to a Baptist church in Mississippi. Madison's veto message stated that he had acted as he did "because the bill . . . comprises a principle and precedent for the appropriation of funds of the United States for the use and support of religious societies, contrary to the article of the Constitution which declares that 'Congress shall make no law respecting a religious establishment.'"[134]

A few years later, Madison cited the vetoed bills as evidence of the "danger of encroachment" upon the "[s]trongly guarded . . . separation between Religion & Govt in the Constitution." "The Constitution of the U.S.," he wrote, "'forbids anything like an establishment of a national religion.'" Now he asserted that the appointment of chaplains to Congress violated this principle because "these are to be paid out of the national taxes. Does not this involve the principle of a national establishment, applicable to a provision for a religious worship . . . conducted by Ministers of religion paid by the entire nation[?]"[135]

Here, it should be noted, Madison took a stricter position than in the Bill of Rights debate. The very Congress that passed the First Amendment voted for congressional chaplains, and Madison voted for the bill involved. Still, as Justice Brennan points out, Madison's later views may have represented his true opinion, as "a detached observer engaged in unpressured reflection." Indeed, says Brennan, "I am not at all sure that Madison's later writings should be any less influential in our deliberations than his earlier vote."[136]

More important, however, than the Rehnquist misuse of history to discover the original intention behind the Establishment Clause is the question of whether, even if he is correct regarding the intent of the framers, the discovery of that intent should be enough to overthrow settled jurisprudence on the matter. The prior analysis has shown, I hope, that Justice Rehnquist's use of history is both inadequate and misleading. Yet even if the judge-turned-historian *had* materialized into another Maitland, that alone would not have justified the course of decision that he advocated.

On a subject such as the Establishment Clause, Rehnquist's *Jaffree* attempt to use history is to ask questions of the past that the past cannot answer.[137] The proponents of the Bill of Rights were men of the eighteenth century, concerned with the problems of their own day—not ours. The intent of Madison and his colleagues can scarcely be a solution to the church-state problems of a society they could not have foreseen.

As Justice Brennan pointed out in an opinion termed by one historian the "closest approach to a sophisticated historical understanding of the problem of church-state relations by any of the Justices in recent years,"[138] our society has been completely transformed over the past two centuries—particularly "our religious composition," which "makes us a vastly more diverse people than were our forefathers."[139] Most of the modern religious-freedom cases turn on issues that did not even exist in 1789.[140] Hence, speaking of the framers, Brennan declares, "I doubt that their view, even if perfectly clear one way or the other, would supply a dispositive answer to the question presented by these cases."[141]

This is all the more true because, by the time of the *Jaffree* case, a whole volume of precedents had been handed down contrary to the Rehnquist position. Even if the Establishment Clause had originally been intended to mean what Justice Rehnquist contended, a prudent judge should still have hesitated to change the meaning acquired by the gloss of half a century. In certain fields of endeavor the palm may go to the boldest innovator, but the bench is hardly one of them. To read the Establishment Clause as Chief Justice Rehnquist has urged is a process that amounts not to interpretation, but to creation, of a constitutional provision.

CONCLUSION

Critics may argue that my effort to demonstrate the fallacies of the original-intention doctrine is akin to battering on an open door, since the doctrine has already been repudiated by most constitutional commentators. The near unanimity of scholarly opinion has not, however, relegated the doctrine to its final deserved repose. Indeed, no matter what the extent of its general repudiation, advocates will continue to urge it, academics will continue to debate it, and more important, judges will continue to invoke it.[142]

Original intention will always have appeal because it appears to furnish the simplicity and certainty that are all too often absent in our constitutional law. But the doctrine is a delusion in the form claimed by its proponents. As *the* key to constitutional construction it is wholly inadequate, both because it is all but impossible, in most cases, to determine with any certainty what the "original intention" of "the

Framers" was, and because even when their intention is clear, it is normally irrelevant to the needs of our society two centuries later.

Those who assert the contrary remind one of the picture of the Supreme Court in a railroad pension case painted some years ago by a leading law professor: "Behold these nine automatons, with minds swept free of every human frailty and every human preference, with no interest in the income of carriers or the well-being of those whose hands are on the throttle and whose eyes are on the track, with no notions of public policy, behold them reading the Constitution with some mechanical instruments of vision and of understanding and finding there between the lines or beneath the words of 1787 and 1789 the answers to the questions of 1935!"[143]

How much more true this assessment is over half a century later! If the history of original-intention jurisprudence has shown anything, it is that the intentions of 1787 and 1789 alone cannot furnish the answers to the questions of 1990. Constitutional interpretation cannot be based on canons of construction developed to construe private instruments such as contracts or wills, where original intention rightly remains the controlling factor.

The mind boggles at the consequences of a contrary view. As we have seen, that could mean a return to an era characterized by Jim Crow, the rack and the pillory, and no paper money. A leading New Right jurist, relying upon original intention, actually asserts that the Supreme Court decision upholding Congressional power to issue paper money "was incorrect."[144] Yet, as Judge Bork himself points out, "[I]f a judge today were to decide that paper money is unconstitutional, we would think he ought to be accompanied not by a law clerk, but by a guardian."[145] Such a decision would take us back to the days when "tons of gold had to be hauled to and fro in drayloads, with horses and heavers doing by the hour what bookkeepers could do in a moment."[146] Despite its delusive simplicity, a jurisprudence that would produce that result should no longer be taken seriously.

35

2

NONENUMERATED RIGHTS AND CONSTITUTIONAL PROTECTION

WHO IS THERE who has not felt a sudden startled pang at reliving an old experience or feeling an old emotion? *'I have done this before. . . .'*[1] A constitutional law commentator all too often has the same sense of déjà vu. The controversy over original intention, most of us believed, had been settled years ago. Yet it has been revived by New Right jurists and placed near the top of their agenda. The same is true of contemporary criticisms of the Supreme Court for not limiting itself to the literal language of the Constitution. More particularly, the Court is faulted for extending constitutional protection to rights not specifically guaranteed in the organic instrument.

One would have thought that the question of literalism had been settled by Marshall's observation that "we must never forget that it is a *constitution* that we are expounding,"[2] an instrument "framed for ages to come, and . . . designed to approach immortality as nearly as human institutions can approach it."[3] Not crabbed pedantry, but the statesmanlike vision of Marshall himself, is what is needed to make constitutional rules more than mere fetters of the past upon the needs of the present. Constitutional construction is bound to be inadequate if it makes a fortress out of the dictionary.[4]

The Marshall aphorism has been accepted as revealed truth by the jurisprudence of almost two centuries. It has been quoted over thirty times by the Supreme Court, and about the same number of times by the other federal courts. But now U.S. Circuit Judge Alex Kozinski, a leading New Right jurist on the bench, has come to tilt a lance against the dictum itself and its consistent use by the judges. Judge Kozinski has said that "had I been there, I would have encouraged [Marshall] to take out that fateful phrase. With the benefit of a century and a half of hindsight, we can see that the phrase has taken on a life of its own and has come to symbolize a theory of constitutional adjudication that Marshall may not have fully envisioned when he wrote it." In practice, says Kozinski, "Almost without exception the phrase is invoked by a judge who wishes to do something that is just not quite found in the Constitution. Sometimes the phrase is used to find new guarantees or rights; other times the phrase is advanced to abridge rights that are already there."[5]

To Kozinski, the Marshall phrase is responsible for the expansive view "that the Constitution must be interpreted in a materially different fashion than other legal instruments, such as statutes, regulations, or contracts." Kozinski flatly rejects this view. To him, only the language of the Constitution is relevant in the decision of cases. "What gives any instrument meaning, be it a constitution, statute, or contract, is not its guiding principles—luminescent or obscure—but its words, words that convey precise and identifiable concepts. . . . The words and concepts of the Constitution ought to be treated the same as words and concepts of other legal instruments, and afforded such specificity or generality as they naturally command." The key principle of constitutional interpretation should be "textual fidelity. Whatever results are reached in a constitutional adjudication must be grounded in the words of the Constitution"[6]—and in them alone.

JUSTICE BLACK AND THE BLACK-LETTER APPROACH

Judge Kozinski's literalist approach to the Constitution is a present-day revival of the view put forth a generation ago by one of the most influential justices ever to sit on the Supreme Court, Hugo L. Black. A famous passage by Holmes has it that the black-letter judge will one day be replaced by the man of statistics and the master of economics.[7] Justice Black was emphatically a judge who still followed the black-letter approach in dealing with the constitutional text. "That Constitution," he said, "is my legal bible. . . . I cherish every word of it from the first to

37

the last."[8] The eminent jurist with his dog-eared copy of the Constitution in his right coat pocket became a part of contemporary folklore. In protecting the sanctity of the organic word, he displayed all the passion of an Old Testament prophet railing against graven idols.

Black would not go beyond the constitutional text in cases involving individual rights. His fundamentalist approach to the Constitution did not permit him to adopt the expansive approach toward individual rights followed by some justices. Black stood his constitutional ground where rights rested on specific provisions, such as the First Amendment or the Fifth Amendment privilege against self-incrimination. But when he could not find an express constitutional base, Black was unwilling to create one to meet a new need. His limited approach would lead him to oppose busing in school desegregation cases. "Where does the word *busing* appear in the Constitution?" Black asked his law clerks while the Court was considering the leading case on school busing orders.[9]

The paradigmatic case illustrating Black's literalist approach to constitutional interpretation is *Griswold v. Connecticut.*[10] The Court there struck down a law that prohibited use of contraceptives and the giving of medical advice in their use. Defendants had given advice to married persons on preventing conception and prescribed contraceptive devices for them. The law was ruled violative of the right to privacy—a right protected by the Bill of Rights even though it is nowhere mentioned in the constitutional text. The opinion of the Court stated "that specific guarantees in the Bill of Rights have penumbras, formed by emanations from those guarantees that help give them life and substance."[11] A constitutional right of privacy is included in these penumbras. As Justice Douglas summarized it in the draft *Griswold* opinion, there is a "regime of privacy which we think the Bill of Rights created."[12]

Justice Black delivered a strong *Griswold* dissent in which he took sharp issue with the majority approach. "The Court," the Black dissent declared, "talks about a constitutional 'right of privacy' as though there is some constitutional provision or provisions forbidding any law ever to be passed which might abridge the 'privacy' of individuals. But there is not."[13] "I like my privacy as well as the next one," Black went on, "but I am nevertheless compelled to admit that government has a right to invade it unless prohibited by some specific constitutional provision"[14] —which was, of course, completely lacking in *Griswold.*

Perhaps the best expression of the Black objection to constitutional protection of rights not specified in the Constitution, such as the right of privacy, is contained in a 1966 memorandum that the justice wrote attacking a draft opinion of the Court,[15] which contained as broad a statement of the right of privacy as any ever made. The Black memo summarized the draft's reliance on the right of privacy as follows: "Describing it as a right 'which the Court derived by implication from the specific guarantees of the Bill of Rights' yet proclaiming that it 'reaches beyond any of its specifics,' the Court holds that this right is so 'basic to a free society' that its invasion can only be 'justified by the clear needs of community living.'"[16]

Black does not "deny that it is an exquisite thing to be let alone when one wants to be." But, he goes on, "[R]egardless of their value, neither the 'right to be let alone' nor 'the right to privacy,' while appealing phrases, were enshrined in our Constitution as was the right to free speech, press and religion."

Black concedes that certain aspects of privacy are protected by the Third, Fourth, and Fifth Amendments. "But," he asserts, "I think it approaches the fantastic for judges to attempt to create from these a general, all-embracing constitutional provision guaranteeing a general right to privacy. And I think it equally fantastic for judges to use these specific constitutional guarantees as an excuse to arrogate to themselves authority to create new and different alleged constitutional rights to be free from governmental control in all areas where judges believe modern conditions call for new constitutional rights. . . . For judges to have such power would amount to authority on their part to override the people's Constitution."

According to Black, what happens when the Court relies upon a right not specifically guaranteed is that "the freedom constitutionally promised, has been transmuted into a debased alloy—transmuted into a freedom which will vacillate and grow weaker or stronger as the Court personnel is shifted from time to time. This means that the scope of . . . freedom is not to be decided by what the Founders wrote, but by what a Court majority thinks they should have written had they been writing now. I prefer to have the people's liberty measured by the constitutional language the Founders wrote rather than by new views of new judges as to what liberty it is safe for the people to have."

For the judges to go beyond the constitutional text in protecting rights, Black writes, means that

> judges are no longer to be limited to their recognized power to make binding *interpretations* of the Constitution. That power, won after bitter constitutional struggles, has apparently become too prosaic and unexciting. So the judiciary now confers upon the judiciary the more "elastic" and exciting power to decide . . . just how much freedom the courts will permit. . . . And in making this decision the Court is to have important leeway, it seems, in order to make the Constitution the people adopted more adaptable to what the Court deems to be modern needs. We, the judiciary, are no longer to be crippled and bobbled by the old admonition that "We must always remember it is a Constitution we are *expounding*," but we are to work under the exhilarating new slogan that "We must always remember that it is a Constitution we are *rewriting* to fit the times."
> I cannot join nor can I even acquiesce in this doctrine which I firmly believe to be a violation of the Constitution itself.

Justice Black notes the attraction of the nonliteral approach. "Though the Constitution requires that judges swear to obey and enforce it, it is not altogether strange that all judges are not always dead set against constitutional interpretations that expand their powers, and that when power is once claimed by some, others are loath to give it up." He also recognizes that "[t]here is . . . a certain surface appeal to the professional concept that the courts should keep our eighteenth century Constitution in tune with the times, adapt it to present-day needs." Yet Black declares that he will have none of that concept: "That doctrine, interpreted out of its legal jargon context, simply means that the best way to amend the Constitution is to let the judges do it. The Founders emphatically did not think so . . . and I am wholly unwilling for judges to change the Founders' handiwork now."

All that has recently been said against judicial protection of rights not specifically guaranteed in the Constitution was said, and said better, in the 1966 Black memo. To Black, only the black-letter approach to the organic text was proper. The alternative, in his view, was to accept "a constitutional theory . . . that this Court is endowed by the Constitution with boundless power under 'natural law' periodically to expand and contract constitutional standards to conform to the court's conception of what at a particular time constitutes 'civilized decency' and 'fundamental liberty and justice.'"[17]

THE JUDGE'S NOTION

A Lincoln anecdote about an Illinois jury has it that the jury foreman asked the judge for help with a question that he had; the judge said that he would be glad to give any help he could. "Well judge," said the foreman, "the jury wanted to know: Was that there you told them the law or just your notion?"[18]

Justice Black's criticism of the decision in a case like *Griswold*, which has been restated in recent years by New Right jurists such as Judge Kozinski, is based precisely upon the claim that the majority justices were applying only their own notions. Black saw *Griswold*[19] as a case in which the Court went beyond the text of the Bill of Rights and arrogated to itself the power to judge what rights should be protected according to the judgment of each individual justice. Is there not in such a subjective approach an element of serious uncertainty, and a temptation to judicial arbitrariness? Declaring himself the servant of the Constitution, the judge becomes, in fact, its creator.

This is the basis of the Black complaint against the protection of rights not specified in the Constitution. It is also the basis of the more recent criticisms of those *Griswold*-type decisions that have elevated rights not mentioned in the Bill of Rights to the constitutional plane. To the recent critics, "[T]he framers' intentions with respect to freedoms are the sole legitimate premise from which constitutional analysis may proceed,"[20] and such intentions may be determined only on the basis of the constitutional text.

The quotation is from a 1984 lecture by Judge Robert H. Bork, perhaps the most eminent critic of the protection of rights not specified in the Constitution. To Bork, such protection of nontextual rights is wholly illegitimate: "[A] judge, no matter on what court he sits, may never create new constitutional rights."[21] Referring specifically to *Griswold*, Bork points out that the opinion there created "an overall right of privacy that applies even where no provision of the Bill of Rights does." Under this approach, Bork asserts, "the Bill of Rights was ex-

41

panded beyond the known intentions of the Framers. Since there is no constitutional text or history to define the right, privacy becomes an unstructured source of judicial power."[22]

What disturbs Bork particularly is that *Griswold* makes for an open-ended Bill of Rights that is given specific content only by the moral values of the individual judge. "Where the Constitution does not embody the moral or ethical choice, the judge has no basis other than his own values upon which to set aside the community judgment embodied in the statute. That, by definition, is an inadequate basis for judicial supremacy."[23]

As Judge Bork sees it, the *Griswold* approach "requires the Court to say, without guidance from the Constitution, which liberties or gratifications may be infringed by majorities and which may not."[24] Since the judge is given no guide other than the constitutional text, which, of course, does not cover a case such as *Griswold*, the question of what nontextual rights should be protected depends completely on the judge's own "notion." "Once we depart from the text of the Constitution," asks Justice Scalia, "just where . . . do we stop?"[25] Or as a much-quoted Bork aphorism has it, "The truth is that the judge who looks outside the historic Constitution always looks inside himself and nowhere else."[26]

Bork points out that protection of a right involves protection of the gratification of those whose right is secured. "When the Constitution has not spoken, the Court will be able to find no scale, other than its own value preferences, upon which to weigh the respective claims to pleasure."[27] Thus, in *Griswold*, Bork says, the anticontraceptive law impaired the married couple's sexual gratification. In a case where an electric utility attacks a smoke-pollution ordinance, the regulation impairs the company's economic gratification. According to Bork, a court cannot properly distinguish between the two types of gratification: "There is no principled way to decide that one man's gratifications are more deserving of respect than another's or that one form of gratification is more worthy than another."[28]

"Why," Bork asks, "is sexual gratification nobler than economic gratification? There is no way of deciding these matters other than by reference to some system of moral or ethical values that has no objective or intrinsic validity of its own and about which men can and do differ."[29]

To Bork, then, there is only a relative difference—no real or objective moral difference—between various acts of gratification.[30] Sexual gratification and other gratifications rest on the same moral plane and there is no principled basis upon which the judge can decide which gratification is entitled to constitutional protection. Value choice is improper when there is no textual foundation and only a relativity between the values involved.

RELATIVISM AND NATURAL LAW

A striking feature of this aspect of the Bork critique is its reliance on the relativism that conservative jurists usually decry. In this century, it cannot be denied that the law has succumbed to the relativism that has come to dominate the physical and social sciences. The law, too, has not proved able to withstand either the facts or the intellectual currents of twentieth-century history. Einsteinian relativist physics, with its challenge of what had been supposed the fixed order of the universe, and Freudian psychology, with its challenge of the fixed order of the mind, have combined with Marxian determinism to undermine the assumptions on which the legal order had been based.[31] Time, distance, and mind lost their absolute values; reality appeared more complex and less stable than had been imagined.[32]

In one of his novels, Kurt Vonnegut tells of education at an American university after World War II: "At that time they were teaching that there was absolutely no difference between anybody. . . . Another thing they taught was that nobody was ridiculous or bad or disgusting."[33] Relativism has become the basic philosophy of a much-divided civilization. "It keeps drumming into our hearts," says Alexander Solzhenitsyn in his Nobel Lecture, "that there are no stable and universal concepts of justice . . . that all of them are fluid." The absolutes of an earlier day appear increasingly out of place in the century of Einstein and Freud.

All of this has had its influence upon juristic thinking. All too often the legal universe, like the physical one, seems to have no center. In law also, everything is seen to be relative: "Nothing is more certain in modern society," declared the Supreme Court at mid-century, "than the principle that there are no absolutes."[34] The world of law, like that of physics, is perceived only as the relativity of one value compared with another.

43

What is surprising, however, is that conservative jurists such as Bork should submit to the century's preoccupation with relativism. To the conservative jurists who drafted our first constitutions and bills of rights, it was self-evident that there were absolute values that government had the duty to further. These values were embodied in the doctrine of natural rights, which was dominant at the time of the founding of the Republic.

The early American judges appealed to natural rights and the social compact in order to limit governmental power, even aside from any express constitutional restrictions. In this sense, the different constitutions were treated as declaratory of natural law, and hence as embodiments of universal precepts to be found at the root of all constitutions.[35] "Though there may be no prohibition in the constitution, the legislature is restrained from committing flagrant acts, from acts subverting the great principles of republican liberty, and of the social compact."[36] The very "nature of society and of government"[37] prescribed essential limits upon legislative power. Those limits, said one court a century and a half ago, rested "upon the broader and more solid ground of natural rights, and [were] not wholly dependent upon these negatives . . . contained in the constitution."[38]

If the shapers of our law in its formative era believed in anything, it was the concept of natural rights that do not depend upon the "negatives contained in the constitution." From this point of view, Justice Black's characterization of the *Griswold* protection of nontextual rights as a natural-law notion is acute. But it is not enough to dismiss *Griswold* as a revival of natural law, for natural law itself has been an essential element of American constitutionalism. As Roscoe Pound writes, it was "natural law which became embodied for us in the Declaration of Independence and is behind our bills of rights."[39]

Indeed, if one belief united the men of 1787 it was that a "higher law" protecting "natural rights" took precedence over positive law. The whole notion of constitutionalism was based on the need to reduce natural rights to written form.[40] "To deduce our rights from the principles of equity, justice and the Constitution, is very well," wrote that important though little-known framer of the Pennsylvania constitution, James Cannon, in 1776, "but equity and justice are no defence against power."

What was needed was to fix the rights of the people in specific fundamental laws. Individual rights, declared Cannon, must be protected and defended "as the apple of your eye"; they must be fixed "on a foundation never more to be shaken"—that is, they must be specified in written documents.[41]

At the same time, the framers recognized that written constitutions could not completely codify the higher law. In the framing of the first constitutions it was widely accepted that there remained unwritten but still binding principles of higher law.[42] In particular, the rights of the people were not limited to those specified in the different bills of rights. Instead, as stated by Justice Chase soon after the founding of the Republic, "I cannot subscribe to the omnipotence of a . . . Legislature, or that it is absolute and without control; although its authority should not be expressly restrained by the constitution." Governmental acts "contrary to the great first principles of the social compact" are invalid even "if they had not been expressly restrained"[43] from violating the rights concerned.

The concept of rights based on "higher law," even though not provided for in the constitutional text, was crucial to the men who wrote and applied our first constitutions. The prevailing view was stated by Chancellor James Kent in an 1811 opinion protecting a nontextual right: "It is not pretended that we have any express constitutional provisions on the subject; nor have we any for numerous other rights dear alike to freedom and justice."[44]

THE FORGOTTEN NINTH AMENDMENT?

It was the intent of the framers to protect rights not specified in the constitutional text that led to the Ninth Amendment. Largely ignored through most of our history, that amendment used to be called the "Forgotten Ninth Amendment."[45] During the past quarter century, however, the amendment has emerged as a textual source for the protection of rights not specifically enumerated in the Constitution.

The Ninth Amendment reads, "The enumeration in the Constitution, of certain rights, shall not be construed to deny or disparage others retained by the people." This seems to confirm that there are individual rights not specified in the constitutional text. Otherwise, why confirm the existence of rights retained by the people even though they are not enumerated in the Constitution?

The concept of individual rights derived not from an organic text, but "vested . . . by the immutable laws of nature,"[46] was widely accepted by the generation that adopted the first constitutions and bills of rights. It had, indeed, been fundamental in the struggle to secure the rights of the colonists that led to the Revolution. The 1768 circular letter sent by the Massachusetts House of Representatives to the colonial legislatures declared that the right to "what a man has honestly acquired" is "an essential unalterable Right in nature." Therefore, "the American Subjects may . . . exclusive of any Consideration of Charter Rights . . . assert this natural and constitutional Right."[47] And the Rights of the Colonists issued by Boston in 1772 listed first the "Natural Rights of the Colonists as Men" and asserted, "Every natural Right not expressly given up or from the nature of a Social Compact necessarily ceded remains."[48]

The history of the federal Bill of Rights supports the concept of nontextual rights that was to be confirmed in the Ninth Amendment. The federal Constitution itself does not, of course, contain any bill of rights, though it does contain some provisions that do protect specific individual rights.[49] Toward the end of the framers' convention, on September 12, 1787, George Mason (author of the Virginia Declaration of Rights) urged that a bill of rights be added to the Constitution, but a motion to that effect was defeated unanimously.[50]

It is difficult to say with any certainty why the Mason proposal for a bill of rights was summarily rejected. That it was made so close to the end of the convention (which finally adjourned on September 17) must have influenced the delegates' almost cavalier rejection. Having sweltered for months over the difficult issues involved in the new Constitution during Philadelphia's hottest summer within memory, they naturally resented the attempt to bring up an important new subject when they were almost at the end of their endeavors. Only one delegate, Roger Sherman, spoke on the merits of the matter. He stated the view that was later to be expressed to justify the omission of a bill of rights: that a federal bill of rights was unnecessary. "The State Declarations of Rights are not repealed by this Constitution; and being in force are sufficient"[51] to protect the rights of their citizens. The new federal government was not given any power to infringe upon the rights thus protected.

Sherman made the same point in reply to a motion on September 14 for a declaration "that the liberty of the Press should be inviolably observed." The motion was defeated after Sherman repeated the argument that the guaranty was unnecessary, since the "power of Congress does not extend to the Press."[52]

As recently summarized in a history of the constitutional convention, Sherman's argument was essentially this: "If a list of rights was enumerated . . . , it might appear that the framers positively meant to exclude some rights that they had just inadvertently overlooked (or they might be forced by a few states to exclude something most states already had and cherished)." The basic proposition on which the Sherman view rested was "All powers not specifically granted to the government were, in any case, reserved to the people." Because of this, a "bill of rights was not necessary," since "the basic rights" possessed by the people "were so deeply ingrained in America."[53]

The Sherman position was based on the premise that there were rights retained by the people even if these rights were excluded (inadvertently or intentionally) from specific constitutional protection. This was the position taken in Hamilton's famous answer in *The Federalist* to the demand for a bill of rights. Hamilton's argument was that a bill of rights was unnecessary because no power was delegated to infringe upon the rights possessed by the people: "Here, in strictness, the people surrender nothing, and as they retain everything, they have no need of particular reservations."[54] The underlying assumption is that the people retain all the fundamental rights that they possessed before the Constitution, except where powers to infringe upon them were delegated by the new organic document.

As is well known, *The Federalist*'s argument that a bill of rights was unnecessary was rejected by the people. Indeed, the Constitution's lack in this respect was a serious obstacle to ratification by the states. In 1788, five of the state ratifying conventions recommended proposed amendments that would add a bill of rights to the Constitution.[55] And it was only because the federalists themselves gave assurances that amendments would be proposed that the Constitution was adopted. As Jefferson stated in a letter in March 1789, "[T]he most important of these amendments will be effected by adding a bill of rights; and even the friends of the Constitution are become sensible of the expediency of such an addition were it only to conciliate the opposition."[56]

There are clear indications that Jefferson agreed that the people possessed rights that might not be included in a bill of rights. In a letter to Madison he answered the objections that had been raised to such a bill. Among them, he wrote was that "[a] positive declaration of some essential rights could not be obtained in the requisite latitude." To this Jefferson responded, "Answer. Half a loaf is better than no bread. If we cannot secure all our rights, let us secure what we can."[57]

How could those rights not included in the Bill of Rights be secured? During the debates on ratification of the Constitution, the idea developed of an amendment that would provide that the Bill of Rights limitations gave Congress no power to infringe upon other rights. The idea first achieved legislative status in the amendments proposed by the Virginia Ratifying Convention on June 27, 1788. The seventeenth Virginia-proposed amendment read, "That those clauses which declare that Congress shall not exercise certain powers, be not interpreted, in any manner whatsoever, to extend the powers of Congress; but that they be construed either as making exceptions to the specified powers where this shall be the case, or otherwise, as inserted merely for greater caution."[58] Similar amendments were proposed by the two remaining ratifying conventions—those in New York and North Carolina.[59]

In his draft of what became the Ninth Amendment Madison changed the language of the proposed amendment so that the focus became not the powers of Congress, but the rights retained by the people. The Madison draft provided, "The exception here or elsewhere in the Constitution, made in favor of particular rights, shall not be so construed as to diminish the just importance of other rights retained by the people, or as to enlarge the powers delegated by the Constitution; but either as actual limitations of such powers, or as inserted merely for greater caution."[60] The House Select Committee changed the language of Madison's amendment to its present formulation as the Ninth Amendment.[61]

Madison himself had been concerned with the problem of how to protect unenumerated rights. During the Virginia Ratifying Convention George Wythe had favored amendments guaranteeing freedom of the press and religion and trial by jury. "With respect to the proposition of

the honorable gentleman to my left, (Mr. Wythe,)," Madison said, "gentlemen apprehend that, by enumerating three rights, it implied there
were no more." The issue of unspecified rights was connected with that
of reserved powers: "[E]very power not granted thereby remains with the
people, and at their will." In addition, "no right, of any denomination,
can be cancelled, abridged, restrained, or modified, by the general
government, or any of its officers, except in those instances in which
power is given by the Constitution for these purposes." To Madison,
"There cannot be a more positive and unequivocal declaration of the
principle of the adoption—that every thing not granted is reserved."[62]

Madison next went back to the subject of unenumerated rights, asking, "If an enumeration be made of our rights, will it not be implied that
every thing omitted is given to the general government? Has not the
honorable gentleman himself admitted that an imperfect enumeration is
dangerous?" He then questioned whether the new government could
exercise powers not granted to it: "Does the Constitution say that they
shall not alter the law of descents, or do those things which would
subvert the whole system of the state laws?"[63]

Madison denied that "what was not excepted would be granted." He
asked, "Does it follow, from the omission of such restrictions, that they
can exercise powers not delegated? The reverse of the proposition holds.
The delegation alone warrants the exercise of any power."[64]

Madison's remarks to the Virginia Ratifying Convention support the
view that, to him, the Ninth and Tenth Amendments were complemen-
tary: the first deals with the *rights* retained by the people, the second
with reserved *powers* that had not been delegated to the new government.[65] The relation between the two was pointed out in a Madison letter
to Washington: "If a line can be drawn between the powers granted and
the rights retained, it would seem to be the same thing, whether the
latter be secured, by declaring that they shall not be abridged, or that
the former shall not be extended."[66]

In presenting his proposed amendments to the House, Madison explained his draft of the Ninth Amendment in terms that answered the
questions regarding unenumerated rights that he had raised at the Virginia convention. He noted the objection he had stated at that convention
"against a bill of rights, that, by enumerating particular exceptions to the
grant of power . . . would disparage those rights which were not placed

in that enumeration; and it might follow, by implication, that those rights which were not singled out, were intended to be assigned into the hands of the General Government, and were consequently insecure." Madison conceded, "This is one of the most plausible arguments I have ever heard urged against the admission of a bill of rights into this system; but, I conceive, that it may be guarded against. I have attempted it, as gentlemen may see by turning to the last clause of the fourth resolution"[67]—the provision in Madison's draft that became the Ninth Amendment.

According to Chief Justice Burger, "Madison's comments in Congress also reveal the perceived need for some sort of constitutional 'saving clause,' which, among other things, would serve to foreclose application to the Bill of Rights of the maxim that the affirmation of particular rights implies a negation of those not expressly defined." The Ninth Amendment thus "served to allay the fears of those who were concerned that expressing certain guarantees could be read as excluding others."[68]

The Virginia-proposed amendment had focused on the powers of Congress; it would have provided for strict construction of congressional authority. Madison shifted the focus to the rights retained by the people. In line with his statement in the Bill of Rights debate, his draft was an attempt to guard against the argument "that those rights which were not singled out, were intended to be assigned into the hands of the General Government." Madison's declaration of the doctrine of nontextual rights was stated, not as a limitation of powers, but as an affirmation of the independent foundation of individual rights.[69]

While the Bill of Rights was before the Virginia legislature, opponents of the Ninth Amendment claimed that the Virginia-proposed amendment had been superior to the version passed by Congress. They argued that "it would be more safe, & more consistent with the spirit of the 1st. & 17th. amendments proposed by Virginia, that this reservation against constructive power, should operate rather as a provision against extending the powers of Congress by their own authority, than as a protection to rights reducable to no definitive certainty."[70] The Madison version and the Ninth Amendment itself, however, appear superior to the Virginia proposal, so far as protecting nonenumerated rights is concerned. Under both the Madison draft and the amendment, the existence of nontextual rights is confirmed. Hence, since the rights of Americans are not created

50

by government, they exist as retained rights, unless they are diminished by the appropriate exercise of an express power:[71] "[And] so by protecting the rights of the people & of the States, an improper extension of power will be prevented & safety made equally certain."[72]

RETAINED RIGHTS: PROPERTY TO MARRIAGE

Both the history and the language of the Ninth Amendment indicate that there are individual rights requiring protection even though they are not enumerated in the Constitution or Bill of Rights. Otherwise, why specify that the enumeration of rights does not "by implication, [mean] that those rights which were not singled out, were intended to be assigned into the hands of the General Government"?[73]

The difficulty, as Hardin Burnley wrote in a letter to Madison, is that "there was no criterion by which it could be determined whither any other particular right was retained or not." Though "the rights declared in the first ten of the proposed amendments were not all that a free people would require the exercise of,"[74] what other rights are retained by the people under the Ninth Amendment?

The men who wrote the Constitution and the Bill of Rights would have answered this question according to the natural rights philosophy of the day. Above all, they would have emphasized the right of property as one that depended more on the nature of man than specific constitutional guaranty. The emphasis in their scale of values was clearly placed upon what Justice Joseph Story, in his Harvard inaugural address, called "the sacred rights of property. . . . I call them sacred because, if they are unprotected, all other rights become worthless or visionary."[75] The members of the framers' convention had repeatedly declared that "property was the primary object of Society."[76]

Thus, to those who established the Republic, "the right of acquiring and possessing property and having it protected, is one of the natural inherent and unalienable rights of man."[77] A legislative act "to take away that security for . . . private property, for the protection whereof the government was established" would be "contrary to the first great principles of the social compact,"[78] whether or not it was prohibited by the Constitution.

In a 1798 case, Justice Samuel Chase declared, "An act of the Legis-

51

lature (for I cannot call it a law) contrary to the great first principles of the social compact, cannot be considered a rightful exercise of legislative authority." He then gave "[a] few instances . . . to explain what I mean." Among them were "a law that destroys, or impairs, the lawful private contracts of citizens, a law that makes a man a judge in his own cause; or a law that takes property from A. and gives to B."[79]

According to Chase, "It is against all reason and justice, for a people to entrust a Legislature with such powers; and, therefore, it cannot be presumed that they have done it. The genius, the nature, and the spirit of our state governments, amount to a prohibition of such acts of legislation; and the general principles of law and reason forbid them." This was true, Chase maintained, even apart from the specific guarantees for individual rights. "To maintain that our federal, or state, Legislature possesses such powers, if they had not been expressly restrained, would, in my opinion, be a political heresy, altogether inadmissible in our free republican governments."[80]

Three quarters of a century later, the same approach was followed in *Loan Association v. Topeka*,[81] where the Court laid down the rule that a tax was not lawful if "not laid for a *public* purpose"[82] and that use of a city's taxing power to make a grant to a company so that it would locate its factory in the city was not a valid public purpose. There was, of course, no constitutional provision limiting the taxing power as stated in the *Loan Association* rule. But the opinion of the Court by Justice Samuel F. Miller found that that was not dispositive. Instead, he asserted, "[t]here are limitations on such power which grow out of the essential nature of all free governments. Implied reservations of individual rights, without which the social compact could not exist, and which are respected by all governments entitled to the name."[83]

That the case turned upon the question of whether the Court could, indeed, invalidate the tax, even though it did not violate a specific guaranty against such a tax, is shown by the dissenting opinion of Justice Nathan Clifford. He argued that "save where those rights are secured by some constitutional provision," the courts might not invalidate a law, "whether the law operates according to natural justice or not in any particular case." Arguing directly against the Miller reasoning, Clifford declared, "Courts cannot nullify an Act of the State Legislature on the vague ground that they think it opposed to a general latent spirit supposed to pervade or underlie the Constitution, where neither the terms nor the implications of the instrument disclose any such restriction."[84]

Justice Miller, like Justice Chase before him, gave examples of legislative acts that would be ruled invalid because they would violate the "[i]mplied reservations of individual rights, without which the social compact could not exist."[85] Thus, according to the Miller opinion, "No court, for instance, would hesitate to declare void a statute which enacted that A and B who were husband and wife to each should be so no longer, but that A should thereafter be the husband of C, and B the wife of D. Or which should enact that the homestead now owned by A should no longer be his, but should henceforth be the property of B."[86]

Comparison of the Miller examples with those stated by Chase supports the view of Dean Pound that, as far as the nontextual rights retained by the people are concerned, "they are not, says the Ninth Amendment, a fixed category of definitely formulated precisely defined expectations of individuals, fixed finally for all times, places and men in the texts of the Bill of Rights."[87] Instead, the rights retained under the Ninth Amendment reflect the values deemed worthy of protection during the different periods of the nation's development.

Each generation has its own scale of values, necessarily reflected in the ends that the legal order seeks to further. In Justice Chase's time the dominant value was the right of property, which, said John Adams, "is . . . as sacred as the laws of God."[88] By the time Justice Miller delivered his opinion, there were signs that the emphasis might shift from property to personal rights.[89] At any rate, the Miller illustrations of retained rights included not only the right of the owner to his land, but also that of the husband and wife in the marital relationship.

There is, of course, no constitutional provision specifically protecting marital rights. Yet few will disagree that there are such rights and that they are beyond the reach of government. Almost half a century ago, the Court spoke of "the private realm of family life which the state cannot enter."[90] Even earlier the Court had stressed the right of parents over the upbringing of their children, striking down laws telling parents what language their children shall learn to speak and what kinds of schools their children shall attend.[91] The cases involving these invalidations were *Meyer v. Nebraska*[92] and *Pierce v. Society of Sisters*,[93] where laws prohibiting teaching of foreign languages in schools and requiring parents to send their children to public, rather than religious, schools were at issue.

Justice Black, who, as shown, completely rejected the concept of nontextual rights, was fully aware of the implications of *Meyer* and *Pierce* and always opposed reliance upon them, or even their citation, by the Court. A striking example occurred in *Bolling v. Sharpe*,[94] the companion case to *Brown v. Board of Education*,[95] where school segregation in Washington, D.C., was challenged. The draft opinion prepared by Chief Justice Earl Warren in *Bolling* asserted the view that racial discrimination might be considered so arbitrary as to constitute a constitutional violation. In support, the draft referred to "analogous situations in the field of education" where the Court "has applied similar reasoning." There was a deprivation "of the liberty protected by the Due Process Clause when the children are prohibited from pursuing certain courses, or from attending private schools or foreign-language schools. Such prohibitions were found to be unreasonable, and unrelated to any legitimate governmental objective. Just as a government may not impose arbitrary restrictions on the parent's right to educate his child, the government must not impose arbitrary restraints on access to the education which government itself provides." The draft then declared, "We have no hesitation in concluding that segregation of children in the public schools is a far greater restriction on their liberty than were the restrictions in the school cases discussed above."[96]

To Justice Black, the problem was that the draft cited both *Meyer* and *Pierce*, which had become anathema to him. Black persuaded Chief Justice Warren to drop the reliance on *Meyer* and *Pierce* and the draft quotes in the last paragraph do not appear in the final *Bolling* opinion. Justice William O. Douglas later stated in an interview, "I think that Black said something to Warren about those cites."[97] To Black, "the reasoning stated in Meyer and Pierce was the same natural law due process philosophy which many later opinions repudiated, and which I cannot accept."[98]

Interestingly, Justice Black did not object to a *Meyer* citation in *Loving v. Virginia*,[99] the case that finally struck down miscegenation laws. According to Benno Schmidt, the Warren law clerk who drafted the opinion, when the chief justice read over the *Loving* draft, he saw that *Meyer* was cited to show that there were fundamental freedoms connected with the family that the states could not restrict. Warren chuckled and said that *Meyer* had been singled out by Justice Black as an example of the old Court acting without any basis in the constitutional text. Citing *Meyer*, said the chief justice, would be like waving a red flag in front of Black. Despite this, he left the *Meyer* citation in, and Black let it pass.[100]

Black's hackles were, however, raised by something else Warren put into the *Loving* opinion. The chief justice wanted the draft to stress that the statute was dealing with a major aspect of the individual's life, that of whom to marry. As Schmidt recalls it, "Justice Black blew up because we were referring to the right to marry, which is nowhere mentioned in the Constitution. . . . So he sent back a statement indicating that he didn't want any sort of natural law notion creeping into the opinion." Warren toned down the right-to-marry language, and Black withdrew his objection.[101] Even so, the *Loving* opinion did refer to marriage as a "fundamental freedom"—"one of the 'basic civil rights of man,' fundamental to our very existence and survival."[102]

GRISWOLD AND PRIVACY

Evaluated from his point of view, Justice Black's objections to *Meyer* and the *Loving* "right to marry" were acute, for *Meyer* and the *Loving* right have served as the foundation for the right of privacy that is the most important nontextual right in contemporary Supreme Court jurisprudence. The right of privacy was elevated to the constitutional plane in *Griswold v. Connecticut.*[103] As mentioned earlier, *Griswold* struck down a law that prohibited use of contraceptives; as Justice Douglas summarized it in the draft *Griswold* opinion, there is a "regime of privacy which we think the Bill of Rights created."[104]

There is no doubt that the right of marital privacy protected by *Griswold* "is not mentioned in explicit terms"[105] in the Bill of Rights. This was, of course, the problem for the Court in deciding the case. The conference on the case found a seven-to-two majority in favor of striking down the contraceptive law. But the majority justices did not articulate a clear theory on which to base the decision. Chief Justice Warren said that he preferred the idea that the act was not narrowly enough written. As he put it, "This is the most confidential relationship in our society. It has to be clear-cut and it isn't." The other majority justices stated different approaches. Justice Tom C. Clark declared, "There's a right to marry, maintain a home, have a family. This is in an area where we have the right to be let alone." Justice Arthur J. Goldberg said, "The state cannot regulate this relationship. There's no compelling state reason in that circumstance justifying the statute."[106]

At the conference, Justice Douglas stated the simplest rationale on which the law could be invalidated, saying that it violated the defendants' First Amendment right of association. The right of association, according to Douglas, is more than a right of assembly. Thus, he reasoned, the right to send a child to a religious school is "on the periphery" of the right of association. As an instance of this peripheral relationship, Douglas cited the *Pierce* case. He used the analogy of the right to travel, which the Court had said "is in radiation of First Amendment and so is this right." There is nothing more personal than this right and it too is "on the periphery" and within First Amendment protection.[107]

The *Griswold* opinion was assigned to Douglas. His draft opinion of the Court followed the approach the justice had urged at the conference. The draft based the decision that the birth control law was unconstitutional on the First Amendment, likening the husband-wife relationship to the other forms of association given First Amendment protection.

It must be conceded that the Douglas draft of the *Griswold* opinion is not legally convincing. At the *Griswold* conference, Justice Black had referred sarcastically to the claim that the challenged Connecticut law violated the defendants' First Amendment right of association. According to the conference notes of one justice, Black stated, "Right of association is for me right of assembly & rt of husband & wife to assemble in bed is new right of assembly to me."[108]

Douglas had shown a copy of his draft opinion to Justice Brennan and asked for suggestions. Brennan sent Douglas a letter urging him to abandon his First Amendment approach. Brennan wrote that association under the First Amendment was not meant to protect grouping or coming together as such, but only to protect such activities that are essential to fruitful advocacy. In Brennan's view, the "association" of married couples had nothing to do with the advocacy protected by the First Amendment.

To save as much of the Douglas draft as possible, Brennan suggested in his letter that the expansion of the First Amendment to include freedom of association be used as an analogy to justify a similar approach in the area of privacy. Privacy itself, Brennan argued, could be brought within the zone of constitutional protection by the approach stated in his concurrence in a case decided just before *Griswold*. Brennan there had stated that "the protection of the Bill of Rights goes beyond the specific guarantees to protect from congressional abridgement those equally fundamental personal rights necessary to make the express guarantees fully meaningful."[109]

Douglas adopted Brennan's suggested approach in his *Griswold* opinion, which stated that "specific guarantees in the Bill of Rights have penumbras, formed by emanations from those guarantees that help give them life and substance."[110] A constitutional right of privacy was included in these penumbras. The right of marital privacy—"older than the Bill of Rights—older than our political parties, older than our school system"[111]—was violated by the Connecticut law.[112]

Why was the right of privacy included in the penumbras emanating from the Bill of Rights guarantees? According to the concurring opinion of Justice Goldberg,[113] the right of privacy is protected ultimately by the Ninth Amendment (which had also been quoted, though not discussed, in the Douglas opinion).[114]

The Goldberg concurrence asserted that, regardless of the paucity of cases relying upon the Ninth Amendment, it is plainly "a basic part of the Constitution"[115] and should be given effect as such.[116] To refuse to recognize a right of marital privacy, Goldberg declared, would be to disregard the amendment: "To hold that a right so basic and fundamental and so deep-rooted in our society as the right of privacy in marriage may be infringed because that right is not guaranteed in so many words by the first eight amendments to the Constitution is to ignore the Ninth Amendment and to give it no effect whatsoever."[117]

Nor is the fact that the right of privacy is not enumerated dispositive. Indeed, says Justice Goldberg, a "judicial construction that this fundamental right is not protected by the Constitution because it is not mentioned in explicit terms by one of the first eight amendments or elsewhere in the Constitution would violate the Ninth Amendment."[118] That is true because "the Ninth Amendment shows a belief of the Constitution's authors that fundamental rights exist that are not expressly enumerated in the first eight amendments and an intent that the list of rights included there not be deemed exhaustive."[119]

Thus, as the Goldberg concurrence sees it, "The Ninth Amendment simply shows the intent of the Constitution's authors that other fundamental personal rights should not be denied such protection or disparaged in any way simply because they are not specifically listed in the first eight constitutional amendments."[120] The amendment shows that there are basic rights not specifically mentioned in the Bill of Rights that are nevertheless protected from governmental infringement. "In sum," Justice Goldberg concludes, "I believe that the right of privacy in the marital relation is fundamental and basic—a personal right 'retained by the people' within the meaning of the Ninth Amendment."[121]

PRIVACY AND AUTONOMY

Griswold is the particular object of attacks by New Right jurists because it rules that "as the Ninth Amendment expressly recognizes[,] there are fundamental personal rights . . . which are protected from abridgement by the Government though not specifically mentioned in the Constitution."[122] More particularly, *Griswold* holds that the right to marital privacy is safeguarded by the Constitution.

But the *Griswold*-created right is broader than a right to *marital* privacy alone. It has since been interpreted as a constitutionally protected zone of privacy not limited to the marital privacy at issue in *Griswold* itself. By 1977 the Court could state, "*Griswold* may no longer be read as holding only that a State may not prohibit a married couple's use of contraceptives."[123] Instead, "If the right of privacy means anything, it is the right of the *individual*, married or single, to be free from unwarranted governmental intrusion into matters so fundamentally affecting a person."[124]

Perhaps the broadest statement of the constitutional right to privacy is contained in an unissued draft opinion of the Court by Justice Abe Fortas. According to the Fortas draft, "There is . . . no doubt that a fundamental right of privacy exists, and that it is of constitutional stature." Nor is the right limited to those of its aspects with a history of protection by the courts.

"It is not just the right of a remedy against false accusation, provided, within limits, by the law of defamation; it is not only the right to be secure in one's person, house, papers and effects, except as permitted by law; it embraces the right to be free from coercion, however subtle, to incriminate oneself; it is different from, but akin to the right to select and freely to practice one's religion and the right to freedom of speech; it is more than the specific right to be secure against the Peeping Tom or the intrusion of electronic espionage devices and wiretapping. All of these are aspects of the right to privacy; but the right of privacy reaches beyond any of its specifics. It is, simply stated, the right to be let alone; to live one's life as one chooses, free from assault, intrusion or invasion except as they can be justified by the clear needs of community living under a government of law."[125]

Thus stated, the right of privacy becomes a virtual right of personal autonomy, one that protects individual independence in making decisions affecting personal life. Freedom of personal choice in matters of family life is thus now treated by the Court as one of the liberties protected by the Constitution.[126] Among the decisions that an individual may make without unjustified governmental interference are personal decisions relating to marriage, procreation, contraception, family relationships, and child rearing.[127]

Perhaps the most controversial application of the *Griswold*-created right was in *Roe v. Wade*,[128] where the Court decided that a state law proscribing most abortions was violative of the right of privacy. That right was held to include the right to terminate pregnancies. The right of privacy was ruled broad enough to encompass the abortion decision.

Justice Douglas issued a *Roe v. Wade* concurrence that stressed the role of the Ninth Amendment as a source of the right protected by the *Roe* decision. As Douglas saw it, this right is one of personal autonomy that "includes customary, traditional, and time-honored rights, amenities, privileges, and immunities that come within the sweep of 'the Blessings of Liberty' mentioned in the preamble to the Constitution." The Douglas concurrence then listed three groups of rights that "come within the meaning of the term 'liberty' as used in the Fourteenth Amendment."[129] The Douglas list was based upon a suggestion contained in a December 30, 1971, letter sent to him by Justice Brennan after the latter had read the Douglas draft concurrence. The letter consisted of a ten-page analysis of the draft and suggestions for improvements. The Douglas draft had found the abortion law violative of the right of privacy. Brennan suggested a broader approach to the privacy concept.

The Brennan letter noted his agreement

> that the right [of privacy] is a species of 'liberty' (although, as I mentioned yesterday, I think the Ninth Amendment . . . should be brought into this problem at greater length), but I would identify three groups of fundamental freedoms that, 'liberty' encompasses: *first*, freedom from bodily restraint or inspection, freedom to do with one's body as one likes, and freedom to care for one's health and person; *second*, freedom of choice in the basic decisions of life, such as marriage, divorce, procreation, contraception, and the education and upbringing of children; and, *third*, autonomous control over the development and expression of one's intellect and personality."[130]

The Brennan list, as adopted by Justice Douglas in his concurring opinion,[131] is the most comprehensive judicial statement of what is included in the right of personal autonomy protected, under *Griswold* and its progeny, by the Constitution. To be sure, none of the liberties in the Brennan-Douglas list is mentioned in the Constitution. Yet all involve freedoms that most Americans rightly believe are protected against governmental intrusion.

The right of personal autonomy comes down to what was stated in classic language by Justice Brandeis: "The makers of our Constitution conferred, as against the Government, the right to be let alone—the most comprehensive of rights and the right most valued by civilized men. To protect that right, every unjustifiable intrusion by the Government upon the privacy of the individual, whatever the means employed, must be deemed a violation of the [Constitution]."[132]

If the individual is not to be overwhelmed by the state, equipped as it is with all the resources of modern science and technology, he or she must be permitted to retain the essential attributes of individuality—that intrinsic element of life that distinguishes not only our species from all others, but all of us within the human community from each other.[133] Above all, in a society where science offers governments a continually refined set of tools for intrusion and surveillance, it is essential that there remain an area of apartness in which the individual may live as

Walt Whitman's "simple separate person"—one that is immune from intervention by the community itself. When man stands in constant danger of being overwhelmed by the machine, he can retain his individuality only if there is preserved for him "a privacy, an obscure nook"[134]— "a liberty of choice as to his manner of life, and neither an individual nor the public has a right to arbitrarily take away from him this liberty."[135]

Even though they are not specifically mentioned in the Constitution, few people would deny that the aspects of autonomy in the Brennan-Douglas list are entitled to constitutional protection. For example, there is what Justice Douglas calls the "freedom from bodily restraint or compulsion, freedom to walk, stroll, or loaf."[136] During a Court conference on a case involving freedom of religion,[137] Douglas stated, "I think we're entitled to our religious scruples, but I don't see how we can make everyone else attune to them. I can't be required to goose-step because eighty or ninety percent goose-step."[138]

More recently, Justice John P. Stevens (at the time a circuit judge) gave the example of "a case in which the sovereign insists that every citizen must wear a brown shirt to demonstrate his patriotism."[139] Would any American judge, no matter how opposed in theory to unenumerated rights, uphold a law requiring people to goose-step or wear a brown shirt?

A comparable illustration is given in Justice Goldberg's *Griswold* concurrence. "Surely," Goldberg writes, "the Government, absent a showing of a compelling subordinating state interest, could not decree that all husbands and wives must be sterilized after two children have been born to them."[140] Would even opponents of nontextual rights say that such a law "would not be subject to constitutional challenge because . . . no provision of the Constitution specifically prevents the Government from curtailing the marital right to bear children and raise a family?"[141] Clearly, as Justice Goldberg puts it, Americans would find it "shocking to believe that the personal liberty guaranteed by the Constitution does not include protection against such totalitarian limitation of family size, which is at complete variance with our constitutional concepts."[142]

The Douglas goose-step illustration bears some explication. The justice was clearly correct in doubting the validity of a law requiring people to walk a certain way. The same would not necessarily be true, however, of a law that governed marching by those in the military or in some other uniformed service. This is borne out by *Kelley v. Johnson*,[143] which upheld a regulation limiting the length of a policeman's hair. The lower courts had invalidated the regulation. At the postargument conference, Chief Justice Warren E. Burger said that they were "dead wrong." The majority, which supported the Burger view, stressed that the plaintiff here was a police officer. As Justice Potter Stewart saw it, the "uniform includes hair dress." Hence, there was "no personal liberty interest if [you] join the police department."

The other majority justices took the same approach. As it was summed up by Justice Rehnquist, who wrote the opinion of the Court, "I'd like to see it said that, whatever liberty interest a civilian may have, it's lesser here and [there is a] legitimate [state] interest here."

This was the core of Rehnquist's reasoning. Though his opinion was not entirely clear—leaving open the question of "whether the citizenry at large has some sort of 'liberty' interest within the Fourteenth Amendment in matters of personal appearance"[144]—it may be assumed that the decision was limited to the police officer, who had (in Rehnquist's conference phrase) a "lesser liberty interest" than an ordinary civilian. This point was the basis for Justice Lewis F. Powell's concurrence, which indicated expressly that what might be a "reasonable regulation to a uniformed police force . . . would be an impermissible intrusion upon liberty in a different context."[145]

Even with regard to the police officer, as Powell expressed it at the conference, "the state can't arbitrarily tell him how to groom his personal appearance." As an example, Powell said, it was "no legitimate interest of the state to satisfy the [police] chief's personal ideas." Even more clearly, there is no legitimate state interest to support a hair or dress code binding upon the community generally. Few would doubt the invalidity of such a code, even though no enumerated right would be violated by it.

OTHER RETAINED RIGHTS

Contrary to the general impression, *Griswold v. Connecticut*[146] is not the first case in which reliance was placed upon the Ninth Amendment by members of the Supreme Court. Two decades earlier, in *United Public Workers v. Mitchell*,[147] the Court considered a federal law that prohibited federal employees from taking an "active part in political management or in political campaigns." In dealing with the claim that such a law was unconstitutional, the Court stated, "We accept appellant's contention that the nature of political rights reserved to the people by the Ninth and Tenth Amendments are involved. The right claimed as inviolate may be stated as the right of a citizen to act as a party official or worker to further his own political views." Thus, the Court affirmed, the law interfered "with what otherwise would be the freedom of the civil servant under the . . . Ninth and Tenth Amendments."[148]

The right at issue in *Mitchell* is plainly a nontextual right; it is not mentioned at all in the Constitution or Bill of Rights. The same is true of most other political rights, including the most basic political right of all—the right to vote. Yet can it be doubted that this right—which the Court has stressed as a "fundamental" right[149]—is protected by the Constitution? The same is true of the other political rights possessed by Americans, such as the right to compete for public office or to engage in political activities. These are still among the basic rights retained by the people, even though they are not specifically included within those enumerated in the Constitution.

It is also true of the right to privacy and personal autonomy discussed in the last section. The example of the hair or dress code applicable to people generally or the Douglas illustration of the goose-stepping requirement would be recognized by most Americans as violations of their constitutional rights, even though the right impinged upon is nowhere mentioned in the Constitution. As one court puts it, "the adult's right to wear his hair as he chooses supersedes the State's right to intrude."[150]

Particularly striking in this respect is a 1987 case which arose out of appellant's arrest for lewd and indecent exposure. His offense consisted of running on a public path in Palm Beach, Florida, without a shirt. This violated an ordinance prohibiting any person from appearing in a public place in Palm Beach with the upper part of his body uncovered. The trial court ruled the ordinance unconstitutional. Instead of appealing, Palm Beach enacted a revised ordinance that continued the topless prohibition. Appellant challenged the revised ordinance in a federal court. The challenge was upheld by the eleventh circuit, which ruled that the ordinance invalidly infringed upon appellant's "liberty interest in personal dress,"[151] since it bore no rational relationship to any legitimate town interest.

Over a century ago, Judge Thomas M. Cooley dismissed laws of the type under discussion with the pithy comment: "The conclusive answer to any such legislation is, that it meddles with what is no concern of the state, and therefore invades private right."[152]

Yet if a "private right" or "liberty interest" is invaded in this type of case, it is surely one that is not enumerated in the Constitution. The original trial court in the Palm Beach case had found the ordinance invalid as a violation of the individual's rights under the Ninth Amendment to dress and to foster health through "athletic expression." In other words, though not mentioned in the text, the rights infringed upon are rights retained by the people and hence entitled to constitutional protection.

Members of the highest Court have indicated that there are other nontextual rights retained by the people. *Richmond Newspapers v. Virginia*[153] presented the issue of public and press access to criminal proceedings. The trial court there had closed a criminal proceeding to the public and the press and refused to grant a newspaper's motion to vacate the closure order. At the postargument conference Chief Justice Burger noted that open trials have always been the practice in our system. "The assumption," he said, "has been that trials must be public. They were taken for granted from 1787 to 1791"—that is, from the drafting of the Constitution to the ratification of the Bill of Rights. Thus, Burger concluded, "[t]here's a common thread for public trials." Yet this still left the question: What's the constitutional handle?

The other justices answered this question in terms of the First Amendment; Burger's answer, however, was different. "I'm not persuaded," he said, "it's in the First Amendment either as an access right or an associational right." The chief justice explained the constitutional approach he would favor: "I would rely on the fact it was part of judicial procedure before adoption of the Bill of Rights. The Ninth Amendment is as good a handle as any."[154]

Had the Burger suggestion of reliance on the Ninth Amendment been followed, *Richmond Newspapers* might have become a leading case in the revival of the amendment. But the chief justice's suggestion was not supported by the others and the Burger *Richmond Newspapers* opinion does not discuss the Ninth Amendment. In the covering memorandum transmitting his draft *Richmond Newspapers* opinion, the chief justice wrote, "I have refrained from relying on the Ninth Amendment but the discussion of its genesis gives at least 'lateral support' to the central theme."[155] The discussion referred to was relegated to a footnote in the Burger opinion.

Yet Burger appears correct in his view that the right of access to trials cannot be based wholly on the First Amendment. Even if freedom of the press includes a right of access to news, that does not necessarily mean that the press has such a right in otherwise nonpublic governmental proceedings.[156] And, even if such a right is protected for the press, how does that give the public any similar right?

The proper analysis is the one given by Chief Justice Burger at the *Richmond Newspapers* conference. Public trials were taken for granted when the Constitution and Bill of Rights were adopted. Since the right to attend such trials was not restricted by the constitutional text, it remained one of the rights retained by the people (including the press) under the Ninth Amendment.

Despite the failure of the *Richmond Newspapers* opinions (including that of the chief justice himself) to adopt the Burger Ninth Amendment conference approach, *Richmond Newspapers* is not inconsistent with the concept of nontextual rights. On the contrary, the Burger opinion there expressly rejects the argument that, since the Constitution nowhere spells out a guaranty for the right to attend trials, no such right is protected. Instead, declares the chief justice, "arguments such as the State makes have not precluded recognition of important rights not enumerated. Notwithstanding the appropriate caution against reading into the Constitution rights not explicitly defined, the Court has acknowledged that certain unarticulated rights are implicit in enumerated guarantees."[157]

The Burger opinion then lists specific examples of nonenumerated rights that are protected: "For example, the rights of association and of privacy, the right to be presumed innocent, and the right to be judged by a standard of proof beyond a reasonable doubt in a criminal trial, as well as the right to travel, appear nowhere in the Constitution or Bill of Rights. Yet these important but unarticulated rights have nonetheless been found to share constitutional protection in common with explicit guarantees."[158]

The right of association was first recognized in *National Association for the Advancement of Colored People v. Alabama.*[159] As originally draft-ed, Justice John M. Harlan's opinion of the Court for this case was based on Alabama's asserted violation of freedom of speech. Justice Frank-furter objected. In a letter to Harlan, he argued that the "liberty" pro-tected by the Fourteenth Amendment "includes my right to belong to any organization I please. . . . To say that such right of association is an ingredient of a person's 'liberty' . . . seems to me a much more accurate and persuasive way of stating what is involved in the N.A.A.C.P. case, what would be involved if it were the American Philosophic Society, than to build up elaborate argumentation that somehow or other what Alabama has done affects free speech."[160] The Frankfurter approach was accepted and the *NAACP* case stands as the first decision holding that there is a constitutional right to organize and join an association for advancement of beliefs and ideas, even though no such right is spelled out in the Constitution.

The right to be presumed innocent has a similar constitutional founda-tion. As the Court stated in a leading case, "The presumption of inno-cence, although not articulated in the Constitution, is a basic component of a fair trial under our system of criminal justice."[161] As such, the presumption is plainly entitled to constitutional protection.

The same approach has been followed with regard to the right to be judged by a standard of proof beyond a reasonable doubt in a criminal trial. Though this standard had long been assumed to be a basic element of fairness, the Court had never ruled on it directly prior to *In re Win-ship.*[162] Justice Brennan's opinion of the Court there categorically affirms the constitutional status of the standard, though it, too, is not mentioned in the Constitution. It should be noted that it was on this holding that the Brennan opinion lost the vote of Justice Black,[163] who could not find "proof beyond a reasonable doubt" in "the words of the written Constitu-tion,"[164] and thus was driven to dissent on this point.

The last enumerated right given as an example in the Burger *Rich-mond Newspapers* opinion is the right to travel. That right was first recognized as a constitutional right over a century ago.[165] In the leading modern case on the subject, the Court stated that it was not necessary to ascribe the source of this right to a particular constitutional provision. Though the "right finds no explicit mention in the Constitution," that is true because it was "so elementary" that it was recognized from the beginning as necessary. "In any event, freedom to travel throughout the United States has long been recognized as a basic right under the Constitution."[166]

JUSTICE HARLAN AND DUE PROCESS

In view of the recent attacks on the concept of nontextual rights, it is significant that the concept was vigorously supported by Justice Harlan, now considered the very model of the true conservative judge. The best statement of Harlan's view in the matter is contained in his dissent in *Poe v. Ullman*,[167] where the Court declined to decide the constitutionality of the ban on contraceptives that it later struck down in *Griswold v. Connecticut*.[168]

At the *Poe* conference, Harlan delivered an emotional statement highly unusual for this most reserved of the Court's justices. "I think," Harlan declared, "the statute is egregiously unconstitutional on its face. . . . The Due Process Clause has substantive content for me. The right to be let alone is embodied in due process. Despite the broad powers to legislate in the area of health, there are limits." Harlan concluded by asserting, "This is more offensive to the right to be let alone than anything possibly could be."[169]

In his *Poe* dissent, Justice Harlan indicated why the right to be let alone was guaranteed even though it was not mentioned in the constitutional text. First of all, said Harlan, the Court must approach "the text which is the only commission for our power not in a literalistic way, as if we had a tax statute before us, but as the basic charter of our society, setting out in spare but meaningful terms the principles of government." For Harlan, "[I]t is not the particular enumeration of rights . . . which spells out the reach of" constitutional protection. On the contrary, the "character of Constitutional provisions . . . must be discerned from a particular provision's larger context. And . . . this context is one not of words, but of history and purposes."[170]

Because of this, Harlan went on,

the full scope of the liberty guaranteed by the Due Process Clause cannot be found in or limited by the precise terms of the specific guarantees elsewhere provided in the Constitution. This "liberty" is not a series of isolated points pricked out in terms of the taking of property; the freedom of speech, press, and religion; the right to keep and bear arms; the freedom from unreasonable searches and seizures; and so on. It is a rational continuum which, broadly speaking, includes a freedom from all substantial arbitrary impositions and purposeless restraints . . . and which also recognizes . . . that certain interests require particularly careful scrutiny of the state needs asserted to justify their abridgment.[171]

It is true that the Harlan recognition of nonenumerated rights was based upon the Due Process Clause rather than the Ninth Amendment. Thus, in the *Winship* case[172] Justice Harlan agreed that the reasonable-doubt standard in criminal trials was mandated by the Constitution. But his recognition of the nontextual right was explained on due process grounds: "I view the requirement of proof beyond a reasonable doubt in a criminal case as bottomed on a fundamental value determination of our society that it is far worse to convict an innocent man than to let a guilty man go free." Under this approach, "due process, as an expression of fundamental procedural fairness, requires a more stringent standard for criminal trials than for ordinary civil litigation."[173]

That Justice Harlan relied upon due process rather than the Ninth Amendment did not detract from his full acceptance of the concept of nonenumerated rights. As Harlan saw it, due process "is a discrete concept which subsists as an independent guaranty of liberty and procedural fairness, more general and inclusive than the specific prohibitions."[174] Except for its terminology, the Harlan approach is essentially similar to the approach that relies on the Ninth Amendment. If the right is a basic right "which [is] fundamental; which belong[s] . . . to the citizens of all free governments,"[175] it is one retained by the people under the Ninth Amendment or, in Harlan's view, included in the "liberty" protected by due process.

JUS NATURALIS REDIVIVUM?

Whether the approach followed on nonenumerated rights invokes the Ninth Amendment or the Due Process Clause, the result is what Chief Justice Burger stated in his *Richmond Newspapers* opinion:[176] that such rights are recognized under the Constitution. As Burger puts it, "The concerns expressed by Madison and others have thus been resolved;

fundamental rights, even though not expressly guaranteed, have been recognized by the Court as indispensable to the enjoyment of rights explicitly defined."[177]

But that brings us back to the point urged by Justice Black and other, more recent critics: who defines the boundaries of nonenumerated rights?

In *Winship*,[178] Justices Harlan and Black gave voice to their disagreement on rights not specifically protected by the constitutional text. "I cannot refrain," Harlan wrote, "from expressing my continued bafflement at my Brother BLACK's insistence that due process . . . does not embody a concept of fundamental fairness as part of our scheme of constitutionally ordered liberty."[179]

On his side, Justice Black was equally adamant in asserting the error of the nonenumerated rights concept. "I shall not," Black declared in his *Winship* dissent, "at any time surrender my belief that that document itself should be our guide, not our own concept of what is fair, decent, and right." To Black, the reliance on nontextual rights was "to put [one's] faith [not] in the words of the written Constitution itself [but] rather . . . to rely on the shifting, day-to-day standards of fairness of individual judges."[180]

The Black animadversion points out the weakness of what is, after all, basically a natural-law notion—whether it is phrased in Ninth Amendment or due-process terms, or as constitutional "penumbras" (that is, the concept relied on in the Douglas *Griswold* opinion[181]). The judge himself must determine, on his individual judgment, whether a particular right is of the very essence of a scheme of ordered liberty, so that it is one retained by the people even if not enumerated, or only some lesser right. Such an approach must inevitably have what Justice Black terms "accordion-like qualities,"[182] expanding and contracting according to the personal notions of the individual judge.

Must we then echo in our day the complaint of seventeenth-century common lawyers against the Court of Chancery, that the justice dispensed by the Supreme Court is so uncontrolled by fixed principles that it might just as well depend on the size of a particular justice's foot? To assume, however, that the conception of nontextual rights must rest wholly on the unfettered discretion of the judge is to go too far. The criticisms of Justice Black and present-day jurists such as Judge Bork prove too much, for they might with equal validity be directed against a large part of the law. What the Court is applying in cases such as *Griswold* is a broad standard rather than a closely defined precept. The same thing is done in most of the important areas of modern law. Indeed, it is in its application of such standards, instead of only mechanical rules, that a developed legal system differs most from a formative one.

Early law, unable to differentiate between varying degrees of the same type of conduct, brands all equally and metes out similar consequences to those concerned. As the law grows more mature distinctions get made, and a judge is allowed to elaborate differences of degree instead of simply punishing with society's vengeance the visible source of any evil result. Thus, to take an obvious example, the mechanical rule of absolute liability for torts, characteristic of the formative period of a legal system, gives way to liability only for culpability, with culpability in each case being judged by the standard of the reasonable man. Certainly the standard of the reasonable man applied in the modern law of torts leaves much to the inclinations and idiosyncrasies of the individual judge or jury; yet few suggest replacing it (except in certain special fields) with the unmoral rule (mechanical though it may be) of liability regardless of the culpability of the actor. As Justice Holmes aptly expressed it, the whole law depends upon differences of degree as soon as it is civilized. Between the differences of degree in a standard such as that of the reasonable man or that of due process, "and the simple universality of the rules in the Twelve Tables or the Leges Barbarorum, there lies the culture of two thousand years."[183]

It is mistaken to assert, as Judge Bork does, that in protecting rights not specifically mentioned "the judge has no basis other than his own values upon which to [act]."[184] "In determining which rights are fundamental, judges are not left at large to decide cases in light of their personal and private notions. Rather, they must look to the 'traditions and [collective] conscience of our people' to determine whether"[185] a right is entitled to protection. The proper posture is that stated by Justice Harlan in his *Poe* dissent. "Each new claim to Constitutional protection," Harlan writes, "must be considered against a background of Constitutional purposes, as they have been rationally perceived and historically developed. Though we exercise limited and sharply restrained judgment, yet there is no 'mechanical yardstick,' no 'mechanical answer.' The decision of an apparently novel claim must depend on grounds which follow closely on well-accepted principles and criteria. The new decision must take 'its place in relation to what went before and further [cut] a channel for what is to come.'"[186]

Justice Harlan quotes the Court's own answer to the Bork-type criticism: "We may not draw on our merely personal and private notions and disregard the limits that bind judges in their judicial function. Even though the concept of [nontextual rights] is not final and fixed, these limits are derived from considerations that are fused in the whole nature of our judicial process."[187] The concept of nontextual rights thus interpreted is not to be derided as resort to a revival of "natural law"[188]—a mere matter of judicial caprice. According to the Bryce truism, "judges are only men."[189] As such, they partake fully of the human sense of justice. "The Foole hath sayd in his heart, there is no such thing as Justice; and sometimes also with his tongue."[190] Like reason, justice derives from the very nature of humanity, urging people to right conduct and diverting them from wrongdoing; this justice became law not when it was written down, but when it first came into existence. "These standards of justice are not authoritatively formulated anywhere as though they were specifics."[191] Instead, the Bill of Rights is "a summarized constitutional guaranty of respect"[192] for those rights recognized by our sense of justice. Those are the "personal immunities which, as Mr. Justice Cardozo twice wrote for the Court, are 'so rooted in the traditions and conscience of our people as to be ranked as fundamental,' . . . or are 'implicit in the concept of ordered liberty.'"[193]

Members of the highest Court are peculiarly placed, both by training and tradition, to determine what rights meet the Cardozo tests. The justices can be expected both to be keenly perceptive to violations of personal rights and to be sufficiently detached to avoid imposing their purely personal notions, not shared by others, upon society. "To practice the requisite detachment and to achieve sufficient objectivity no doubt demands of judges the habit of self-discipline and self-criticism, incertitude that one's own views are incontestable and alert tolerance toward views not shared. But these are precisely the presuppositions of our judicial process. They are precisely the qualities society has a right to expect from those entrusted with ultimate judicial power."[194]

It is not realistic to fear that the judge using the concept of nontextual rights will apply merely erratic, capricious, or idiosyncratic standards. "Our judges are products of our society, and . . . they will generally think along with the beliefs of some substantial segment of the citizenry. A man who uses a moral standard that no one shares in a population of 150 million probably does not belong at large, much less on the bench."[195] To be sure, there will be individual variations and even accordionlike expansions and contractions of the rights protected. But that is the very essence of a system of case law, which enables it to adjust itself to the ebbs and flows of the civilization it is supposed to regulate.

3

ECONOMIC LIBERTIES
AND THE CONSTITUTION
LOCHNER REDIVIVUS?

THE TITLE of this chapter is taken from a book written by Bernard H. Siegan,[1] one of the most influential of the New Right jurists, who was nominated to a federal appellate judgeship by President Reagan.[2] Professor Siegan's book is an attack upon the Supreme Court jurisprudence during the last half century in cases involving economic regulation. Siegan condemns the Court for what he considers its abdication in the area of economic rights. At the outset of his book he states, "I shall attempt to . . . persuade the reader that contemporary construction of the Federal Constitution that prevents its application to restrictions upon economic activity is erroneous and should be corrected."[3]

The major theme of Siegan's work is "the great need under our governmental system for judicial oversight of economic legislation."[4] As Siegan sees it, "In a society that extols private property and private enterprise, those who engage in economic activities in reliance on existing laws are entitled to be secure against arbitrary and confiscatory governmental actions. . . . This is one of the major reasons that we have a Supreme Court and that we grant it enormous power over lawmakers."[5]

In his dissent in *Roe v. Wade*[6]—perhaps the most controversial judicial decision during the past quarter century—Justice Rehnquist (as he then was) accused the majority of reviving the approach followed in the 1905 case of *Lochner v. New York*.[7] "While the Court's opinion," Rehnquist asserted, "quotes from the dissent of Mr. Justice Holmes in Lochner v. New York . . . the result it reaches is more closely attuned to the majority opinion of Mr. Justice Peckham in that case. As in *Lochner* and similar cases applying substantive due process standards to economic and social welfare legislation, the [approach followed in *Roe*] will inevitably require this Court to examine the legislative policies and pass on the wisdom of these policies."[8]

Rehnquist claimed that the *Roe* Court was in effect striking down state abortion laws because it disagreed with the legislative policies behind those laws. This, says Rehnquist, was what the *Lochner* Court had done in invalidating the regulatory law at issue there because the justices found it unreasonable and hence violative of due process.

Yet even Justice Rehnquist did not seek to defend the "deliberately discarded" *Lochner* doctrine.[9] That is exactly what Siegan does, however, in urging the Court to return to its earlier posture of protecting property rights under the Due Process Clause. Indeed, urges Siegan, *Lochner* "has as solid a constitutional basis as numerous contemporary decisions that have elicited little criticism and, frequently, lavish praise."[10]

THE *LOCHNER* CASE

Joseph Lochner had been convicted for violating a New York law by requiring a worker in his bakery to work more than sixty hours in one week. The statute prohibited bakery employees from working more than ten hours a day, or sixty hours a week. In reviewing this law the Court subjected it to the reasonableness test of the Due Process Clause. According to the Court, the question to be determined in cases involving challenges to legislation on due process grounds is: "Is this . . . fair, reasonable and appropriate . . . or is it an unreasonable, unnecessary and arbitrary interference with the right of the individual?"[11]

In answering this question, the *Lochner* Court indicated that the reasonableness of a challenged statute, under the Due Process Clause, must be determined as an objective fact by the judge upon his own independent judgment. In holding the *Lochner* law invalid, the Court in effect substituted its judgment for that of the legislator, and decided for itself that the statute was not reasonably related to any of the social ends for which the police power might validly be exercised.

This interpretation of reasonableness, as an objective criterion to be determined by the judge himself, permeates the *Lochner* opinion. "We think," said the Court, "that a law like the one before us involves neither the safety, the morals nor the welfare of the public, and that the interest of the public is not in the slightest degree affected by such an act."[12] Hence, if it is to be upheld, it must be as a law pertaining to public health. But the mere assertion that the subject relates to health, though in remote degree, is not enough. The relationship to public health must be direct enough for the Court itself to deem it reasonable.

In *Lochner*, the required relationship was found lacking: "There is, in our judgment, no reasonable foundation for holding this to be necessary or appropriate as a health law to safeguard the public health or the health of the individuals who are following the trade of a baker."[13] The trade of baker, in the Court's view, was not an unhealthy one, so as to justify legislative interference with the right of contract. Of course, almost all occupations may be said more or less to affect health. Yet that alone does not mean that such occupations must be subject to any police-power regulation on public-health grounds. "There must be more than the mere fact of the possible existence of some small amount of unhealthiness to warrant legislative interference with liberty."[14] Labor, in and of itself, may carry with it the seeds of unhealthiness. "But are we all, on that account, at the mercy of legislative majorities?"[15]

Lochner is, of course, remembered mostly for its now classic dissent by Justice Holmes, celebrated for its oft-quoted aphorisms. In addition to the Holmes dissent in *Lochner*, however, there was also a dissenting opinion by Justice Harlan, which (more pedestrian though it doubtless was) in many ways probed more deeply into the issue at stake. According to Harlan, it was not for the Court to consider whether any particular view of the economic issues involved presented the sounder theory. If there were reasons to support the view that excessive hours worked by bakers might endanger their health, that should end the matter. "It is," urged the Harlan dissent, "enough for the determination of this case, and it is enough for this court to know, that the question is one about which there is room for debate and for an honest difference of opinion."[16] Where the propriety of the challenged law as a health measure was open to discussion, it should at the least be deemed reasonable.

The *Lochner* Court, in striking down a law whose reasonableness was, at a minimum, open to debate, in effect determined upon its own judgment whether such legislation was desirable. Critics argued that the Court, in applying due process in such a manner, came close to exercising the functions of a "super-legislature"[17]—to being what an English observer termed "a third chamber in the United States."[18] Under the *Lochner* approach, the Supreme Court was able to set itself up as almost the supreme censor of the wisdom of regulatory legislation.

LOCHNER MORALITY PLAY

Lochner today stands near the top of any list of discredited Supreme Court decisions. When commentators discuss the case at all, they use it as a vehicle to illustrate the drastic change in Supreme Court jurisprudence during the present century, which has seen the Holmes dissent become elevated to established doctrine.

"There was a time," the Court tells us, citing *Lochner*, "when the Due Process Clause was used by this Court to strike down laws which were thought unreasonable, that is, unwise or incompatible with some particular economic or social philosophy."[19] Justice Holmes strongly objected to "[t]his intrusion by the judiciary into the realm of legislative value judgments."[20] The Holmes objection ultimately prevailed. "The doctrine that prevailed in *Lochner* . . . that due process authorizes courts to hold laws unconstitutional when they believe the legislature has acted unwisely—has long since been discarded. We have returned to the original constitutional proposition that courts do not substitute their social and economic beliefs for the judgment of legislative bodies, who are elected to pass laws."[21]

This morality-play version of *Lochner* has now been subjected to its first serious challenge by New Right jurists such as Bernard Siegan. They assert that it was the *Lochner* majority who were right and Holmes and the recent Court who were wrong in their approach to the constitutionality of laws providing for economic regulation.

"This case," asserted the Holmes *Lochner* dissent, "is decided upon an economic theory which a large part of the country does not entertain."[22] The *Lochner* Court struck down the statute as unreasonable because a majority of the justices disagreed with the economic theory on which the state legislature had acted. This is precisely the approach to judicial review that the Court has now rejected. There may, in the given case, be economic arguments against a challenged regulatory law. According to the contemporary Court, however, "such arguments are properly addressed to the legislature, not to us. We refuse to sit as a 'superlegislature to weigh the wisdom of legislation,' and we emphatically refuse to go back to the time when courts used the Due Process Clause 'to strike down state laws, regulatory of business and industrial conditions, because they may be unwise, improvident, or out of harmony with a particular school of thought.'"[23] It is not for the court to intervene because it disagrees with the economic theory upon which a law is based. "Whether the legislature takes for its textbook Adam Smith, Herbert Spencer, Lord Keynes, or some other is no concern of ours."[24]

According to Professor Siegan, however, that is exactly what should be the concern of a reviewing court. If a law is based upon what the judge considers an unsound economic theory, the judge should, Siegan urges, hold the law contrary to due process. To Siegan, also, *Lochner* is a morality play; but his heroes and villains are the opposites of those in the now accepted version.

In Siegan's view, the *Lochner* Court was correct, both in its approach to review of economic regulation and in its decision invalidating the maximum-hours law for bakers. In the first place, says Siegan, the *Lochner* Court was right in determining the reasonableness of the law on its own independent judgment. That is what is required in cases involving judicial review and there is no valid reason for following a different approach where only economic rights are at issue. When that approach is followed, Siegan asserts, a law like that in *Lochner* should be stricken down, for it is based upon an economic theory of regulation that economists now reject.

DICHOTOMY DENIED

The Siegan posture on the proper scope of review in the *Lochner*-type case is, of course, contrary to the now settled jurisprudence on the subject. For half a century, our public law has been based upon a dichotomy between property rights and personal rights, with the judges far more ready to find legislative invasion when personal rights were involved than in the sphere of economics.[25] As Siegan himself summarizes it, "The Court generally observes this hierarchy of rights: At the top are the rights of expression, religion, sexual privacy, and voting; at the bottom are economic rights."[26] But Siegan himself rejects this dichotomy, urging that the lower valuing of property upon which it is based is contrary both to history and the logic of judicial review.

From a historical point of view, the subordinate status of property rights in the constitutional scheme is a relatively recent development. Certainly, as Siegan stresses, "A major objective of the Constitution's Framers was protecting and preserving the right of property."[27] If anything is clear from the words and actions of the men who wrote the Constitution, it is that, to them, property was as important as liberty. "The preservation of property . . . ," declared a member of the first Supreme Court, who had been one of the framers of 1787, "is a primary object of the social compact."[28] Without property rights, the framers well knew, the rights of a person would be devoid of practical content. "Property must be secured," affirmed John Adams, "or liberty cannot exist."[29]

It is also true that, until half a century ago, property predominated in the trilogy of rights protected by the Constitution. The Due Process Clause, declared the American Bar Association president in 1892, "puts property upon precisely the same footing of security that it puts life and liberty. It binds them each and all indissolubly together."[30] By the end of the last century, however, the most striking aspect of our public law was not the treatment of property as an equal member of the constitutional triad, but its elevation to a position of dominance. Louis D. Brandeis gave contemporaneous expression to this development: "Property is only a means. It has been a frequent error of our courts that they have made the means an end."[31]

During the first part of this century, the emphasis remained on the rights of property. All this, of course, has changed over the past fifty years. Merely to repeat the 1922 statement of a federal judge "that of the three fundamental principles which underlie government, and for which government exists, the protection of life, liberty, and property, the chief of these is property"[32] is to show how far out of line such a statement is with the present scale of legal values. If, at the turn of the century, unrestricted acquisition and use of property was at its broadest, it became progressively narrowed as the century went on. Some years ago, Rudolf von Ihering, one of the greatest of modern jurists, formulated the matter thus: "Formerly high valuing of property, lower valuing of the person. Now lower valuing of property, higher valuing of the person."[33]

Now Siegan and his confreres repudiate this dichotomy. They assert that the framers' scale of values in this respect should still prevail. More than that, they challenge the whole notion of a hierarchy of rights as not provided for in the Constitution and contrary to the logic of judicial review. As Siegan states it, "Establishing the priority of liberties is a political judgment. Not being provided for in the Constitution, it is beyond the authority of the High Court."[34] The review power extends equally to all cases coming within Article III. "Although Justices cannot be expected to treat every interest and concern the same, excising from constitutional protection liberties that affect substantial numbers of people is a judgment exceeding the bounds of discretion inherent in judicial decision-making. The judiciary lacks legitimacy to discriminate against certain liberties."[35] Hence, Siegan concludes, "Judicial withdrawal from the protection of economic activity violates Article III."[36]

REHABILITATING *LOCHNER*?

Professor Siegan does not stop with the argument that denies the legitimacy of the Court's personal-rights/property-rights dichotomy, and asserts that economic rights may not be placed upon a lower level in the constitutional scale of values. Instead, he goes further and seeks to accomplish the result stated in the title of his law review article *Rehabilitating Lochner*.[37]

Interestingly, in the same law review issue there is an address by Justice Stevens that declares, "When the Court repudiated the line of cases that is often identified with *Lochner v. New York*, it did so in strong language that not only glittered but seemed to foreclose forever any suggestion that the due process clause of the fourteenth amendment gave any power to federal judges to pass on the substance of the work product of state legislatures."[38] To Stevens, as to other commentators, the post-*Lochner* jurisprudence "seemed to foreclose" any possible *Lochner* revival. And so it appeared until the recent writings of jurists such as Siegan. To Siegan, the uniform case law during the past half century does not justify *Lochner*'s continued relegation to constitutional limbo. On the contrary, Siegan asserts, "The evidence is very persuasive that *Lochner* was a legitimate interpretation. . . . Full rehabilitation may be in order."[39]

For Siegan, *Lochner* was not only correct in its approach to judicial review; it was also correct in its decision on the merits of the case, as a matter both of law and economics. In this he opposes the ruling of the present Court, which says that it is not for judges to decide the proper economic posture for the legislature: "[W]e emphatically refuse to go back to the time when courts used the Due Process Clause 'to strike down state laws because they may be unwise, improvident, or out of harmony with a particular school of thought.'"[40]

Siegan rejects this approach and argues that even if Holmes was correct in his claim that *Lochner* was decided upon the Court's own economic theory,[41] that need not mean that the decision was wrong. On the contrary, Siegan argues, the *Lochner* justices were only doing what judicial review requires when they invalidated the law because it was based upon what they considered an incorrect economic theory.

BRANDEIS AND REGULATION

Critics of *Lochner* have taken their legal cue from the Holmes dissent in that case. But they have taken their economic lead from Justice Louis D. Brandeis, who, with Holmes, formed the most famous dissenting team in judicial history. Yet though both shared a similar posture on the proper approach to judicial review of regulatory laws, they differed on the merits of economic regulation. Justice Frankfurter once wrote that Holmes "privately distrusted attempts at improving society by what he deemed futile if not mischievous economic tinkering. But that was not his business."[42] Yet it was emphatically Brandeis's business throughout his career.

Brandeis firmly believed that "[r]egulation . . . is necessary to the preservation and best development of liberty. . . . We have long curbed the physically strong, to protect those physically weaker. More recently we have extended such prohibitions to business. . . . the right to competition must be limited in order to preserve it."[43]

Both on and off the bench, Brandeis was a leader in the movement to ensure that law mirrored society at large in its transition from laissez faire to the welfare state. His Brandeis brief[44] replaced the black-letter judge with the statistician and the economist as judicial guides. Though it was not realized at the time, the Brandeis method of advocacy sounded a clarion that heralded the end of the *Lochner* doctrine. Compare the Brandeis brief, with its emphasis throughout on the economic and social conditions that called forth the challenged statute, with *Lochner*, where those factors were all but ignored. The difference is as marked as that between the poetry of T.S. Eliot and Alfred Austin.

On the Supreme Court, the Brandeis approach to regulation was best expressed in his dissent in the 1932 case of *New State Ice Co. v. Liebmann.*[45] At issue there was a state law requiring a certificate of convenience and necessity for entry into the business of manufacturing and selling ice. The licensing agency was forbidden to issue a license to any applicant except upon proof of the necessity for a supply of ice at the place where it was sought to establish the business, and was to deny the application where the existing licensed facilities "are sufficient to meet the public needs therein."

The Supreme Court ruled the licensing requirement for the ice business invalid. The business of manufacturing and selling ice, like that of the grocer, the dairyman, the butcher, or the baker, was said to be an ordinary business, essentially private in its nature, and hence not so charged with a public use as to justify the licensing restriction. In the Court's view, engagement in the ice business was not a privilege to be exercised only in virtue of a public grant, but a common right to be exercised independently by any competent person.

In his *New State Ice* dissent, Justice Brandeis spelled out the legal and economic bases for licensing regulation such as the requirement at issue. Regulation, he contended, was necessary to ensure the proper working of the competitive system. "The introduction in the United States of the certificate of public convenience and necessity marked the growing conviction that under certain circumstances free competition might be harmful to the community, and that, when it was so, absolute freedom to enter the business of one's choice should be denied."[46]

In this case, Brandeis asserted, the license requirement could be imposed because of the nature of the business involved. "The business of supplying ice is not only a necessity, like that of supplying food or clothing or shelter, but the Legislature could also consider that it is one which lends itself peculiarly to monopoly."[47] Duplication of ice plants was wasteful and led "to destructive and frequently ruinous competition," which was "ultimately burdensome to consumers."[48] There was a need of some remedy for the evil of destructive competition. "Can it be said in the light of these facts that it was not an appropriate exercise of legislative discretion to authorize the commission to deny a license to enter the business in localities where necessity for another plant did not exist?"[49]

Nor, according to Brandeis, is this type of regulation objectionable because it curbs competition. In such a case, as he had written years earlier, "Regulation is essential to the preservation and development of competition."[50] The necessary conclusion is that "where, as here, there is reasonable ground for the legislative conclusion that, in order to secure a necessary service at reasonable rates, it may be necessary to curtail the right to enter the calling, it is, in my opinion, consistent with the due process clause to do so, whatever the nature of the business. The existence of such power in the Legislature seems indispensable in our ever-changing society."[51]

The rejection of *Lochner* has meant the acceptance of both the Holmes-Brandeis approach to review of regulatory laws and the Brandeis economic justification of regulation. With regard to the former, the prevailing theme has been that stated in the Brandeis *New State Ice* dissent: "Our function is only to determine the reasonableness of the Legislature's belief in the existence of evils and in the effectiveness of the remedy provided. In performing this function we have no occasion to consider whether all the statements of fact which may be the basis of the prevailing belief are well-founded; and we have, of course, no right to weigh conflicting evidence."[52]

Though the Brandeis rationale for regulation in the *New State Ice* dissent had all but taken over the field during the past half century, it has now been repudiated by the legal New Right. Perhaps the most influential writer to reject the Brandeis dissent and support the economic theory behind *Lochner* is Judge Richard A. Posner. He notes that the prevailing view in recent years has been that *Lochner* and similar decisions earlier in the century "reflected a weak grasp of economics" and cites the *New State Ice* dissent as "based on this view."[53]

According to Posner, however, the Brandeis economic analysis was seriously flawed: "In viewing the case as one in which Liebmann's economic rights were pitted against the interests of the poor people of Oklahoma who could not afford refrigerators, Justice Brandeis got it backwards. The right he would have vindicated was the interest of New York Ice and other established ice companies to be free from competition. The people actually wronged by the statute were the poor, who were compelled to pay more for ice; the well-to-do, as Brandeis pointed out, were more likely to have refrigerators."[54]

To Posner, laws like those at issue in *Lochner* and *New State Ice* "were attempts to suppress competition under the guise of promoting the general welfare."[55] Such attempts are all but heresy to advocates of Chicago School economics, which Posner himself has done so much to translate into legal doctrine. That school has never reconciled itself to the fact that, in this century, the invisible hand of Adam Smith has increasingly been replaced by the "public interest" as defined in regulatory legislation and administration. To the Chicago School, the overriding goal of law, as of economics, should be that of efficiency. The law should intervene "to reprehend only that which is inefficient," and even then the law's role should be limited, since the "market punishes inefficiency faster and better than the machinery of the law."[56]

LOCHNER AND LAISSEZ FAIRE

Those jurists who rely on Chicago School economics to resuscitate *Lochner* are essentially repeating the justification for that case by its proponents when it was decided. *Lochner* used the newly developed tool of substantive due process to immunize the economy from interference by the machinery of the law. *Lochner* was the culmination of the developing jurisprudence that identified due process with the doctrine of vested rights drawn from natural law, a doctrine that had been developed to protect property rights. This meant that due process itself was the great substantive safeguard of property; its protective umbrella included all the constitutional limitations, express and implied, upon governmental interference with the rights of property.[57]

How the Supreme Court would use substantive due process to protect corporate enterprise from governmental restraints was foreshadowed in the *Income Tax Case*.[58] The Court there ruled invalid the federal income tax law of 1894, even though a similar statute had previously been upheld. The decision can be explained less in legal terms than in terms of the personal antipathies of the justices. Opposing the statute, Joseph H. Choate depicted the income tax as "a doctrine worthy of a Jacobin Club," the "new doctrine of this army of 60,000,000—this triumphant and tyrannical majority—who want to punish men who are rich and confiscate their property."[59]

Such an attack upon the income tax (though, technically speaking, irrelevant) found a receptive ear. "The present assault upon capital," declared Justice Stephen J. Field, "is but the beginning. It will be but the stepping-stone to others, larger and more sweeping, till our political contests will become a war of the poor against the rich; a war constantly growing in intensity and bitterness." If the Court were to sanction the income tax law, "it will mark the hour when the sure decadence of our present government will commence."[60]

The judges who felt this way about a tax of two percent on annual incomes above $4,000 now had at their disposal the newly fashioned tool of substantive due process. *Lochner* is the classic case in which the tool was used.

It should, however, be stressed that judicial utilization of the *Lochner* approach to substantive due process was not mere control of state legislation in the abstract. Court control was directed to a particular purpose— the invalidation of state legislation that conflicted with the doctrine of laissez faire that dominated thinking at the turn of the century.[61] What Justice Frankfurter termed "the shibboleths of a pre-machine age . . . were reflected in juridical assumptions that survived the facts on which they were based. . . . Basic human rights expressed by the constitutional conception of 'liberty' were equated with theories of *laissez-faire*."[62] The result was that due process became the rallying point for judicial resistance to the efforts of the states to control the excesses and relieve the oppressions of the rising industrial economy.[63]

"The paternal theory of government," declared Justice David J. Brewer, one of the principal architects of the doctrine of substantive due process, "is to me odious. The utmost possible liberty to the individual, and the fullest possible protection to him and his property, is both the limitation and duty of government."[64] To courts that adopted the Brewer philosophy, the "liberty" protected by due process became synonymous with a governmental hands-off policy in the field of private economic relations. "For years the Court struck down social legislation when a particular law did not fit the notions of a majority of Justices as to legislation appropriate for a free enterprise system."[65]

Lochner set a pattern, both as to doctrine and method, that prevailed for a generation. The pattern was not always adhered to; but it constituted the prevailing current in Supreme Court jurisprudence. In truth, had not that current been altered and "[h]ad not Mr. Justice Holmes' awareness of the impermanence of legislation as against the permanence of the Constitution gradually prevailed, there might indeed have been 'hardly any limit but the sky' to the embodiment of 'our economic or moral beliefs' in that Amendment's 'prohibitions.'"[66]

FREEDOM OF CONTRACT

In its *Lochner* opinion the Court declared, "It is a question of which of two powers or rights shall prevail—the power of the state to legislate or the right of the individual to liberty of person and freedom of contract."[67] *Lochner*, of course, came down strongly on the side of the individual right. "There is no reasonable ground for interfering with the liberty of person or the right of free contract, by determining the hours of labor, in the occupation of a baker."[68]

Lochner was decided the way it was because of the extremes to which the law of the day carried the doctrine of freedom of contract: The judges had begun with an unpretentious assertion of the freedom to follow one's calling. By the turn of the century, "that innocuous generality was expanded into the dogma, Liberty of Contract."[69] A paper delivered at the 1900 meeting of the American Bar Association proclaimed, "[T]here is . . . complete freedom of contract; competition is now universal, and as merciless as nature and natural selection."[70]

A broadside freedom of contract was now considered the basic part of the liberty safeguarded by the Due Process Clause. The result was an unprecedented accent on the autonomy of private decision-makers; the law was devoted to providing legal tools, procedures, and compulsions to create the framework of reasonable expectations within which economic growth could take place.[71]

The right of free contract as a fundamental natural right first appears, in its late-nineteenth-century sense, in Herbert Spencer's *Justice*.[72] Spencer stressed the unrestricted right to make promises, rather than the natural force of promises when made, which was emphasized by earlier writers such as Hugo Grotius. Justice required that each individual be at liberty to make free use of his natural powers in bargains, exchanges, and promises. Contract law was conceived of negatively, as a hands-off system that allowed men to do things.[73] Freedom of contract became a chief article in the creed of those who sought to minimize the functions of the state; to them, the only legitimate governmental function was to enforce obligations created by private contract.[74] "Men in industrial societies must have intercourse and commerce by means of the contrivance of contract; the State surrenders its control over them more and more, and they outgrow legal lines until they come to the full stature of free men."[75]

To Spencer, freedom of contract was a prime instrument of social progress. He adopted it as a means; his American disciples, however, made it an end. Contract, they said, "gives to liberty its content and its interpretation."[76] The right to contract was regarded, not as a phase of freedom, but as the essence of liberty, posited as permanent and absolute.[77] Impairment was not to be suffered, except within the most rigorous limits. Conceptions were fixed; basic premises were no longer to be examined. The system became a closed circle; the slightest dent was a subtraction from its essence.

"The Constitution," said Chief Justice Charles Evans Hughes, "does not speak of freedom of contract. It speaks of liberty and prohibits the deprivation of liberty without due process of law."[78] It was, nevertheless, settled by the end of the last century that liberty of contract was included within the "liberty" guaranteed by the Constitution. "At present," wrote Judge Learned Hand in 1908, "the construction which includes within it the 'liberty' to make such contracts as one wishes has become too well settled to admit of question without overturning the fixed principles of the Supreme Court."[79]

Freedom of contract was first declared a fundamental constitutional right in the 1897 case of *Allgeyer v. Louisiana*,[80] where the concept of substantive due process itself was raised to the status of accepted doctrine. In *Allgeyer* the Supreme Court stated specifically that the liberty mentioned in the Fourteenth Amendment embraces "the right of the citizen to . . . enter into all contracts which may be proper, necessary and essential."[81]

The principle of freedom of contract thus articulated was by then dominant throughout the law. Wealth in the commercial and industrial society was largely made up of promises.[82] In such a society, the social interest in the freedom to make promises was of the first importance. Contract became both a realization of the idea of liberty and a means of promoting the maximum of individual self-assertion. The basic goal was that of unshackling men and allowing them to act as freely as possible.[83] "If there is one thing more than another which public policy requires it is that men of full age and competent understanding shall have the utmost liberty of contracting."[84] The law existed to secure the right to contract freely, not merely against aggression by other individuals, but even more against invasion by society.[85] Whatever the state might do in other areas, it might not limit contractual capacity, because this capacity was derived from nature itself.[86]

Today it is hard to comprehend a system grounded upon an all-but-inexorable adherence to freedom of contract. Yet in order to obtain a true picture of American law at the time, it is necessary at least to appreciate the extent to which such freedom dominated thought and writing at the turn of the century. The noted English legal observer Sir Henry Maine, giving his impression of the American system just prior to that time, could state, "It all reposes on the sacredness of contract and the stability of private property, the first the implement, and the last the reward, of success in the universal competition."[87]

Maine himself had all but anointed freedom of contract in post–Civil War society by his celebrated generalization of society's progress. In as famous an epigram as appears in legal literature,[88] Maine summarized the course of legal development: "[W]e may say that the movement of the progressive societies has hitherto been a movement *from Status to Contract*."[89] In other words, legal progress goes from institutions where rights, duties, and liabilities flow from a condition in which the individual is defined without reference to his will, to those where they flow from exertion of individual will. Looked at this way, the movement stated by Maine is one from subjection to freedom[90]—and the instrument of freedom is the right of contract.

This theory of the course of legal development fitted in so well with the dominant Spencerian philosophy that it soon gained possession of the field. "Contracts," said the Supreme Court in 1878, "mark the progress of communities in civilization and prosperity."[91] Maine's generalization was almost universally accepted in this country.[92] "American civilization," Brooks Adams asserted, "is based upon the theory of freedom of contract."[93] It was taken for gospel that law was moving and must move in the direction of individual self-determination by free contract.[94] "The juridical history of every people," declared the American Bar Association president-elect in 1896, "which has passed from a rude state to an enlightened one begins with laws referable to status, and ends with laws explained by contract."[95] Any limitation on abstract freedom of contract was a step backward and hence arbitrary and unreasonable.[96] To judges imbued with a genuine faith in the progress from status to contract, the strongest presumption existed against any and all restrictions on the freest possible bargaining. Since social progress itself was intimately connected with the extension of contractual liberty, the Maine dictum could be violated only at the peril of social retrogression. Due process itself was violated by legislative attempts to restore status and restrict the contractual powers of free men by enacting that men of full age and sound mind in particular callings should not be able to make agreements that other men might make freely.[97]

LABOR AND THE LAW

Those who would take the law back to its position at the time of *Lochner* forget how inadequate the law then was from labor's point of view. "From my own experience," wrote Jane Addams at the beginning of this century, "I should say, perhaps, that the one symptom among workingmen which most definitely indicates a class feeling is a growing distrust of the courts."[98]

Labor's legal grievances at the time were numerous and real. The law took little account of the inequality in bargaining power that had come to exist between capital and labor. Traditional jealousy of organizations stood in the way of effective employment of collective action through unions. Enormously increased danger to life and limb in industrial employment was inadequately secured against by the common law, as administered by courts hampered by the traditional law of master and servant. The legal situation put the worker in an intolerable condition.[99]

Reaction was inevitable. The abuses inherent in post–Civil War galloping industrialism led to legislative attempts to protect the worker by laying down minimum standards governing the conditions of employment. Such laws could not, however, successfully run the freedom-of-contract gantlet, for they "illustrate the exercise of the 'police power,' so strongly denounced by the . . . disciples of Herbert Spencer and the *laissez-faire* school."[100] As Judge Learned Hand pointed out, they could not be squared with the theory of freedom of contract, "for they indubitably 'deprived' the worker of his 'liberty' to work under such conditions as he saw fit. The only process of law accorded him was the fiat of the legislature which forbade him and his employer to contract as they pleased."[101]

In a 1909 article, Roscoe Pound summarized the decisions employing freedom of contract to strike down legislative intervention in the relations between employer and employee. Legislation thus invalidated included: laws forbidding employers from interfering with union membership; laws prohibiting imposition of fines upon employees; laws providing for the mode of weighing coal in fixing miners' compensation; laws requiring payment of wages in money; laws regulating hours of labor; and laws prohibiting contracts by railway employees releasing their employers in advance from liability for personal injuries.[102]

The Pound list conforms closely to Herbert Spencer's enumeration a decade and a half earlier of legislation found objectionable because it "tended continually to narrow the liberties of individuals."[103] The American judges agreed with Spencer that "the real issue" posed by such laws "is whether the lives of citizens are more interfered with than they were." In the Spencerian calculus, "the liberty which a citizen enjoys is to be measured . . . by the relative paucity of the restraints [government] imposes on him." Laws that "increase such restraints beyond those which are needful . . . for maintaining the liberties of his fellows against his invasions of them" must inevitably fail the test.[104]

The decisions that so strictly employed freedom of contract to strike down laws regulating the relations between employer and employee seem incomprehensible to most of us today. In an age of pervasive regulation designed to ensure minimum standards and fair dealing for workers, cases that uphold the right to contract above all else appear mere aberrations. A society controlled by regulation from cradle to grave may look back with nostalgia, but scarcely with understanding, upon an era that opted in favor of unlimited freedom of contract.

True, the same judges who applied freedom of contract to invalidate laws regulating labor conditions acknowledged situations where contractual liberty might properly be restricted. Thus the courts recognized that usury laws might be enacted, even though they contravened the theoretical freedom to contract of those affected.[105] Usury laws were reconciled with freedom of contract "upon the theory that the lender and the borrower of money do not occupy towards each other the same relations of equality that parties do in contracting with each other in regard to the loan or sale of other kinds of property, and that the borrower's necessities deprive him of freedom in contracting, and place him at the mercy of the lender."[106]

In other words, freedom of contract depends upon the position of basic equality that exists between the parties to ordinary private contracts. "Free contract presupposes equals behind the contract in order that it may produce equality."[107] When the condition of the parties is not equality, it cannot truly be said that an agreement between them is the result of a free meeting of minds. In such a case, the mind of the inferior may be overborne as much as if actual duress had been used. To restore the balance, society may intervene.

If the judges at the turn of the century could concede this protection, however, why did they fail to recognize the legitimate interest of society in protecting the worker?

The answer given was that the community had no legitimate interest in the regulation of labor because the condition of inequality between the parties that justifies infringement of freedom of contract did not exist. "The right of a person to sell his labor upon such terms as he deems proper," declared the Supreme Court, "is, in its essence, the same as the right of the purchaser of labor to prescribe the conditions upon which he will accept such labor from the person offering to sell it. So the right of the employé to quit the service of the employer, for whatever reason, is the same as the right of the employer, for whatever reason, to dispense with the services of such employé. . . . In all such particulars the employer and the employé have equality of right, and any legislation that disturbs that equality is an arbitrary interference with the liberty of contract."[108]

Assuming equality between employer and employee, the conclusion regarding legislative interference with that equality follows without too much difficulty. "As between persons sui juris," asks an 1899 opinion, "what right has the legislature to assume that one class has the need of protection against another?"[109] To the courts of the time, laws regulating the conditions of employment could be portrayed as putting laborers under guardianship,[110] as making them wards of the state,[111] as stamping them as imbeciles,[112] and as "an insulting attempt to put the laborer under a legislative tutelage . . . degrading to his manhood."[113]

These characterizations now seem quaintly ludicrous, for the theory upon which they were based was wholly out of line with reality. The 1909 Supreme Court dealt with the relation between employer and employee in railway transportation as if the parties were individual farmers haggling over the sale of a horse.[114] Such an approach was rendered obsolete by modern industrial society.[115] The helplessness of the individual employee, unaided by government or collective action with his fellows, has been a basic fact of labor history since the industrial revolution. "Men are not free while financially dependent."[116] Such dependence makes "freedom of contract . . . a misnomer as applied to a contract between an employer and an ordinary individual employee."[117] As an English judge stated two centuries ago, "[N]ecessitous men are not, truly speaking, free men, but, to answer a present exigency, will submit to any terms that the crafty may impose upon them."[118] This remark is particularly relevant to the industrial employee's position: he is compelled to bargain, alone and unaided, for whatever terms of employment he can secure. "There is grim irony in speaking of the freedom of contract of those who, because of their economic necessities, give their services for less than is needful to keep body and soul together."[119]

LOCHNER AND LEGAL DARWINISM

On November 9, 1882, Delmonico's in New York City was the scene of a dinner in honor of Herbert Spencer, then ending a visit to the United States. William M. Evarts, popularly known as "the Prince of the American Bar," made a speech praising the guest. In all areas of social life, declared Evarts, "we acknowledge your labors, Mr. Spencer, as surpassing those of any of our kind. . . . The faculty of laying on a dissecting board an entire nation or an entire age and finding out all the arteries and veins and pulsations of their life is an extension beyond any that our medical schools afford."[120]

In his *Lochner* dissent, Justice Holmes delivered his famous protest that "The Fourteenth Amendment does not enact Mr. Herbert Spencer's Social Statics."[121] But the Evarts tribute was closer to the truth of the day. Justice Rufus W. Peckham (himself the author of the *Lochner* opinion and hence the architect, in large part, of the due process approach of the day) once pointed out that a judge was "naturally and necessarily affected by the atmosphere of the times in which he lived." His views on the propriety of governmental interferences with private rights were bound to be "colored by the general ideas as to the proper function of government then existing."[122] During the latter half of the nineteenth century Spencer's application of the theory of evolution to human society became the accepted social gospel. Despite the Holmes stricture, Spencer's Social Darwinism became the dominant legal philosophy. Temporary theories were translated into legal absolutes; abstract conceptions concerning liberty and justice were erected into constitutional dogmas.[123] The Fourteenth Amendment was treated as a legal sanction of the survival of the fittest.

The tenor of the times was set forth in Mark Twain's *The Gilded Age*,[124] particularly in the character of Colonel Beriah Sellers—he of the magical tongue, grandiose dreams, and flexible ethics. The Twain book stamped its title on the whole period between the Civil War and the turn of the century.[125]

The American of that day is described by Henry Adams: "The American thought of himself as a restless, pushing, energetic, ingenious person, always awake and trying to get ahead of his neighbors." All his energies "were oriented in one direction"—the making of money.[126] "It is the desire to earn money," asserted a member of the Supreme Court in 1893, "which lies at the bottom of the greatest efforts of genius. . . . The motive which prompted Angelo to paint . . . the frescoes of the Sistine Chapel was essentially the same as that which induces a common laborer to lay brick or dig sewers."[127] Even Herbert Spencer was shocked at the "sole interest—the interest in business" that he found in the United States of 1882.[128]

Yet it was Spencer who furnished the philosophical foundation for the American devotion to materials ends. To Americans Spencer resembled Saturn returned to earth, bringing back the freedom of contract that the politicians had banished.[129] The Golden Age was to be the reign of justice, governed by its first principle: "Every man has freedom to do all that he wills, provided he infringes not the equal freedom of any other man." The essential function of government was to administer this principle, and in doing so it must keep its hands off the economic system. "In putting a veto upon any commercial intercourse, or in putting obstacles in the way of any such intercourse, a government . . . directly reverses its function." In regulating commerce, "the State is transformed from a maintainer of rights into a violator of rights." It was, indeed, "criminal in it to deprive men, in any way, of liberty to pursue the objects they desire."[130]

This simplistic version of laissez faire received what its contemporaries considered an unshakable scientific base when it was grounded in Darwinism. Spencer's *Social Statics* was originally published in 1851. But it was not until "the greatest of prophets in the most evolutionary of worlds"[131] provided a scientific justification in his *Origin of Species* that Spencerian sociology took over the field. The concept that species evolved by adapting to the environment was seen as applicable to social, as well as natural, life. There, too, the struggle for existence was similar to that which Darwin had discerned among plants and animals;[132] progress resulted from the "survival of the fittest" (Spencer's term). The corollary was a strong bias against human interference with the operation of Darwin's natural laws. When Spencer proclaimed that "[p]rogress . . . is not an accident, but a necessity,"[133] the implication—especially to his American disciples—was that tampering with the balance set by nature would only impair progressive evolution.[134]

To the American lawyer, the "law in all its aspects and evolution presents so many analogies to the biological world" that "translation of it into post-Darwinian language" became appropriate.[135] The judges who decided cases like *Lochner* virtually elevated what Joseph H. Choate called "Darwin's great theory of the survival of the fittest"[136] into the law of the land.

Legal Darwinism permeates the jurisprudence of the day. A New York precursor of *Lochner* stresses "the unceasing struggle for success and existence which pervades all societies of men." Through it, a man "may be deprived of that which will enable him to maintain his hold, and to survive." But the operation of the evolutionary struggle must not be interfered with by government. "Such governmental interferences disturb the normal adjustments of the social fabric, and usually derange the delicate and complicated machinery of industry and cause a score of ills while attempting the removal of one."[137]

Justice Peckham followed a similar approach as a member of the New York court before his elevation to Olympus. As he saw it, the "liberty" protected by due process "is deemed to embrace the right of man to be free in the enjoyment of the faculties with which he has been endowed by his Creator, subject only to such restraints as are necessary"—plainly a paraphrase of Spencer. This principle is violated by "legislation . . . of that kind which has been so frequent of late, a kind which is meant to protect some class in the community against the fair, free and full competition of some other class, the members of the former class thinking it impossible to hold their own against such competition, and therefore flying to the legislature."[138]

Lochner itself reflected the same Spencerian philosophy. "The liberty of the citizen to do as he likes so long as he does not interfere with the liberty of others to do the same, which has been a shibboleth for some well-known writers,"[139] provided the true basis for the *Lochner* decision. Laws regulating occupations such as that of bakers violate "the liberty of the individual in adopting and pursuing such calling as he may choose. . . . Statutes of the nature of that under review, limiting the hours in which grown and intelligent men may labor to earn their living, are mere meddlesome interferences with the rights of the individual."[140]

The judges who wrote these opinions echoed the common view of the legal profession, itself a manifestation of the dominant philosophy of the day. Legal writings and addresses toward the turn of the century are replete with applications of Spencerian Darwinism. Christopher G. Tiedeman virtually wrote Spencer's doctrines into his influential *Unwritten Constitution of the United States*. Tiedeman states the natural-rights doctrine that underlies American law in Spencerian terms as "a freedom from all legal restraint that is not needed to prevent injury to others."[141] The law, like nature itself, must proceed on the natural selection principle: "[S]ociety, collectively and individually, can attain its highest development by being left free from governmental control." The notion "that government has the power to banish evil from the earth" is nothing but the revival of an "old superstition."[142]

The prevalence of this view may be seen from the speeches made at bar meetings, particularly those of the newly organized American Bar Association. As the ABA president put it in 1897, "Under our system, the gates and avenues . . . are open to all who will run the course . . . ; there is no favor for any, and the best wins."[143] To the profession, "Natural Selection seemed a dogma to be put in the place of the Athanasian creed; it was a form of religious hope; a promise of ultimate perfection."[144] Spencerian doctrine was elevated to "the vital and mighty fact of modern Christian civilization; the integrity of every human soul and its right to the possession, exercise and enjoyment of all its faculties, capabilities and activities as to it seems good and in such full measure as is consistent with the same right of others."[145]

Legal Darwinism thus came to permeate all aspects of the legal order. Laissez faire and Spencerism became touchstones throughout the law— the fundamental principle being "that the less the law-making power has to do with controlling [man] in his business methods, the better."[146] Nor was this type of assertion put forth defensively. The prosperity and growth of the country appeared to demonstrate the potential in an environment free of legal controls; the frontier experience was seen as a proving ground for Darwinist arguments.[147] "Experience seems to justify the reckless American confidence, which has decided that the forces which make for growth shall be absolutely free to act."[148]

THE LION AND THE OX

During the *Lochner* era, Louis D. Brandeis tells us, courts "continued to ignore newly arisen social needs," such as those of labor in the new industrial society. Instead, "They applied complacently eighteenth century conceptions of the liberty of the individual and of the sacredness of private property. Early nineteenth century scientific half-truths, like

'The survival of the fittest,' which translated into practice meant 'The devil take the hindmost,' were erected by judicial sanction into a moral law."[149]

Looking back, we can see that the emphasis on the rights of the property owner and his virtually unlimited freedom from public interference with his will went too far. "Nothing, it has been said," declared a federal judge in 1942 "exceeds like excess. Laissez-faire went too far."[150] By the turn of the century, "[f]reedom had become individualism, and individualism had become the inalienable right to preempt, to exploit, to squander."[151] In the law as elsewhere, utterly unrestrained individualism becomes self-devouring.[152] If unlimited freedom of contract alone is to prevail, in practical terms the individual may be forced to part, by the very contract he is allowed to make, with all real freedom.[153] "One law for the Lion & Ox," says William Blake, "is Oppression." The same is true of one law for the mammoth corporation and its employee. Survival of the fittest had turned the Gilded Age into brass.

Even at the time, there were those who saw the tarnish. In a law school lecture early in this century, Brooks Adams stated that "freedom of contract is an effect of unrestrained economic competition." Its ultimate effect would be that it "induces an unstable equilibrium by encouraging over-competition among its members. When the moment of over-competition is reached, a period of transition begins. I am inclined to believe that the United States is now entering upon such a period."[154]

Most observers today would agree that Adams's analysis was accurate. In his discussion of laissez faire, James Bryce noted that, even in America, "[n]ew causes are at work . . . tending not only to lengthen the arms of government, but to make its touch quicker and firmer." Unlimited competition, he went on, pressed too hard on the weak, and to restrain its abuses the action of government was being carried into ever-widening fields. This was true even though "the process of transition to this new habit [was] so gradual . . . that for a long time few but lawyers and economists became aware of it."[155]

Now, half a century after the repudiation of *Lochner* and the Spencerian philosophy on which it was based, New Right jurists such as Professor Siegan proclaim that once again "substantive due process becomes a policy of laissez faire."[156] But history itself gives the lie to the complacent vision of a wholly unrestrained economy held by these pseudo-Spencerians.

If, as Siegan urges, we rehabilitate *Lochner*, we would be going back to a time when "it was unconstitutional to intrude upon the inalienable right of employees to make contracts containing terms unfavorable to themselves, in bargains with their employers."[157] In those days, "[a]n ordinary worker was told, if he sought to avoid harsh contracts made with his employer . . . that he had acted with his eyes open, had only himself to blame, must stand on his own feet, must take the consequences of his own folly."[158] And if, as in *Lochner*, a law sought to equalize the situation, it was ruled an invalid interference with freedom of contract. To return to *Lochner* is to return to the abuses that inevitably accompany complete laissez faire. Few will agree with Professor Siegan that such a return is desirable.

4

TAKINGS AND PUBLIC POWER

NEW RIGHT jurists think of themselves as spearheading a conservative revival in jurisprudence. They are, however, conservative only in a Pickwickian sense. In reality, their approach to constitutional law is a radical one; they aim to uproot established doctrine and replace it with principles long repudiated by a settled line of case law.

This is particularly true of the work of Richard A. Epstein, one of the most influential and scholarly of the New Right jurists who have tilted a lance against the established law. Epstein's approach is even broader in scope than that of Bernard Siegan. It would make for a quantum change in constitutional jurisprudence that would completely transform the relations between public power and property rights. Far-reaching though it is, however, it is based entirely on one simple clause in the Constitution—the Takings Clause of the Fifth Amendment.[1]

TAKINGS: THE CONSTITUTIONAL CENTER?

Professor Epstein sees the Takings Clause as the true center of the constitutional universe. At first glance his Copernican enterprise appears doomed to failure, for the Takings Clause, on its face, seems a relatively narrow one, dealing with only one basic governmental power and its limitations. The clause provides, "[N]or shall private property be taken for public use, without just compensation." By implication it confirms the power of eminent domain—that is, the governmental authority to acquire property compulsorily. It is, the Supreme Court tells us, "a tacit recognition of a preexisting power to take private property for public use, rather than a grant of new power."[2] But the clause also limits compulsory acquisition to property taken for a "public use" and for which "just compensation" must be paid.

To Epstein, however, the reach of the Takings Clause is far broader than its literal language. The clause, in his view, is not confined to cases in which property is acquired by eminent domain. Instead, he starts with the Blackstone definition of property as "that sole and despotic dominion which one man claims and exercises over the external things of the world, in total exclusion of the right of any other individual in the universe."[3] According to Blackstone, property ownership includes a trilogy of rights: "The third absolute right, inherent in every Englishman, is that of property, which consists in the free use, enjoyment, and disposal of all his acquisitions, without any control or diminution, save only by the laws of the land."[4]

For Epstein, "Blackstone's account of private property explains what the term means in the eminent domain clause."[5] The key Epstein premise is that *any* diminution in the Blackstone trilogy of rights is a "taking" within the meaning of the Fifth Amendment.[6] Under this approach, the scope of the Takings Clause is expanded exponentially so that it covers virtually every governmental interference with the right to possess, use, and dispose of any property. The concept includes interferences with property rights by regulation and taxation, as well as acquisitions of property by eminent domain in the traditional sense. To Epstein, regulations and taxes are "takings" no less than compulsory transfers of title, for they also impinge upon the Blackstone trilogy of rights.

Such a radical expansion of the Takings Clause makes it *the* guaranty for property rights in the Constitution. More than that, it renders superfluous the other constitutional protections for property, such as those contained in the Contract Clause, the Due Process Clause, and the Equal Protection Clause. Why rely on these clauses, when the Takings Clause bars all governmental interferences with property rights unless just compensation is paid?

This chapter will deal with the implications of Professor Epstein's expansive view of the Takings Clause. Is Epstein a latter-day Copernicus whose discovery of the true center of the constitutional universe will transform the protection of property rights in American law, or does his work belong "with the output of the constitutional lunatic fringe . . . a travesty of constitutional scholarship"?[7] Before we try to answer this question, a word should be said about Epstein's attack on the broadening of the "public use" concept during the past century.

PUBLIC USE: THE INVISIBLE LIMITATION?

Under the Takings Clause, eminent-domain power may be exercised only when the property is taken for a "public use." As Justice Story stated, in classic language, "Although the sovereign power in free governments may appropriate all the property, public as well as private, for public purposes, making compensation therefore; yet it has never been understood, at least, never in our republic, that the sovereign power can take the private property of A. and give it to B., by the right of 'eminent domain'; or, that it can take it at all, except for public purposes."[8]

The Supreme Court has continued to assert that the "public use" requirement remains an essential limitation on the eminent-domain power.[9] Despite this, Professor Epstein terms the relevant provision "The Invisible Public Use Clause" and asserts that the Supreme Court "gave the limitation a mortal blow" in the leading modern case on the subject.[10]

It can hardly be denied that there has been a tremendous expansion in the public-use concept during the past century. We can see this clearly from *Shoemaker v. United States*,[11] the first case in the Supreme Court involving the question of whether a taking was for a public use. The Court there at the very outset of its opinion asserted, "In the memory of men now living, a proposition to take private property, without the consent of its owner, for a public park . . . would have been regarded as a novel exercise of legislative power."[12]

If, in 1893, the Court could characterize the use of the eminent-domain power to acquire land for a park as "a novel exercise" of such power, what would the members of that tribunal say about the extension that has since occurred in the public-use concept? For, if one thing is certain, it is that the notion of public purpose has undergone an expansion fully comparable to that characterizing the police power during the past century. The reasons behind both expansions are basically similar.

100

The necessities of modern industrial society have required that judges give ever-broadening scope to the social interests that the community may vindicate through the police power. What is true of regulation is also true of taking. The courts have been obliged to recognize that the need of present-day society to acquire public property is not as limited as that of our essentially agricultural society of a century ago. The public purposes that may be achieved through the power of eminent domain have had to be broadened to correspond with present-day expanded notions of the proper reach of governmental power.

It should not be forgotten that both the police power and the eminent-domain power are only different weapons in the governmental arsenal, all of which are intended to enable government to serve the great public needs that the prevailing thought of the day deems essential to the welfare of society. In an era dominated by an ever-expanding police power, it would be anomalous if an equally vital governmental power were confined within the narrower range permitted to it when the police power itself was more rigidly construed.

The burgeoning conception of the public welfare, which has been of such consequence to the police power, has been of equivalent importance to the eminent-domain power. "The law of each age," says a state judge, "is ultimately what that age thinks should be the law."[13] The same is the case with regard to the proper reach of governmental authority. An age that permits the police power to be employed whenever it is deemed to be in the interest of the public health, safety, morals, or welfare will hardly do less for the power of eminent domain.

The proper approach in these cases was taken half a century ago by the New York Court of Appeals:

> The fundamental purpose of government is to protect the health, safety and general welfare of the public. All its complicated activities have that simple end in view. Its power plant for the purpose consists of the power of taxation, the police power and the power of eminent domain. Whenever there arises, in the State, a condition of affairs holding a substantial menace to the public health, safety or general welfare, it becomes the duty of the government to apply whatever power is necessary and appropriate to check it. . . . if the menace is serious enough to the public to warrant public action and the power applied is reasonably and fairly calculated to check it, and bears a reasonable relation to the evil, it seems

to be constitutionally immaterial whether one or another of the sovereign powers is employed.[14]

Under this approach, the public purpose for which eminent domain power may be exercised merges into the concept of public welfare itself. If that is true, public use may be defined as broadly as was done in a Connecticut case: "[P]ublic use means public usefulness, utility, or advantage, or what is productive of general benefit, so that any appropriating of private property by the state under its right of eminent domain, for purposes of great advantage to the community, is a taking for public use."[15]

If we go so far, we are in effect saying that where government has the authority to undertake the purposes for which land is sought to be condemned, then the use is a public one for which the power of eminent domain may be exerted. "If the Federal Government, under the Constitution, has power to embark upon the project for which the land is sought, then the use is a public one."[16]

This means that the scope of eminent domain today is as far-reaching as the radius of governmental power itself. Or, as it was put in the most recent Supreme Court statement on the matter, "The 'public use' requirement is thus coterminous with the scope of a sovereign's police powers."[17] It follows that whatever government may do through its police power, it may also seek to accomplish through use of condemnation authority. All the ends that may be attained by exercise of the police power may be attained as well through employment of the power of eminent domain, where that can be done through the acquisition of property. If the purpose for which land is sought by the state bears a reasonable relationship to the public health, safety, morals, or welfare, then the use is a public one.[18]

Professor Epstein strongly disagrees with this expansion of the public-use concept, which in effect equates eminent-domain power with the police power. "There is good reason," Epstein asserts, "to believe that the received wisdom, which trivializes the public use limitation, is incorrect."[19] As an example of the incorrect approach, he cites *Berman v. Parker*,[20] the leading modern case on the expanded meaning of "public use." At issue in *Berman* was the District of Columbia Redevelopment Act. As more recently explained by the Court, "That Act provided both for the comprehensive use of the eminent domain power to redevelop slum areas and for the possible sale or lease of the condemned lands to private interests."[21] A public agency was authorized to condemn property in substandard areas and then to sell the property to private persons for development by them in accordance with slum-clearance or redevelopment schemes.

To Epstein, the *Berman v. Parker* scheme was "a perversion of the public use doctrine. . . . [T]he programs depend on the taking of private property for private use, here on a massive scale."[22] To the Court, on the other hand, the taking was clearly for a public use. Slum clearance bears a reasonable relationship to the ends that may be attained by the state's police power; hence, the land involved is being taken for a public use. "Once the object is within the authority of congress, the right to realize it through the exercise of eminent domain is clear." Nor, according to the Court, did the fact that private enterprise was used for redevelopment make the taking one for private use: "The public end may be as well or better served through an agency of private enterprise than through a department of government—or so the Congress might conclude. We cannot say that public ownership is the sole method of promoting the public purposes."[23]

Berman v. Parker involves another extension of the public-use concept that runs contrary to the earlier, more limited concept approved by Professor Epstein. The lower court there had upheld the use of eminent-domain power in the District of Columbia for slum clearance purposes. Its opinion indicated, however, that eminent-domain power might not be employed solely for aesthetic purposes. Referring to the redevelopment plan at issue, the court conceded that "it would enhance the beauty . . . of the area. If undertaken by private persons the project would be most laudable. It would be difficult to think of a village, town or city in the United States which a group of artists, architects and builders could not improve vastly if they could tear down the whole community and rebuild the whole of it. But as yet the courts have not come to call such pleasant accomplishments a public purpose which validates Government seizure of private property."[24]

The Supreme Court expressly disagreed. It candidly recognized that the redevelopment plan was motivated as much by aesthetic considerations as by any others. Such a motivation, it ruled, could justify exertion of condemnation authority: "It is within the power of the legislature to determine that the community should be beautiful as well as healthy." Ugly housing may constitute a "sore, a blight on the community which robs it of charm, which makes it a place from which men turn."[25] Under *Berman*, the public use becomes one that may be aesthetic as well as material.

Berman v. Parker is Professor Epstein's particular bête noire. The question it raises, however, is this: Would society be better off with the restricted notion of public use that the courts used to follow? A critic could write then, "What we have reason to complain of is an undue restriction of the right of eminent domain . . . ; this restriction is due to a too narrow interpretation of public purpose, an interpretation which in turn is due to an excess of individualism in the law."[26] In particular, should we return to the restricted view of public power that prevailed when neither eminent domain nor the police power could be employed to accomplish aesthetic objectives? "Aesthetic considerations," declared a leading 1905 case, "are a matter of luxury and indulgence rather than of necessity, and it is necessity alone which justifies the exercise of the police power."[27] Critics referred to European uses of governmental authority to make cities "beautiful and attractive in the interest of rich and poor" and asked, "Why should we struggle so long to secure the recognition of beauty as a public concern?"[28] But the law then was summed up in an 1897 article by Sir Frederick Pollock, which categorically denied that Anglo-American law took cognizance of aesthetic considerations: "Robust good sense is the merit of our common law, but the fine taste— the aesthetic sensibility which is the birthright of the Frenchman, as it was of the Greek, is denied to the Anglo-Saxon." Acceptance of this doctrine would mean going back to the day when, to support this assertion, Pollock could quote Hood's lines:

Nature which gave them the goût
Only gave us the gout.[29]

TAKINGS CLAUSE: LANGUAGE AND INTENT

The most far-reaching aspect of Professor Epstein's interpretation of the Takings Clause is his assertion that any diminution by government of the rights of a property owner constitutes a "taking" under the Fifth Amendment. Before the implications of the Epstein analysis are discussed, a word should be said about the language used in the Takings Clause and whether it supports Epstein's interpretation. I shall examine this question by looking first at the history of protections against takings without compensation enacted before the Fifth Amendment was adopted.

The Fifth Amendment's Takings Clause was, of course, not the first provision in American law prohibiting takings without compensation. The very first enactment in this country safeguarding the rights of the people contained such a prohibition. The enactment in question was the Massachusetts Body of Liberties of 1641. It was enacted, we are told by John Winthrop, then governor of Massachusetts Bay, because the "people had long desired a body of laws, and thought their condition very unsafe, while so much power rested in the discretion of magistrates."[30] Bearing in mind its early date, both the scope and specific provisions of the Massachusetts enactment are striking. Many of the fundamental rights later to be protected in American constitutions were either safeguarded or anticipated in the 1641 enactment.

Among the rights thus protected was that against takings without compensation. The relevant provision read: "No mans Cattel or goods of what kinde soever shall be pressed or taken for any publique use or service, unlesse it be by warrant grounded upon some act of the generall Court, nor without such reasonable prices and hire as the ordinarie rates of the Countrie do afford."[31] This language indicates that the property must actually be used in the public service before any right to compensation exists.

The first constitutional protection against takings was in the Vermont Declaration of Rights of 1777. Under it, "private property ought to be subservient to public uses, when necessity requires it; nevertheless, whenever any particular man's property is taken for the use of the public, the owner ought to receive an equivalent in money."[32] This language, too, indicates that the property must be acquired by government before the clause applies—an interpretation supported by a later provision of the Vermont Bill of Rights that "no part of a man's property can be justly taken from him, or applied to public uses, without his own consent, or that of his legal representatives."[33]

The implication in this respect is even clearer in the next constitution-

105

al guaranty on takings to be enacted, in the Massachusetts Declaration of Rights of 1780. Under it, "whenever the public exigencies require, that the property of any individual should be appropriated to public uses, he shall receive a reasonable compensation therefore."[34] For property to "be appropriated to public uses," there would have to be a governmental takeover of the property concerned.

There was also a provision on takings in the Northwest Ordinance of 1787, the most important enactment of the federal government before the Constitution. The ordinance's second article provided that "should the public exigencies make it necessary for the common preservation to take any persons property, or to demand his particular services, full compensation shall be made for the same."[35] Here, too, the implication is that the property must be acquired before the compensation requirement becomes applicable.

We come now to the Takings Clause of the Fifth Amendment itself. The federal Bill of Rights was, of course, essentially the work of James Madison. It was his draft, introduced in the House of Representatives on June 8, 1789, that was the basis for the amendments passed by the First Congress. As authored by Madison the Takings Clause read: "No person shall . . . be obliged to relinquish his property, where it may be necessary for public use, without a just compensation."[36] The Madison language is even clearer than the earlier provisions discussed in this section. It indicates that Madison "intended the clause to apply only to direct, physical taking of property."[37] It is hard to see how one can "be obliged to relinquish his property" unless the property is actually acquired for the public use.

Madison himself did not say exactly what he meant by his draft Takings Clause. None of the statements he made in the House debate had anything to do with the clause. Nor, so far as the report of the debate in the *Annals of Congress* tells us, was there discussion of the Takings Clause by any other House member.

We do know that Madison's proposed amendments were referred to a Select Committee of eleven members (one of whom was Madison himself).[38] The committee changed the language of the Takings Clause to the version that passed both the House and Senate and became the clause in the Fifth Amendment as ratified.[39] But there is no legislative history on why the change was made or on its meaning either in the committee or on the floor in either House.

It is, however, most unlikely that the change in language was intended to change the meaning of Madison's draft Takings Clause. The substitution of "taken" for Madison's original "relinquish" did not mean that something less than acquisition of property would bring the clause into play. That was, indeed, the meaning of a "taking" with which the men of 1789 were familiar. Samuel Johnson's *Dictionary*[40] (the only one in existence when the Bill of Rights was adopted) contains sixty-six meanings of the verb "to take." Those relevant to its use in the Takings Clause are: "To seize what is not given"; "To snatch; to seize"; "To get; to have; to appropriate"; "To get; to procure"; and "To fasten on; to seize." All of these are consistent with the Takings Clause as requiring an appropriation or acquisition of property. None of the meanings listed by Dr. Johnson indicates any acceptance of the Epstein view that an interference with property short of acquisition can constitute a taking.

REGULATION VERSUS TAKING

Both the prior provisions on which it was based (from the Massachusetts Body of Liberties to Madison's draft clause) and the Fifth Amendment's Takings Clause itself indicate that an acquisition or appropriation of property is required before the just-compensation guaranty is applicable. Despite this, Richard Epstein contends that the reach of the Takings Clause is far broader. He argues that the clause applies whenever governmental action involves a diminution in the Blackstone trilogy of rights—that is, whenever there is a governmental interference with an owner's right to possess, use, and dispose of his property. In particular, Epstein asserts that the Takings Clause comes into play whenever governmental regulation interferes with the rights of the property owner.

Epstein points out that governmental regulation of the possession, use, and disposition of private property "is a perfectly commonplace affair in modern American life." He then refers to different types of regulations: those that require owners to allow access and entry; land-use regulations; and regulations that limit the goods that can be sold and the prices charged for them. Epstein notes that there may be important differences among these various forms of regulation. "Yet," he argues, "these protean forms of regulation all amount to partial takings of private property."[41]

The first thing to note about this assertion is that it extends the Takings Clause far beyond the meaning normally given to the clause's language. In the ordinary meaning of the term, a "taking" of property is "a physical takeover of a distinct entity, with an accompanying transfer of the legal powers of enjoyment and exclusion that are typically associated with rights of property."[42] This was also the meaning given to the term by both the drafters of the Takings Clause and those who drew up earlier protections against uncompensated takings. The idea that regulation involving only a diminution in the owner's rights and not any takeover of the property concerned constitutes a partial taking within the Fifth Amendment appears supported only by Epstein's own ipse dixit.

Such an assertion is also completely contrary to the established law on the matter. The law has always made a sharp distinction between the power of eminent domain and regulatory action taken under the police power. Epstein to the contrary, it is not true that whenever governmental action results in the deprivation of property or diminution of its value, there is a taking for which just compensation must be paid. The exercise of the police power may in many cases (particularly those concerned with public health and safety) involve a drastic impact upon the value of property being regulated, and may, in extreme cases, virtually destroy the value of the property. Yet there is no taking in such cases under the settled jurisprudence on the matter.

The extreme impact of the police power in appropriate cases may be illustrated by *Miller v. Schoene*.[43] Acting under a state statute authorizing the destruction of red cedar trees infected with rust, the relevant official had ordered the cutting down of plaintiff's ornamental cedars, to prevent the contamination of neighboring apple orchards. This turned out to be the only practical method of protecting the orchards, in a state where apple-growing constituted one of the principal agricultural pursuits.

There is no doubt that the effect upon plaintiff in *Miller v. Schoene* was as drastic as though his trees had been taken under eminent domain. Yet if there had been a taking, plaintiff would clearly have been entitled to just compensation. *Miller v. Schoene*, on the other hand, upheld the destruction of the trees even though there was no provision whatever for compensation to their owner. As the Court has more recently explained it, in *Miller v. Schoene* "it was clear that the State's exercise of its police power to prevent the impending danger was justified, and did not require compensation."[44]

To Professor Epstein, *Miller v. Schoene* is a case in which the state took private property, even though the claimant was left in possession of the cut timber. In effect, the state paid for the standing trees with cut timber of far less value. According to Epstein, the decision really involved a "transformation of eminent domain law." That is because the Court allowed the state, under the guise of the police power, to decide "upon the destruction of one class of property in order to save another which, in the judgment of the legislature, is of greater value to the public." Under such an approach, says Epstein, "The confusion between police power and public necessity is complete. The price paid for the error is that the just compensation requirement becomes legislative instead of constitutional."[45]

To Epstein, the *Miller v. Schoene* reasoning "is wholly inconsistent with any theory of property rights. . . . In the absence of any wrong by the owner of the cedar trees, the decision not to compensate is nothing more than authorization to transfer property illicitly from one class of citizens to another, as the owner of the cedar trees is left with neither the thing nor its value, when he has done no wrong."[46]

The whole point about *Miller v. Schoene*, however, is that there is no right to compensation unless there is a "taking" under the eminent-domain power. When the value of property is diminished by regulatory action taken under the police power, the same right does not arise—even though, as *Miller v. Schoene* expressly recognized, preferment of the public interest over the property interest of the individual is an essential characteristic of every exercise of the police power that affects property.[47]

The requirement that compensation be made for property taken for public use imposes no restriction upon the governmental power, by reasonable regulation, to protect the health, safety, morals, and welfare of the community.[48] It may well be true that there is "no set formula to determine where regulation ends and taking begins."[49] As a general proposition, nevertheless, it is safe to say that eminent domain takes property and applies it to a use that is beneficial to the public, while the police power restricts the owner in the use or enjoyment of his property because unrestricted exercise of the rights of ownership is deemed contrary to the public interest.[50]

The distinction in this respect was well stated by a federal court: "The distinction between an exercise of the eminent domain power that is compensable under the fifth amendment and an exercise of the police power is that in a compensable exercise of the eminent domain power, a property interest is taken from the owner and applied to the public use because the use of such property is beneficial to the public and in the exercise of the police power, the owner's property interest is restricted or infringed upon because his continued use of the property is or would otherwise be injurious to the public welfare."[51]

The application of this distinction is shown by *Goldblatt v. Hempstead*.[52] Appellant there owned and operated a thirty-eight-acre tract of town land, which he used for mining sand and gravel. The town had expanded around the excavation, so that the mining site was now located directly in the midst of a substantial residential area. The town naturally desired to stop further mining on the tract. Had it done so by taking over the property, compensation would have had to be paid. Instead, the town promulgated an ordinance prohibiting any excavating below the water table. Since the excavation in question was already well below the water table, the practical effect of the ordinance was to require the end of further mining by appellant.

The Court ruled that the ordinance was a valid exercise of the police power because of the relationship between excavations and the public safety, particularly so far as children were concerned. That being the case, it made no difference that the ordinance completely prohibited a beneficial use to which the property had previously been devoted. Nor could it be claimed that this was a "taking" without compensation: "A prohibition simply upon the use of property for purposes that are declared, by valid legislation, to be injurious to the health, morals, or safety of the community, cannot, in any just sense, be deemed a taking or an appropriation of property for the public benefit. Such legislation does not disturb the owner in the control or use of his property for lawful purposes, nor restrict his right to dispose of it, but is only a declaration by the State that its use by any one, for certain forbidden purposes, is prejudicial to the public interests."[53]

It is thus clear that government may diminish property values by assertion of the police power without having to make compensation for the loss.[54] It is only when property is actually transferred to government to be enjoyed and used by it as its own, or (as we shall see) when its value is destroyed, that there is a taking for which compensation must be paid.[55]

PARTIAL TAKING AND ZONING

Our conception of property has moved from "that sole and despotic dominion" of which Blackstone speaks[56] to "the bundle of rights that are [now] commonly characterized as property."[57] The fact that some sticks in the bundle may be shortened or even removed by governmental restrictions does not bring the Takings Clause into operation. "At least where an owner possesses a full 'bundle' of property rights, the destruction of one 'strand' of the bundle is not a taking, because the aggregate must be viewed in its entirety."[58]

It is, at the same time, erroneous to assume that for a "taking" to occur there must be a transfer of full ownership in the property concerned—that is, all the sticks in the bundle must be taken from the property owner. It is, on the contrary, settled, in the words of one case, that "[a]cquisition of title is not [always] essential to 'taking.'"[59] The governmental assertion of the right to use another's property, or to subject it to burdensome servitudes that limit or destroy the owner's beneficial use, is sufficient. "Property is taken in the constitutional sense when inroads are made upon an owner's use of it to an extent that, as between private parties, a servitude has been acquired either by agreement or in course of time."[60]

The principle that a taking may occur even without the physical acquisition of the property concerned[61] has been applied most frequently in cases involving the flooding of adjoining lands by government-constructed dams and comparable projects.[62] The established rule has become that the destruction of privately owned land by flooding is a taking to the extent of the destruction caused. To the extent that the owner's right to use and enjoy his land is destroyed by the governmental act, his loss is the same as if the government concerned had entered upon the land and taken possession of it.[63]

Other cases involve governmental action that in effect amounts to

111

acquisition of an easement on private property. A leading case dealt with an action to recover for an alleged taking resulting from the noise and glare of lights from planes landing at or leaving a military airport. The planes flew below the parameters of navigable airspace, as defined by federal law; the noise and glare caused plaintiff to stop using his neighboring farm for raising chickens, and otherwise seriously impaired his use and enjoyment of his land. The Court held that the government had so disturbed the peace of the occupants, and so altered the ability of the owner to use his land as a chicken farm, that there had been a "taking," in the constitutional sense, of an air easement, for which compensation had to be paid.[64] In a later case, a similar decision was rendered with regard to an airport operated by a state, where low landing and take-off flights made neighboring property "undesirable and unbearable for . . . residential use."[65]

These decisions, ruling that air easements were "taken" for a public use, rest upon the fact that the property owner owns not only the surface of the land, but also the "superadjacent airspace"[66] that may reasonably be used by the owner. Yet it is clear from the example of *Goldblatt v. Hempstead* that if the owner's right to use the space above his land had been eliminated by a reasonable regulation promulgated under the police power (as by a zoning ordinance or an ordinance restricting building heights), he would not be entitled to any compensation.

Professor Epstein is particularly troubled that zoning restrictions are included in the principle that a regulation limiting the use of property does not come within the Takings Clause. The leading case is, of course, *Euclid v. Ambler Realty Co.*[67] The Court there for the first time sustained a comprehensive zoning ordinance of the type that has become basic in modern efforts at town planning. The decision was based on a recognition that the realities of modern city life have made such regulation essential: "Until recent years, urban life was comparatively simple; but with the great increase and concentration of population, problems have developed, and constantly are developing, which require, and will continue to require, additional restrictions in respect of the use and occupation of private lands in urban communities."[68] Zoning regulations, like traffic regulations, must now be deemed to bear a reasonable relationship to the public safety and welfare, though, a half century earlier, they might well have been rejected as arbitrary and oppressive.

112

To Professor Epstein, the *Euclid* decision was all wrong. Plaintiff alleged that the restriction of its land to residential uses reduced its value by seventy-five percent. Because of this, Epstein argues, "the restrictions on use were a partial taking." Epstein asserts that the comprehensive zoning was not supported by the police-power ends relied on by the Court. More specifically, he denies that any of those ends supports a need to segregate residential from commercial areas. "The police power has always functioned where the two were integrated, and there is no obvious connection between the degree of separation and the degree of injury avoided. Any desired separation can be achieved by private means." Yet the whole point about zoning is that the market may not be adequate in this respect. Government may consequently intervene to ensure effective urban planning. Epstein, however, sees the entire *Euclid* zoning scheme "as an ill-concealed effort to transfer wealth from one set of landowners to another through the medium of regulation."[69]

To Epstein, indeed, "*Euclid*, at the birth of zoning, represents a virtual abandonment of efforts to monitor the overbreadth question in land use cases. The insistence upon the 'rational relation,' here as elsewhere, carries a legal message that is at variance with ordinary usage. Any fit between ends and means, however weak, will suffice even when superior alternatives are available."[70]

Epstein's animadversion notwithstanding, the *Euclid* decision remains a landmark in the legal transformation of property that has taken place during this century, under which the virtually absolute right of the owner to use his property as he chooses has given way to the principle of reasonable use, as defined by the relevant authorities. From this point of view, few decisions have been of greater practical import than that rendered in *Euclid*. A decision the other way would have all but rendered effective urban planning impossible in this country. Despite Epstein, *Euclid* did not really go beyond the traditional police-power approach, relying essentially upon the proposition that zoning "bears a rational relation to the health and safety of the community."[71]

In the more recent case of *Agins v. Tiburon*,[72] the Court affirmed specifically that a valid zoning ordinance does not effect a "taking" for which compensation is required. Appellants had acquired five acres of unimproved land for residential development in an area where land "has greater value than any other suburban property in the State of California." The land was then zoned to permit appellants to build only between one and five single-family residences on their tract. The Court rejected appellants' claim that the zoning took their property without compensation. "The specific zoning regulations at issue are exercises of the city's police power to protect the residents of Tiburon from the ill effects of urbanization."[73] A zoning regulation that constitutes a valid exercise of the police power does not effect a "taking," even though it restricts the right to develop property in the given area.

Professor Epstein compares the *Agins* zoning ordinance to a restrictive covenant created by private agreement. In both cases, he argues, "a property interest [is] taken from the owner of the burdened land." There may, Epstein goes on, be differences between covenants and zoning on the benefit side.[74] But that is not relevant to the taking question: "[T]he takings question asks only what has been taken; the nature and distribution of the benefits conferred become relevant only after the initial taking is acknowledged." In Epstein's view, "The well-nigh conclusive presumption that regulations are 'reasonable' simply does not begin to address the hard issues in takings cases. The eminent-domain clause does not say, 'The private rights of disposition and use are in the public domain.' But that is how it is now read."[75]

In a case like *Agins*, however, the right of disposition and use is, like other economic rights, subject to valid regulation under the police power. That the regulation restricts the property owner's rights, and by so doing lessens the value of his land, does not convert the regulation into a taking for which compensation must be paid. "That the loss is heavy and that [plaintiff] must bear more than its proportionate share of the burden for the sake of the general welfare, however, did not convert the regulation into a taking."[76]

What is especially striking about the zoning and land-use cases is that while their property restrictions are upheld because of an ostensible relationship to police-power factors such as health and safety, that relationship may be a fiction most of the time. As a zoning expert once remarked, "The whole thing is really a matter of aesthetics and traffic, isn't it?—that is, apart from keeping out a few nuisance industries."[77] The principal concern in typical zoning and town-planning regulation is how an area looks.[78] In the courts, nevertheless, the arguments and decisions still turn almost entirely upon considerations of health and safety.[79]

The most common type of zoning requirement whose aim is almost entirely aesthetic is the requirement of conformity to a building line. Such a requirement was sustained against due-process objections in a 1927 Supreme Court decision, which went on grounds of public health and safety.[80] Yet it is apparent, as Justice Holmes once conceded, that a building-line requirement has "aesthetic considerations in view more obviously than anything else."[81]

The same is true of zoning restrictions laying down minimum lot size and minimum floor space, as well as those which seek to ensure architectural design in conformity with existing structures. The latter may involve an attempt to prevent substantial variance from "the exterior architectural appeal" of existing houses in a neighborhood,[82] or it may seek to preserve the distinctive architectural tradition of a city like New Orleans.[83] In either case, the regulation seeks to promote aesthetic objectives; yet both types of restrictions on building design have been upheld.[84] In one of the cases so holding, the highest court of Wisconsin, after alluding to the older rule that the zoning power may not be exercised for purely aesthetic considerations, stated that "such rule was undergoing development. In view of the latest word spoken on the subject by the United States supreme court in Berman v. Parker . . . this development of the law has proceeded to the point that renders it extremely doubtful that such prior rule is any longer the law."[85]

The Supreme Court decision in *Berman v. Parker*[86] to which the Wisconsin court referred is now the seminal decision on the subject. The statute there authorized "the redevelopment of blighted territory in the District of Columbia and the prevention, reduction, or elimination of blighting factors or causes of blight." Appellant attacked the inclusion of his property in a slum-clearance scheme on the ground that the property was not a slum, and that it violated due process for a man's property to be taken to develop a better balanced, more attractive community.

As seen in our previous discussion of the case,[87] the Court upheld the challenged slum-clearance plan even though it conceded that the details of the plan were motivated as much by aesthetic, as by other, considerations. The land-use power was stated in expansive terms to include values that "are spiritual as well as physical, aesthetic as well as monetary." Under such an approach, "If those who govern the District of Columbia decide that the Nation's Capital should be beautiful as well as sanitary, there is nothing in the Fifth Amendment that stands in the way."[88]

From this point of view, Professor Epstein has a basis for his complaint that the police-power justifications usually stated in zoning cases are largely fictitious. Epstein shows, for example, how the police-power ends of public health and safety relied on by the *Euclid* Court were not supported by the facts in the case.[89] Even if the Epstein criticism is valid, however, the *Euclid* type of zoning ordinance is supported by the *Berman v. Parker* reasoning: "It is within the power of the legislature to determine that the community should be beautiful as well as healthy."[90] What was said by the Louisiana court as early as 1923 is so relevant in this connection that it deserves to be quoted:

> The beauty of a fashionable residence neighborhood in a city is for the comfort and happiness of the residents, and it sustains in a general way the value of property in the neighborhood. It is therefore as much a matter of general welfare as is any other condition that fosters comfort or happiness, and consequent values generally of the property in the neighborhood. Why should not the police power avail, as well to suppress or prevent a nuisance committed by offending the sense of sight, as to suppress or prevent a nuisance committed by offending the sense of hearing, or the olfactory nerves?[91]

Beauty is so basic a value in any society—To make us love our country, said Burke, our country ought to be lovely—that it should support the *Euclid-Berman* type of comprehensive zoning or urban-clearance regulation.

HOLMES VERSUS BRANDEIS

The principal case that appears to lend support to the Epstein interpretation of the Takings Clause is *Pennsylvania Coal Co. v. Mahon.*[92] That case presented the unusual spectacle of an articulated difference of opinion between Justices Holmes and Brandeis in a case involving economic regulation. At issue was a Pennsylvania law—usually called the

Kohler Act—forbidding the mining of coal in such a manner as to cause the subsidence of any structure used as a human habitation. The statute contained an exception for land where the surface was owned by the owner of the underlying coal. The coal company had conveyed the surface of the land involved in the case to plaintiff, but had expressly reserved the right to remove all the coal beneath the plot. The company served notice that their mining beneath the premises would soon cause subsidence in the surface. Relying on the Kohler Act, plaintiff sued to enjoin mining that would cause any subsidence of their house.

To Justice Brandeis, the case involved a simple application of the principle that an otherwise valid regulation does not constitute a taking: "Every restriction upon the use of property imposed in the exercise of the police power deprives the owner of some right theretofore enjoyed, and is, in that sense, an abridgment by the State of rights in property without making compensation. But restriction imposed to protect the public health, safety or morals from dangers threatened is not a taking."[93]

But Brandeis spoke only for himself in dissent. The majority of the Court, with Holmes delivering the opinion, ruled the Kohler Act invalid as a taking of property without compensation. In the Court's view, the police power might not be pushed so far as to destroy the previously existing rights of property and contract. While property may be regulated, if regulation goes too far it must be recognized as a taking for which compensation must be paid.[94]

To Professor Epstein, of course, the *Pennsylvania Coal* decision is wholly correct. "Owing to the clarity of the grant, . . . the case is an easy one. Before the statute the coal company was in possession of a mineral estate. After the statute was passed, the interest itself was lost. All else is superfluous; the case is easy."[95]

The Epstein agreement with the *Pennsylvania Coal* decision follows naturally from his interpretation of the Takings Clause. For those who reject that interpretation, *Pennsylvania Coal* is a more difficult case. According to the Holmes opinion, the Kohler Act could not be justified as a safety measure, since that "could be provided for by notice."[96] Yet all that Holmes himself said on other occasions about the propriety of judicial substitution of judgment on the mode chosen to deal with an evil might, with equal fitness, be said in answer to his assertion here. Certainly, it cannot be denied that a measure enacted to prevent subsidence

117

of dwelling houses bears a reasonable relationship to public safety. Why, to paraphrase Justice Brandeis in his dissent, may not the state prohibit one from digging so deep or excavating so near the surface as to expose the community to danger?[97]

Where the safety of society is so plainly involved, it should be for the legislator to determine whether mere notice of intention to mine would adequately protect the public or whether prohibitory power should be exercised. Where the connection with public safety is so patent, the power to regulate should exist—and that regardless of the impact on preexisting rights. In Brandeis's apt phrase, "If public safety is imperiled, surely neither grant, nor contract, can prevail against the exercise of the police power."[98]

The more recent case of *Keystone Bituminous Coal Ass'n v. DeBenedictis*[99] indicates that the Supreme Court itself now agrees more with the Brandeis than with the Holmes *Pennsylvania Coal* view. At issue in *Keystone* was the Pennsylvania Subsidence Act of 1966. It prohibits coal mining that causes subsidence damage to public buildings, dwellings, and cemeteries. Under regulations issued by the Pennsylvania Department of Environmental Resources, fifty percent of the coal beneath protected structures must be kept in place to provide surface support. The act authorizes the department to revoke a mining permit if the removal of coal causes damage to a protected structure or area and the operator has not within six months repaired the damage, satisfied any claim arising therefrom, or deposited the sum that repairs will reasonably cost as security. Petitioners, who owned substantial coal reserves under property protected by the subsidence act, filed suit claiming that the statute, as implemented by the fifty-percent rule, violated the Takings Clause.

Keystone appears to involve a present-day version of the *Pennsylvania Coal* case. But this time the Court held that the subsidence act did not constitute an invalid taking. The Court did so without overruling *Pennsylvania Coal*. According to the *Keystone* Court, the Holmes ruling on the validity of the Kohler Act "rested on two propositions. . . . First, because it served only private interests, not health or safety, the Kohler Act could not be 'sustained as an exercise of the police power.' . . . Second, the statute made it 'commercially impracticable' to mine 'certain coal' in the areas affected by the Kohler Act."[100]

Holmes had found that the Kohler Act served only private interests because the case was only "the case of a single private house": "A source of damage to such a house is not a public nuisance even if similar damage is inflicted on others in different places. The damage is not common or public." On the other side, Holmes stated that the company's mining right was worthless under the Kohler Act if the company could not remove its coal: "The right to coal consists in the right to mine it."[101] To make it commercially impracticable to mine the coal, Holmes asserted, had the same effect for constitutional purposes as appropriating the coal. Hence, there was a taking without compensation.[102]

Of course, Holmes was wrong in assuming that because the case involved only damage to a single private house, it was a mere dispute between private litigants. The Kohler Act had not been passed for the private benefit of plaintiff Mahon. The law stated specifically that it was passed "as remedial legislation, designed to cure existing evils and abuses." These were *public* evils and abuses, identified in the preamble as "wrecked and dangerous streets and highways, collapsed public buildings, churches, schools, factories, streets, and private dwellings, broken gas, water and sewer systems, the loss of human life." Thus, as Chief Justice Rehnquist stated in his *Keystone* dissent, "There can be no doubt that the Kohler Act was intended to serve public interests."[103]

In *Pennsylvania Coal*, Justice Holmes had stressed that the statute had destroyed the company's right to mine coal under the Mahon property. In *Keystone*, it was conceded that the 1966 act required the plaintiff companies to leave twenty-seven million tons of coal in place. But the Court compared that amount to the total coal in plaintiff's mines (1.46 billion tons) and concluded that the statute "requires them to leave less than 2% of their coal in place." So far as was shown, plaintiffs' mining operations continued to be profitable despite the coal required to be left in place. Hence, *Keystone* differed from *Pennsylvania Coal* because plaintiffs had not shown "that they have been denied the economically viable use of that property."[104]

What the *Keystone* Court was doing here was to adopt the dissenting view urged by Justice Brandeis in *Pennsylvania Coal*—that coal lands affected by the statute should be viewed as a totality. To the Holmes assertion that the Kohler Act destroyed the value of the right to mine under the Mahon house, Brandeis answered, "[V]alues are relative. If we are to consider the value of the coal kept in place by the restriction, we should compare it with the value of all other parts of the land."[105] The *Keystone* Court engaged in just such a totality view of plaintiffs' properties to support the conclusion that the subsidence act "places a burden on the use of only a small fraction of the property that is subjected to regulation."[106]

Had the same totality approach been followed in *Pennsylvania Coal*, the result would have been that reached in the Brandeis dissent. Hence it is fair to say, as does one commentator, "*Keystone* involved almost exactly the same situation and in the same state as *Mahon*; only the result changed."[107] The *Keystone* Court's attempt to distinguish the case before it from *Mahon* is unconvincing. The *Keystone* result is exactly the opposite of that reached in *Pennsylvania Coal*. Despite the Court's disclaimer, then, *Keystone* in effect overrules *Pennsylvania Coal*. At the least, it indicates that a subsidence law, such as that at issue in both cases, will normally be held not to constitute a taking for which compensation must be paid. The totality approach used in *Keystone* will almost always lead to the result reached by Brandeis rather than that by the Holmes *Pennsylvania Coal* opinion.

DIMINUTION IN VALUE TEST

Despite its effective reversal by *Keystone*, there is one aspect of *Pennsylvania Coal* that continues to play an important part in the law on the subject. In the opinion he delivered in the case, Justice Holmes indicated that there was a line beyond which a regulation might not go without violating the Takings Clause. Holmes started by repeating the general rule: "Government hardly could go on if to some extent values incident to property could not be diminished without paying for every such change in the general law." This means that property "values are enjoyed under an implied limitation and must yield to the police power."[108]

But, Holmes stated, "obviously the implied limitation must have its limits." Holmes noted that one factor "for consideration in determining such limits is the extent of the diminution. When it reaches a certain magnitude, in most if not in all cases there must be an exercise of eminent domain and compensation to sustain the act."[109]

Under the *Pennsylvania Coal* opinion, "The general rule at least is, that while property may be regulated to a certain extent, if regulation goes too far it will be recognized as a taking."[110] When does the regulation go too far? When the diminution in value caused by the regulation is great enough effectively to deprive the owner of his property. Regulation does not require compensation whenever it results in impairment of property value. But where the decline in value goes as far as Holmes thought it did in *Pennsylvania Coal*, the Takings Clause comes into play. As Holmes saw it, the Kohler Act made it impossible for the company to mine the coal beneath the Mahon property. "To make it commercially impracticable to mine certain coal has very nearly the same effect for constitutional purposes as appropriating or destroying it."[111]

The "diminution in value" theory stated by Holmes has remained as a limitation upon regulatory power. It has been referred to by the Court in cases down to the present day.

But that does not mean that the law has accepted Professor Epstein's view that regulation resulting in *any* diminution in the rights of a property owner comes within the Takings Clause. On the contrary, it is only where the regulation goes as far as the Kohler Act did in the Holmes analysis that the line between regulation and taking is crossed. And that, in turn, means that the regulation must destroy the essential rights of the property owner before the Holmes "diminution in value" theory becomes applicable.

The "diminution in value" theory does not support the extreme Epstein view that any diminution of property rights constitutes a taking. "Unlike physical invasions, which are relatively rare and easily identifiable without making any economic analysis, regulatory programs constantly affect property values in countless ways, and only the most extreme regulations can constitute takings."[112]

The justification for equating the extreme regulation with a taking was stated a decade ago by Justice Brennan: "Police power regulations such as zoning ordinances and other land-use restrictions can destroy the use and enjoyment of property in order to promote the public good just as effectively as formal condemnation or physical invasion of property. From the property owner's point of view, it may matter little whether his land is condemned or flooded, or whether it is restricted by regulation . . . [so as] to deprive him of all beneficial use of it."[113]

121

The analogy here, as Justice Brennan points out, is the case involving flooding of adjoining lands by a government dam or other project. In the leading decision holding that a taking had occurred in such a case, the Court said that "it would be a very curious and unsatisfactory result if . . . it shall be held that if the government refrains from the absolute conversion of real property to the uses of the public it can destroy its value entirely, can inflict irreparable and permanent injury to any extent, can, in effect, subject it to total destruction without making any compensation, because, in the narrowest sense of that word, it is not *taken* for the public use."[114]

There is a taking in the flooding case even though there has been no physical appropriation of the property because the flooding operates to "destroy its value entirely." The same is true of a taking by regulation under the "diminution in value" theory. "It is only logical, then, that government action other than acquisition of title, occupancy, or physical invasion can be a 'taking,' and therefore a *de facto* exercise of the power of eminent domain, where the effects completely deprive the owner of all or most of his interest in the property."[115]

The difference between Professor Epstein's view and the settled law on the matter can be seen from analysis of *Andrus v. Allard*.[116] The Eagle Protection Act makes it unlawful to "take, possess, sell, purchase, barter, offer to sell, purchase or barter, transport, export or import" eagle parts. Regulations prohibit sales of any objects containing eagle feathers, even those from birds legally killed before the act. Plaintiffs, who sold Indian artifacts containing eagle feathers, brought suit to have the statute and regulations ruled invalid. The district court held that the act and regulations violated plaintiffs' Fifth Amendment property rights because the prohibition wholly deprived them of the opportunity to earn a profit from their artifacts.

To Professor Epstein, the district court decision was plainly correct. Indeed, he writes, "On its facts the case is a simple one. The right of sale is part (perhaps the most valuable part) of the right of disposition. The loss of this right is not merely a diminution in value but is the deprivation of a property right, a partial taking for which compensation is prima facie required."[117] In other words, if government deprives plaintiffs of their right to sell their eagle feathers, that is a taking, even if the owners still have the rights to possess and use the feathers.

A unanimous Supreme Court rejected the Epstein reasoning in their *Andrus* decision. The Court recognized that "a significant restriction has been imposed on one means of disposing of the artifacts." Indeed, concedes the opinion, "It is . . . undeniable that the regulations here prevent the most profitable use of appellees' property." But, said the Court, "that is not dispositive. When we review regulation, a reduction in the value of property is not necessarily equated with a taking." In this case, plaintiffs still retained all aspects of ownership, except the right to sell: "[A]ppellees retain the rights to possess and transport their property, and to donate or devise the protected birds." Hence, "it is not clear that appellees will be unable to derive economic benefit from the artifacts; for example, they might exhibit the artifacts for an admissions charge."[118]

It must be admitted that plaintiffs in *Andrus* were deprived of the key right in the "bundle" of property rights that they had in the eagle feathers. They had purchased the artifacts only to be able to sell them at a profit. From a legal point of view, however, the *Andrus* regulation did not constitute a taking because it did not "completely deprive the owner of all or most of his interest in the property."[119] There was a substantial diminution in value, but the beneficial interest in the property was not destroyed, as it was, for example, in the flooding case.

As the Court summarized it in 1987, "[O]ur test for regulatory taking requires us to compare the value that has been taken from the property with the value that remains in the property."[120] Traditional regulation, "short of that which totally destroys the economic value of property,"[121] does not work a taking. Only where the value that remains is negligible—that is, the major portion of the property's value has been destroyed[122]—has the line between regulation and taking been crossed.

Adoption of the Epstein argument that any diminution in value caused by a regulation makes for a taking would make effective regulation under the police power all but impossible. Economic regulation always involves adjustment of property rights. "Often this adjustment curtails some potential for the use or economic exploitation of private property. To require compensation in all such circumstances would effectively compel the government to regulate by *purchase*."[123] All regulation would have to be "purchased regulation,"[124] involving costs that would hamstring effective use of the police power.

This point is forcefully made by Judge Posner, whose economic analysis of the law is usually taken as gospel by New Right jurists. Posner points out that, despite *Pennsylvania Coal Co. v. Mahon*, "most regulatory measures that reduce the value of property without the government's taking possession of it are held not to require payment of compensation. Is this economically correct?" Posner notes that it has been argued that "if the market value of a home fell by $10,000 as a result of some government regulation the owner should be entitled to the same compensation as if the government had taken a corner of the property worth $10,000."[125]

According to Posner, however, "[T]here are economic differences between these cases. When the government regulation affecting property values is general in its application, as will normally be the case, the costs of effecting compensation would be very high. . . . Imagine the difficulties involved in identifying, and then transacting with, everyone whose property values were . . . lowered by government regulation of the price of natural gas or heating oil."[126]

REDUCTIO AD EPSTEINUM

The Epstein view of the Takings Clause would make economic regulation virtually impossible, for it considers any regulation that imposes any limits on the rights of the property owner a taking for which compensation must be paid. But Professor Epstein does not stop with this expansive interpretation of the Takings Clause. Instead, he advocates a view of the clause that would go far to eliminate the power of the purse that is the foundation of the modern welfare state.

By now the concept of the welfare state has come to dominate the polity, though it came relatively late (by comparison with other countries) to the American scene. Legally speaking, the trend toward the welfare state in the United States began with the factory laws and workmen's compensation laws passed at the beginning of this century. More recently, such laws, designed to protect the worker against the hazards incident to industrial employment, have proved inadequate. Our society has also sought to safeguard the individual against the uncertain nature of modern employment. It has come to be recognized that the costs of maintaining superannuated workers and of unemployment, like the costs of industrial accidents, should be distributed as part of the costs of production, instead of being borne immediately by the individuals concerned. This has led to legislation establishing retirement and pension systems, as well as unemployment insurance programs.

These new laws were contrary to the restricted conception of governmental power that prevailed during the first part of the century. As late as 1935, the Supreme Court ruled an old-age pension law to be an invalid interference with freedom of contract. Such a law "is an attempt for social ends to impose by sheer fiat non-contractual incidents upon the relation of employer and employee . . . as a means of ensuring a particular class of employees against old age dependency."[127]

This decision was one of the first casualties of the constitutional revolution of 1937. The *Social Security Act Cases*[128] of that year definitely settled the constitutional authority to enact social legislation, such as that stricken down in 1935. The fundamental premise that has since governed judicial consideration of all such legislation is that society may take care of its human wastage, whether owing to accident, age, or some other cause.[129]

The Social Security Act of 1935 brought the federal government extensively into the field of social insurance. It established a nationwide system of old-age benefits to workers, as well as an extensive system of unemployment insurance. The systems were financed by taxes on both employers and employees. In the series of 1937 cases,[130] the Supreme Court upheld the constitutionality of both the old-age and unemployment benefit provisions. In so ruling, the Court gave the broadest scope to the congressional power to tax and spend, holding that the Social Security Act provisions were valid exercises of that power. The 1937 decisions put an end to fears that unemployment insurance and old-age benefit laws might prove beyond the power of government in this country. Henceforth the United States was not to be the one great nation powerless to adopt such measures.

The significance of the *Social Security Act Cases*, however, extends far beyond the statute at issue. The opinions delivered furnished the doctrinal basis for the developing state. That state was characterized above all by the geometric growth of government largess. "Government is a gigantic siphon. It draws in revenue and power, and pours forth wealth: money, benefits, services, contracts, franchises, and licenses."[131] The field of benefactions came to occupy an increasingly large proportion of the efforts of government. The political order itself was known compendiously as the welfare state.

The key instrument of the welfare state is the fisc, its motive force the power of the purse. The 1937 decisions construed that power broadly. If Congress chooses to tax and spend to operate schemes of old-age benefits and unemployment insurance, that is a matter within its discretion. Under the *Social Security Act Cases*, the power of the purse may be utilized for whatever social purpose the legislature chooses. The only restriction on that power in the Constitution is that it be exercised "to . . . provide for the common Defence and general Welfare." The *Social Security Act Cases* allow the legislature to determine whether a given exercise of the power of the purse will promote the general welfare: "The line must still be drawn between one welfare and another, between particular and general. . . . There is a middle ground or certainly a penumbra in which discretion is at large. That discretion, however, is not confided to the courts. The discretion belongs to Congress."[132]

All of this law, which has served as the jurisprudential foundation for the social welfare programs provided during the past half century, would be done away with by Professor Epstein, who considers it contrary to the Takings Clause. In Epstein's view, the clause applies to both taxation and transfer payments of the type provided under welfare assistance programs.

Epstein starts with the proposition that taxation comes within the Takings Clause. "With a tax, the government takes property in the narrowest sense of the term, ending up with ownership and possession of that which was once in private hands." Hence, "[A]ll taxes . . . are takings of private property prima facie compensable by the state."[133] It follows that the approach used by Epstein in other cases involving government interference, particularly those involving regulation, apply as well to taxation.

To Epstein this means, first of all, that progressive taxation is constitutionally invalid. The benefit received from taxation is not proportionate to the amount where the percentage taxed increases with the amount of income. Only the flat tax imposes a proportionate burden on all income and thus passes the disproportionate impact test that is, in Epstein's view, critical to the Takings Clause. Hence, the clause should be read "as requiring the flat tax."[134]

126

Professor Epstein is, however, not content with simply asserting the unconstitutionality of the progressive tax. He also contends that all taxes that have a redistributive effect violate the Takings Clause. He even reaches that result with regard to unemployment compensation taxes, which have appeared beyond constitutional challenge for over half a century.[135] According to Epstein, underlying unemployment compensation is "the concealed but implicit redistribution of wealth within the class of covered employees. As structured, the tax is levied upon the total payroll, so employers and employees in stable work forces end up paying a net subsidy to employees (and of course employers) who worked in high-turnover industries."[136]

In substance, Epstein here is repeating the objection to the unemployment tax made by Justice George Sutherland, in dissenting from the decision upholding the tax. Sutherland pointed out that the employer who had not discharged a single worker was taxed just as was the employer who had fired half his workers, even though the former had contributed nothing to the evil of unemployment.[137] Yet, as the Court pointed out in ruling the unemployment tax valid, "Nothing is more familiar in taxation than the imposition of a tax upon a class or upon individuals who enjoy no direct benefit from its expenditure, and who are not responsible for the condition to be remedied." As the Court tells us, "A tax is not an assessment of benefits. It is . . . a means of distributing the burden of the cost of government."[138] Hence, a tax is not a taking requiring compensation merely because the taxpayer does not derive benefits commensurate with the amount of tax paid. Any other view would unduly dilute the specific power of government to levy taxes to "provide for the . . . general Welfare."

It is not only unemployment insurance that falls under Professor Epstein's interpretation. His analysis applies to all governmental redistributive programs, particularly those for welfare assistance. As Epstein sees it, "Welfare transfers, whether in cash or in kind, aid the poor at the expense of the rich." To Epstein, then, it is obvious that taxes to provide for welfare payments involve takings within the Fifth Amendment. But, he asserts, welfare and other transfer payments do not meet the compensation requirement. "Welfare remains a transfer system whose tiny insurance component does not furnish adequate compensation to those who are taxed to support it." Indeed, according to Epstein,

127

"It is not possible to design a stable set of institutional arrangements for transfer payments to satisfy the just-compensation requirement of the eminent domain clause."[139]

To sum up Epstein's views on the matter, taxing a rich person to fund welfare payments to a poor person is unconstitutional. When such a tax is imposed, there is a taking and the state must make compensation, which must be a real equivalent of the value taken. Under the Epstein approach here, not only welfare but all redistributive programs, including progressive taxation, are proclaimed unconstitutional. "The basic rules of private property are inconsistent with any form of welfare benefit,"[140] or other redistributive programs.

The implications of the Epstein approach here are far-reaching. The most important affirmative powers of government become either invalid or powers to be exercised only by purchase. To Epstein, it is not enough that the police power would become merely the power of purchased regulation; his approach would drastically limit the power to tax and spend. And this would be done under a clause that was put into the Constitution only to confirm government authority to acquire property by eminent domain—as "a tacit recognition of a preexisting power to take private property for public use."[141] The Takings Clause, limited on its face to eminent domain cases, would be used to all but nullify the most essential powers granted by Article I, section 8. The result would be a quantum change in constitutional jurisprudence that would completely transform both our law and our society.

EPSTEIN IN INCREMENTS?

Richard Epstein is usually considered one of the leaders of the new conservative jurisprudence. Yet his conception of the Takings Clause would effect the most radical change in public law that has ever taken place. The Takings Clause would become the center of a new constitutional cosmology, with its rays protecting property to a hitherto unheard-of extent. Property rights would be immunized against the police power and redistributive taxation. Public power would be reduced to a power to proceed by purchase. At the same time, all the other constitutional protections for economic rights would become superfluous. They would be swallowed up by the Takings Clause, which would serve as the only necessary guaranty for property.

Under the Epstein interpretation, the controversy over *Lochner*[142] discussed in the last chapter would become irrelevant. Whether the *Lochner* review approach is revived or not becomes less significant if the *Lochner*-type regulation comes within the Takings Clause, since this regulation diminishes the property rights of those regulated. Even if the given economic regulation is upheld, it becomes effective under the Epstein view only when the compensation requirement is met. This, as already stressed, would reduce the most important public powers to the power to act only by purchase.

Neither the language of the Takings Clause nor the settled jurisprudence under it supports the expansive Epstein interpretation. But more important, his view would have the most baneful effect on our public law, for it would call into question most exercises of the power to regulate and the power to tax, and by doing so would undermine the constitutional foundation of the welfare state.

Even Professor Epstein recognizes that his approach is so far-reaching that it cannot, practically speaking, be fully implemented. Referring to transfer and welfare programs, he states that had his interpretation been followed at their inception, "the only proper remedy would have been their invalidation, because the just-compensation requirement cannot be satisfied." However, Epstein concedes, "That easy remedial option is effectively foreclosed today because of two social facts. First, a whole host of taxes and regulations, which necessarily offend the eminent domain clause, have long been in operation. Second, virtually all recipients have acted, often over a period of years, if not decades, in reliance on the present legal order." This leads Epstein to conclude that the vast network of present-day social and economic programs cannot entirely be dismantled. The most that can be expected is that adoption of his "correct theory at the very least can lead to incremental changes in the proper direction, even though it cannot transform the world."[143]

Must we, therefore, conclude that Professor Epstein is, in his own words, only engaged in "a quixotic effort to turn back the clock, to repeal the twentieth century?"[144]

It is all too easy to dismiss Epstein's work as but one more tilting of the lance against the jurisprudence of the past half century. Few today share the social vision that is the foundation for his restricted view of public power and his exaltation of property rights. Those who approve the changed role of government during this century know that when Epstein asserts that the Takings Clause makes much of this change in role unconstitutional, he is surely wrong. But in making the assertion, Epstein has already begun to alter the terms of the constitutional debate. As one commentator puts it, "[I]n the very act of asking ourselves that question [that is, whether the Epstein approach can be correct] . . . something has changed. Epstein has created a question where none existed before. This is a small but direct step toward the world of his social vision."[145]

It is in this respect that Epstein speaks of the "incremental changes in the proper direction" that can result from his work—since, as he sees it, "the present structure of constitutional law does admit a high degree of play at the joints."[144] Ever since Epstein's advocacy of his takings approach, a slow evolution of takings law has begun.

CHANGING CASE LAW

Before Epstein's *Takings* was published, even the most conservative justices had accepted the settled case law on the matter. Two cases that Epstein singles out for criticism are *PruneYard Shopping Center v. Robbins*[147] and *Hawaii Housing Authority v. Midkiff*.[148] In *PruneYard*, the Court ruled that a state could require a shopping center to allow entry to its premises by students soliciting signatures against a United Nations resolution. In *Hawaii Housing*, the state was allowed to use eminent domain to break up a concentration of land ownership by transferring title to long-term tenants. In Epstein's view, *PruneYard* involved a deprivation of the property owner's right to exclude persons from his property and was, as such, a partial taking. In *Hawaii Housing*, according to Epstein, the law provided for the state "to arrange a set of coerced transfers between A and B when voluntary markets can arrange the same transfers without the abuses of faction." To Epstein, "Legislation (like that challenged in *Hawaii*) that simply takes land and transfers it from landlords to tenants, or the reverse, constitutes the paradigmatic transaction that the eminent domain clause was designed to prohibit. So when the Court sustained the Hawaiian statute, it declared the central wrong to be perfectly legal. The justices stood the Constitution on its head."[149] For Epstein it was clear that in none of the Hawaii takings "is the property used for a pure public good." The Hawaii type of land reform "thus runs afoul of the public use limitation."[150]

The *PruneYard* and *Hawaii Housing* opinions were, however, written by the two leading conservatives on the Burger court, Justices Rehnquist and Sandra Day O'Connor. The Rehnquist *PruneYard* opinion specifically rejected the Epstein notion that the case came within the Takings Clause. Restriction of the "right to exclude others" did not so diminish "the use or economic value of their property that . . . it amounted to a 'taking.'"[151] In *Hawaii Housing*, Justice O'Connor followed the expanded view of public use that has prevailed in this century. Indeed, she affirmed what is in some ways the broadest conception of "public use," equating it to the police power itself: "The 'public use' requirement is thus coterminous with the scope of a sovereign's police powers." In addition, O'Connor specifically confirmed the extremely limited review in cases challenging takings as not for a public use: "[W]here the exercise of the eminent domain is rationally related to a conceivable public purpose, the Court has never held a compensated taking to be proscribed by the Public Use Clause."[152]

Since Epstein's expansive view of takings was published, however, there have been cases in which members of the Supreme Court may have begun to adopt a broader view of the Takings Clause. In recent years there have been several cases that support this conclusion.

In *First English Church v. Los Angeles County*,[153] the Court held that an owner whose land was "taken" by a regulatory taking could recover damages for the period between enactment of the regulation and the determination that the regulation resulted in a taking. *Nollan v. California Compensation Commission*[154] ruled that the grant of a permit to build a larger house on a beachfront lot upon condition that the public be allowed an easement to pass across the lot's beach involved a taking so far as the condition requiring the easement was concerned. Finally, in *Hodel v. Irving*,[155] the Court struck down as a taking without compensation a statute providing that no undivided fractional interest in Indian lands should descend by intestacy or devise, but instead should escheat to the tribe, if it represented less than two percent of the tract concerned and earned its owner less than one hundred dollars per year.

The opinions in the three cases were written by the three leading conservatives on the Court: Chief Justice Rehnquist and Justices Antonin Scalia and O'Connor. Even more significant, however, than the decisions in these cases are the indications by some of the justices that they have begun to move toward Professor Epstein's view on when regulation constitutes a taking. In *Hodel v. Irving*, Justice Scalia, with the concurrence of Chief Justice Rehnquist and Justice Powell, went out of his way to assert that the statute at issue, "insofar as concerns the balance between rights taken and rights left untouched, is indistinguishable from the statute that was at issue in *Andrus v. Allard*." According to Scalia, "[T]hat comparison is determinative of whether there has been a taking [and], in finding a taking today our decision effectively limits *Allard* to its facts."[156]

The implication is that *Allard* was wrong in its application of the "diminution in value" test and that the restriction of the right to sell involved a diminution of property rights sufficient to result in a regulatory taking. This is, of course, the Epstein view on takings by regulation rather than that followed in the cases until now, including *Allard* itself. That three members of the Court asserted a similar view in *Hodel v. Irving* indicates that the Epstein call for a new approach to the Takings Clause is starting to be heard within the marble palace itself.

In *Pennell v. San Jose*,[157] Justice Scalia went further and applied the same approach to rent control. The rent control ordinance at issue permitted various factors to be considered in determining whether a proposed rent increase was reasonable, including "the hardship to a tenant." It was claimed that the tenant hardship provision resulted in a forced subsidy for poor tenants in violation of the Takings Clause. The Court held that the claim was premature, since there was no evidence that the provision had been used in an actual case to reduce the rent. Justice Scalia, joined by Justice O'Connor, dissented, stating that he would decide on the merits and would hold that the Takings Clause was violated.

To Scalia, the hardship provision has no relation to the purpose of rent control, which is to eliminate exorbitantly priced housing. The owners receive benefits from such housing that government may legitimately reduce to a reasonable level. Here, however, says Scalia, the hardship provision is aimed at the problem of poor tenants, which has nothing to do with the landlords who are regulated. Instead, the landlords are compelled to subsidize those who cannot pay reasonable rents, for reasons unconnected with the rents they pay. Here, Scalia concludes, rent regulation is being used "to establish a welfare program, privately funded by those landlords who happen to have 'hardship' tenants."[158]

Professor Epstein points out that the Scalia opinion has ramifications far beyond the immediate case. "Scalia's approach cannot be confined to the objectionable 'hardship' features of the San Jose law. His . . . objection to the San Jose ordinance applies to all forms of rent control—indeed to all forms of regulation generally." The Scalia subsidy reasoning can be used to undermine all rent control laws. "Rent control always involves at least an implicit subsidy of some tenants by some landlords. Even if tenants as a class are entitled to the subsidy, why should unwilling landlords alone provide it?"[159]

In *Hodel v. Irving* and *Pennell v. San Jose*, Justice Scalia spoke for only a small minority of the Court. But the expansive takings view has also begun to influence decisions in the lower federal courts. Judge Posner, the paradigmatic example of a New Right judge, recently indicated that the Epstein takings posture should be taken seriously. At issue in the case before him was a Chicago ordinance requiring landlords to pay interest on security deposits, authorizing rent withholding for landlord lease violations, and prohibiting charges of more than ten dollars a month for late payment of rent. In his opinion, Judge Posner rejected Contract Clause and substantive due process attacks against the ordinance because of the Supreme Court jurisprudence on the matter. But he went on to point out that the landlords had not raised what he termed their "most promising" challenge—"that the ordinance . . . violates the eminent domain clause of the Fifth Amendment . . . by taking away an important part of a landlord's property rights without compensation."[160]

An even more striking illustration of the Epstein influence in the lower federal courts is contained in *Hall v. Santa Barbara*,[161] a ninth circuit case. The City of Santa Barbara enacted a rent control ordinance applicable to mobile home parks. Plaintiffs were mobile park operators who provided tenants a plot of land and access to certain amenities such as water and electricity. Tenants installed the mobile homes, paying rent for use of the land and facilities. The ordinance permitted tenants to sell their mobile homes and assign the leases on the same terms as they had enjoyed.

Plaintiffs claimed that the ordinance effected a taking of their property that was neither for a public purpose nor justly compensated. The court characterized plaintiffs' claim as "a novel one."[162] Plaintiffs argued that, by giving tenants the right to a perpetual lease at a below-market rental rate, the ordinance transferred to them a possessory interest in the land on which their mobile homes were located. Plaintiffs claimed that the rise in prices of mobile homes in parks subject to the Santa Barbara ordinance reflected the transfer of a valuable property right to occupy mobile home parks at below-market rates.

Professor Epstein terms the *Hall* ordinance "a manifest constitutional travesty."[163] The court agreed, holding that the rent control ordinance worked a taking within the meaning of the Takings Clause. The opinion distinguishes between regulatory taking cases and physical occupation cases. According to it, "Regulatory taking cases are those where the value or usefulness of private property is diminished by regulatory action not involving a physical occupation of the property."[164] This definition is very close to the Epstein approach in the matter.

Yet the ninth circuit went even further in its decision. According to the court, the allegations of the complaint (to be taken as true on defendant's motion to dismiss) "present a claim for taking by physical occupation." That was true because "the tenant is given an economic interest in the land that he can use, sell or give away at his pleasure; this interest (or its monetary equivalent) is the tenant's to keep or use, whether or not he continues to be a tenant. If the Halls' allegations are proven true, it would be difficult to say that the ordinance does not transfer an interest in their land to others."[165]

Under the ordinance, "landlords are left with the right to collect reduced rents while tenants have practically all other rights in the property they occupy." In the court's view, "this oversteps the boundaries of mere regulation and shades into permanent occupation of the property for which compensation is due."[166] Nor, according to the ninth circuit, does the fact that this was a rent control ordinance change the result: "[W]e cannot indulge the notion that a city may eviscerate a property owner's rights and shield its action from constitutional scrutiny by calling it rent control."[167]

The ninth circuit follows a far-reaching approach. In effect, the court holds that the economic regulation at issue has somehow become a "physical invasion." This is a notion that is supported neither by logic nor precedent. It gratuitously casts doubt on rent control regulation, where limitation of the landlord's profit has never been held a taking, so long as a reasonable return on investment is allowed.[168] Professor Epstein does not approve entirely of the court's reasoning, but he plainly agrees with the result. "*Hall* reaches the right result, but only because all rent control statutes are unconstitutional, not because this statute is any worse than the others."[169]

Similarly, the Scalia opinion in *Pennell v. San Jose* calls into question economic regulation that effects wealth transfers. What Scalia says could apply equally to other comparable regulatory measures, such as those providing for price control and wage and hour regulation. Indeed, the Scalia opinion is reminiscent of the ruling striking down a minimum wage law in *Adkins v. Children's Hospital.*[170] According to Chief Justice Taft's opinion there, "To the extent that the sum fixed exceeds the fair value of the services rendered, it amounts to a compulsory exaction from the employer for the support of a partially indigent person, for whose condition there rests upon him no peculiar responsibility, and therefore, in effect, arbitrarily shifts to his shoulders a burden which, if it belongs to anybody, belongs to society as a whole."[171] This is, of course, similar to the Scalia objection to the hardship provision in the San Jose rent control ordinance.

The constitutional approach urged by New Right jurists such as Professors Siegan and Epstein thus means a return to the public law of the first part of this century, with all the abuses that accompanied it— abuses before which government was legally powerless under the prevailing jurisprudence of the time. Under the Siegan view discussed in the last chapter, the law would be returned to the days of *Lochner*,[172] when the Constitution was construed as the embodiment of Social Darwinism and laissez faire. But the Epstein approach to the Takings Clause would go even further. It would completely undermine the jurisprudential foundation of the welfare state, reducing the most important public powers to powers exercisable only by purchase in most cases.

And all under a constitutional clause intended merely to confirm the power of eminent domain, subject only to the public-use and just-compensation requirements. To read the Takings Clause as Professor Epstein does is to work a veritable revolution in our public law—one justified neither by the history, language, or intent of the clause, nor by the practice or precedents under it. As Judge Bork has recently conceded, Epstein may have "written a powerful work of political theory . . . , but has not convincingly located that political theory in the Constitution."[173]

It is most unfortunate that the incremental approval of the Epstein view has already begun. Even the conservative judges who have recently urged an expanded view of the Takings Clause may not realize the full implications of an acceptance of Epstein's approach. Do they really want to turn back the clock to *Lochner*, when the law embodied the extreme individualism of the day, and thus repeal the jurisprudence of an entire century? Even those judges, such as Justice Scalia, who have started to write the Epstein position into our public law should hesitate before going further in that direction.

5

DISASTER BY DECREE?
RACIAL DISCRIMINATION AND
THE CONSTITUTION

O NCE AGAIN the title of this chapter is taken from a book written by
one of the leaders of New Right jurisprudence—here *Disaster by
Decree* by Lino A. Graglia,[1] which is subtitled *The Supreme Court Deci-
sions on Race and the Schools*. The book is a violent polemic against the
Court's decisions on school segregation, starting with the landmark
Brown case.[2]

I became personally acquainted with Professor Graglia's work when he
wrote an essay review[3] of my book on the *Swann* case.[4] The Court there
had upheld broad judicial remedial power in desegregation cases, including the power to order busing to help attain the goal of a "unitary
[school] system in which racial discrimination would be eliminated root
and branch."[5] In this respect, *Swann* did go further than prior cases. Yet
it was anything but a radical decision; on the contrary, *Swann* was simply
the culmination of the Court's desegregation decisions, its holding issu-
ing logically from the by-then settled jurisprudence on the subject.

The Graglia review is a lengthy diatribe against both the *Swann* decision and authors who write about the case without condemning the
Court. Indeed, Graglia goes so far as to assert with regard to *Swann*,
"Legal historians will almost surely one day see it as the *Dred Scott*[6] of
the twentieth century, the outstanding example of improper judicial be-
havior resulting in a decision of disastrous consequences. No decision
better illustrates both the magnitude of the Court's policymaking power

and the lack of scruple—the essential irrelevance to the Court of logic and fact—in the Court's exercise of that power."[7]

It is difficult to see how even one who strongly differs with *Swann* can excoriate the decision "with hatred so malignant that it seems obscene."[8] A case that only seeks to give effect to the *Brown* ruling is compared to the most discredited decision ever rendered by the Supreme Court.

But New Right disagreement with the jurisprudence in this area is not limited to the *Swann* case. Instead, it extends to the whole range of Supreme Court decisions on racial discrimination, beginning with *Brown* itself. *Brown* can therefore conveniently be taken as the starting point for a discussion of the subject.

BROWN AND SEGREGATION

New Right commentators on *Brown* start with the proposition that the framers of the Fourteenth Amendment did not intend to abolish school segregation.[9] "For this writer," declares Bernard H. Siegan, "the case is strong that the Thirty-ninth Congress did not seek to adopt an amendment that would affect racial segregation in the schools."[10]

Despite their conclusion "that the framers had no intention of striking down segregation,"[11] New Right jurists now generally concede that *Brown* was correctly decided. Reference has been made to Attorney General Meese's agreement[12] that *Brown* "earned all the plaudits it received" and that the *Brown* Court was only "correcting the damage done 50 years earlier" by the erroneous decision in *Plessy v. Ferguson.*[13] Other New Right legal theorists agree that the bare decision in *Brown* deserves approval, not censure. Even Graglia writes, "The appeal and general acceptance of a simple prohibition of all official racial discrimination are so great, indeed, that it is hardly possible to quarrel with the *Brown* decision."[14]

Graglia stresses that this statement applies only to "the *Brown* decision—as distinct from the opinion."[15] Chief Justice Warren's opinion is criticized as wholly inadequate to support the far-reaching *Brown* ruling. As a Reagan-appointed federal judge puts it, "Their problem was that *Brown* never explained—indeed, never tried to explain—its crucial conclusion that segregated schools, however equal their facilities, still intangibly harmed black children. True, *Brown* kept repeating this conclusion, at least five separate times. But the Court essentially asked the country to take it on faith: that because nine justices thought segregation wrong, it must be so."[16]

In particular, *Brown* is censured as a "Sociological Decision" that relied "more on the social scientists than on legal precedents. . . . The Court's opinion reads more like an expert paper on sociology than a Supreme Court opinion."[17] This characterization is based on the fact that the *Brown* opinion rested not so much on legal reasoning as on the conclusion that segregation denoted black inferiority and also that it lessened the motivation to learn. Whatever may have been the extent of psychological knowledge at the time of *Plessy*, the *Brown* opinion asserted, these conclusions were "amply supported by modern authority." This assertion was backed by a footnote—the celebrated footnote 11, which became the most controversial note in Supreme Court history.[18]

In this note, Graglia tells us, "The Court . . . cited . . . several psychological and sociological writings on questions of race."[19] But this effort by the Court to support its decision is, in Graglia's view, "badly mistaken." It shows "a serious misapprehension by the justices of the limits of their competence." According to Graglia, "For judges to presume to decide such questions as the determinant of 'the motivation of a child to learn' or of the 'educational and mental development of negro children' is to be disrespectful of both the difficulty and the possibility of gaining useful knowledge about such matters. The dangers involved in such presumption could hardly be better illustrated than by *Brown* itself. . . . [T]he 'finding' that school segregation had adverse educational effects on blacks was not in fact 'amply supported,' if supported at all, by scientific knowledge."[20]

However, critics such as Graglia who focus intensively on the controversial *Brown* footnote have acted out of a less than complete understanding of the manner in which Supreme Court opinions are prepared. Chief Justice Warren himself always stressed that it was the decision, not the citations, that was important. "It was only a note, after all," he declared to an interviewer.[21] Warren normally left the citations in opinions to his law clerks. He considered them among the minutiae of legal scholarship, which could, in the main, be left to others.

In the *Brown* case, the fleshing out of the opinion with footnotes was left primarily to one of Warren's clerks, Richard Flynn. As he recalls it, there was no specific method in the organization of footnote 11. When it came time to cite supporting authority, the works listed were, to Flynn, the "obvious" things to list. When asked by me if there was any method in the way he organized the note, he answered, "I don't recall any, that's just the way it fell."

It has been said that footnote 11 provoked concern among several justices, particularly its gratuitous citation of Gunnar Myrdal's *An American Dilemma*,[22] which had, in the decade since its publication, become a red flag to the white South. In 1971, Justice Tom C. Clark, then retired from the Court, told an interviewer, "I questioned the Chief's going with Myrdal in that opinion. I told him—and Hugo Black did, too—that it wouldn't go down well in the South. And he didn't need it."[23]

Clark's recollection appears now to have been inaccurate. Over the years, he may have come to feel that in view of the storm in the South caused by the Myrdal citation, he should have said something at the time; this may, years later, have become a blurred recollection that he and Black had expressed concern. In all likelihood, however, if Justices Black and Clark had objected, the Myrdal reference would have been taken out. The citation was just not important enough to Warren to withstand even a mild expression of concern by any of the justices.

There was, in fact, no controversy over "psychological knowledge" or footnote 11 in the Court itself. So far as we know, the draft *Brown* opinion was speedily approved by the justices, and without significant changes. The general attitude among Warren's colleagues was expressed in a handwritten note by Justice Douglas: "I do not think I would change a single word. . . . You have done a beautiful job."

One wonders, indeed, whether criticisms of the *Brown* opinion, whether by New Right jurists or others, are not by now completely beside the point. It may be unfortunate that the *Brown* opinion was not written by a Marshall or a Cardozo. Great cases deserve nothing less than opinions by the consummate giants of legal craftsmanship. But the criticism reminds me of a comment made by Warren E. Burger shortly after he succeeded Warren as chief justice. Seated before the fire at the elegant Elizabethan manor where international conferences are held in Ditchley, England, the new chief was distressed by critics who contended that he did not have the qualifications of a Cardozo. "Who is there today who does?" he wryly asked.

The same can be asked of those who have urged that the *Brown* opinion deserved a Holmes or a Cardozo as its author. One can go further and wonder whether those virtuosos of the opinion could possibly have secured the unanimous decision that was the Warren forte. If we take the *Brown* opinion as it is written, it certainly ranks as one of the great opinions of judicial history. Perhaps the opinion did not demonstrate as well as it might have that the mere fact of segregation denies educational equality. But *Brown* is so clearly right in its conclusion in this respect that one wonders whether additional labor in spelling out the obvious would really have been worthwhile. Considerations of *elegantia juris* and judicial craftsmanship are largely irrelevant to the truism that segregation was intended to keep blacks in a status of inferiority.

Over three decades after the *Brown* case, it has become apparent that criticisms of the Court's performance there have lost their relevancy. What is plain is that *Brown* has taken its place at the very forefront of the pantheon of historic decisions. In the light of what Justice Arthur J. Goldberg has termed the American commitment to equality,[24] and of *Brown's* part in helping to fulfill that commitment, the case will occupy a paramount position long after current criticisms cease to have any more significance than those voiced against the great decisions of the Marshall Court at the outset of the nation's constitutional development.

BROWN II: JUDICIAL ENFORCEMENT POWER

New Right commentators on *Brown*, such as Professors Graglia and Siegan, are really concerned not so much with the decision that segregation is unconstitutional as with the Court's holding on judicial remedial power. Though the original *Brown* decision established the unqualified principle that school segregation violated the Equal Protection Clause, it did not discuss the remedial question of how the principle was to be enforced. A separate decision—in *Brown II*—dealt with that issue a year after *Brown I* was decided.[25]

Brown II is remembered today mainly because of the statement in the opinion there that the *Brown I* no-segregation principle was to be enforced by the nondiscriminatory admission of blacks to schools "with all deliberate speed."[26] This oxymoronic phrase, so untypical of Chief Justice Warren's normal mode of expression, led to learned controversy on the origins of the phrase. Papers recently made available indicate definitely that the phrase was used by Warren in response to a suggestion by Justice Frankfurter.[27]

More important than the origin of the phrase or even the phrase itself, however, was *Brown II*'s provision for what Justice Harold H. Burton called decentralized enforcement of *Brown I*.[28] The Supreme Court would not itself perform the enforcement function. Instead, *Brown II* delegated that function to the federal district courts. It was those courts that were directed by *Brown II* "to take such proceedings and enter such orders and decrees . . . as are necessary and proper" to secure the admission of blacks "to public schools on a racially nondiscriminatory basis."[29]

The key factor in *Brown I* enforcement under the *Brown II* decision was the discretion vested in the federal courts. It is true, said the *Brown II* opinion, that the primary responsibility for resolving the problems "arising from the transition to a system of public education freed of racial discrimination" was to be in the school authorities. But the courts would have to consider whether actions of the authorities constituted good-faith implementation. The "courts which originally heard these cases can best perform this judicial appraisal,"[30] and they were vested with the broad discretion of courts of equity in exercising their enforcement function.

"These cases," declared the *Brown II* opinion, "call for the exercise of these traditional attributes of equity power." To effectuate the interest of blacks in admission to schools on a nondiscriminatory basis "may call for elimination of a variety of obstacles." Courts of equity may act to vindicate "the public interest in the elimination of such obstacles in a systematic and effective manner."[31]

It is on the judicial enforcement power recognized by *Brown II* and applied in the later desegregation cases that critics such as Graglia and Siegan have focused their censure. "In applying its equity powers," Siegan writes,

> the Court was charting a new course—a fact evident from its failure to cite supporting precedent in constitutional law. Equitable principles are an integral part of American jurisprudence when applied to private and public disputes enabling judges to achieve a just result notwithstanding existing judicial rules. They do not entitle the judiciary to override the

constitutional authority of the states or other branches of government. Nor does equitable enforcement seem necessarily required when the Constitution specifically authorizes a mode of political implementation, as it does in section 5 of the fourteenth amendment. [32]

The *Brown* justices themselves had been united in the view that *Brown I* enforcement should be by courts vested with traditional equity enforcement powers. At the *Brown II* postargument conference, Warren had stressed that "this is a court of equity." As such, the enforcing court should be given "as much latitude as we can but also as much support as we can." [33] In a memorandum a few days earlier, Justice Frankfurter had stressed that enforcement "would take due . . . account of considerations relevant to the fashioning of a decree in equity." [34] And, as already seen, the *Brown II* opinion specifically provided for enforcement of the *Brown I* decision by the "traditional attributes of equity power."

The Siegan notion that enforcement through traditional equity remedial power is improper in the *Brown*-type case was also the position that Chief Justice Burger tried to have the Court adopt in the *Swann* case. The Burger draft opinion of the Court there took a restricted view of the judicial remedial power in this type of case. The draft itself recognized the far-reaching authority traditionally possessed by courts of equity, conceding, "Once a right and a violation have been shown, the scope of equitable remedies to redress past wrongs is broad for in the nature of equitable remedies breadth and flexibility are essential." But then the chief justice drew a gratuitous distinction between remedial power in this desegregation case and what the draft termed "a classical equity case"— for example, where removal of an illegal dam or divestiture of an illegal corporate acquisition is ordered. "Here, however," the draft declared, "we are not confronted with a simple classical equity case, and the simplistic, hornbook remedies are not necessarily relevant. Populations, pupils or misplaced schools cannot be moved as simply as earth by a bulldozer, or property by corporations." [35]

Though equity judges have normally had power to do whatever they deem necessary to redress a violation, here, the *Swann* draft asserted, only a more limited remedial power should be approved. According to Burger, all the district court could do in such a case was to act to bring about a "system functioning on the same basis as school systems in which no discrimination had ever been enforced."[36] The implication was that affirmative measures to secure integration were not approved, even though the district judge deemed them to be the only effective measures to correct the constitutional violations proved by plaintiffs.

But the other *Swann* justices categorically refused to accept the restricted Burger conception of remedial power. The united opposition led the chief justice to give way[37] and his final *Swann* opinion specifically stated that "a school desegregation case does not differ fundamentally from other cases involving the framing of equitable remedies. . . . As with any equity case, the nature of the violation determines the scope of the remedy. In default by the school authorities of their obligation to proffer acceptable remedies, a district court has broad power to fashion a remedy that will assure a unitary system."[38]

This was a complete change from the restricted conception of judicial authority contained in the Burger first draft. Now it was made clear that once a constitutional violation was found, the remedial authority of the district court was as broad as necessary to correct the violation, including any measures needed to "assure a unitary system." Under the final *Swann* opinion, "There is no suggestion of an intention to restrict those powers or withdraw from courts their historic equitable remedial powers."[39]

The united refusal of the justices to accept the restricted Burger conception of remedial power is of great significance. The refusal was not confined to the liberal Douglas-Brennan-Marshall wing of the Court. Even those justices from whom Burger normally expected support— Justices Harlan, Stewart, White, and Blackmun—vigorously opposed the Burger view. Except for Justice Black, the Chief Justice received no backing for his attempt to narrow the scope of judicial remedial power in desegregation cases.

There is no support, either in precedent or history, for the restricted view of remedial power in desegregation cases urged by Professor Siegan and Chief Justice Burger. Equity jurisprudence has always rested upon the principle that the power of the chancellor is coextensive with the needs of justice in the given case.[40] In this respect, as the final *Swann* opinion recognizes, "a school desegregation case does not differ fundamentally from other cases involving the framing of equitable remedies to repair the denial of a constitutional right."[41] That Justice Harlan strongly opposed the restricted view of remedial power[42] indicates that even the model conservative on the Court saw no basis for treating desegregation cases differently from other cases calling for invocation of equitable authority.

THE CHANGING TRAFFIC LIGHT: FROM *BROWN* TO *GREEN*

Although New Right jurists generally concede the correctness of the *Brown* decision, they direct their criticism at the later desegregation cases, particularly the *Green*[43] and *Swann*[44] cases.

Green v. County School Board[45] arose in a rural Virginia county in which blacks comprised some fifty-seven percent of the school population. The county had two schools; one had been a white school, the other had been the school for blacks. For a decade after *Brown*, the situation remained unchanged. In 1965, in order to remain eligible for federal funds, the county adopted a "freedom of choice" plan. Under it, each pupil might choose each year between the two schools. If no choice was made, they were assigned to the school previously attended. In the three years in which the plan was in operation, not a single white child chose to attend the black school, and eighty-five percent of the black children in the county still attended the all-black school.

At the *Green* conference, Chief Justice Warren asserted that "freedom of choice is violative of constitutional rights." As he saw it, the "purpose of *Brown* was to break down segregation" and the county's plan failed to do that. Except for Justice Black, who voted to affirm the decision upholding freedom of choice, the remaining justices agreed with Warren that the plan, as it operated, invalidly maintained a segregated school system. Ultimately, Black agreed to go along with the majority, enabling the Warren Court to maintain its record of unanimity on the merits in school desegregation cases.[46]

The *Green* opinion was written by Justice Brennan, who had expressed himself at the conference as strongly as had Warren against the freedom of choice plan. Brennan decided to write a *Green* opinion that would deal with the problem as forcefully as possible, and, at the same time, take its model from the *Brown I* opinion itself, "short, pungent, and to the point."[47]

Justice Brennan circulated a strong draft *Green* opinion. As the chief justice had done in *Brown*, he emphasized the "inferiority" of education in segregated schools: "The stigma of inferiority which attaches to Negro children in a dual system originates with the State that creates and maintains such a system. So long as the racial identity ingrained, as in New Kent County, by years of discrimination, remains in the system, the stigma of inferiority likewise remains."[48]

Brennan recognized, however, the need to continue the tradition of unanimity in school segregation cases. The *Green* draft was circulated on May 16, 1968, the eve of the fourteenth anniversary of the first *Brown* decision. At the conference the next day, Justices White and Harlan advised Brennan that they could not join the opinion so long as it contained the references to "inferiority." They said that the references risked angering desegregation opponents even further and rendering compliance even harder to obtain. White also said that in his view modern sociological and psychological data did not support the notion of "stigma" relied on by the *Brown I* opinion. Had he been on the Court, White said, he would not have agreed with *Brown I*'s famous footnote 11. Both White and Harlan urged Brennan to avoid raising the footnote 11 controversy again and to leave the notion of stigma "implicit" in the opinion.[49]

After consulting the other members of the Court, Justice Brennan agreed to delete the "inferiority" language; the passage quoted above does not appear in the final *Green* opinion. Brennan also made some changes in the draft that were suggested by Justice Black and enabled the latter to join the opinion despite his original dissenting vote.[50] The result was a unanimous *Green* opinion striking down freedom of choice plans.

Though Justice Brennan had to tone down his *Green* opinion, the opinion as issued is still unusually forceful—indeed, the strongest Supreme Court opinion on the subject since *Brown*. The key factor requiring the freedom of choice plan to be invalidated was its failure to bring about elimination of the "dual [school] system, part 'white' and part 'Negro.' It was such dual systems that 14 years ago *Brown I* held unconstitutional and a year later *Brown II* held must be abolished."[51]

The *Green* opinion declares that the question for a court in a school segregation case is whether the school authorities have "achieved the 'racially nondiscriminatory school system' *Brown II* held must be effectuated." It was not enough for school boards, such as that in the Virginia county before the Court, merely to remove the legal prohibitions against black attendance in white schools. Instead, "School boards such as the respondent then operating state-compelled dual systems were . . . clearly charged with the affirmative duty to take whatever steps might be necessary to convert to a unitary system in which racial discrimination would be eliminated root and branch."[52]

The Court stressed that it was no longer willing to countenance the South's "deliberate perpetuation of the unconstitutional dual system." Delays "are no longer tolerable" and the "time for mere 'deliberate speed' has run out." The courts were no longer to tolerate school plans that might bring about desegregation at some future time. On the contrary, "The burden on a school board today is to come forward with a plan that promises realistically to work, and promises realistically to work now."[53]

Nor was it enough for the lower courts to find that a given school board had met this burden. The judicial responsibility did not end with approval of a plan that appeared to discharge the school authority's affirmative duty to convert to a unitary system. The plan must also "prove itself in operation." Thus, "[W]hatever plan is adopted will require evaluation in practice, and the court should retain jurisdiction until it is clear that state-imposed segregation has been completely removed."[54] Under *Green*, the district courts were expressly vested with the affirmative duty to supervise the operation of desegregation plans. The clear implication was that they should do whatever they deemed necessary to ensure that those plans proved effective in practice. Discharge of the judicial duty here might well involve the courts in the intimate details of school administration. Perhaps, under the *Brown II* approach, the Supreme Court itself avoided the danger of acting as what Justice Frankfurter had termed "a super-school board."[55] But the same would not necessarily be true of the district courts now charged with the affirmative mandate imposed by the *Green* opinion.

The justices themselves clearly understood the significance of the *Green* decision. When Warren joined the opinion, he wrote Brennan, "When this opinion is handed down, the traffic light will have changed from *Brown* to *Green*. Amen!"[56]

Critics such as Lino Graglia, on the other hand, charge that *Green* "worked a revolution in the law of school segregation comparable to, indeed more drastic than, that effected by *Brown.*" Indeed, Graglia declares, "With the *Green* decision, . . . the *Brown* era was brought to a close. Purporting to do no more than apply the holding of *Brown* to the cases at hand, the Court changed the constitutional mandate from a prohibition to a requirement of racial discrimination in school assignment."[57]

According to Graglia, this is true because *Green* provided for "compulsory integration, even though this would mean abandoning the very principle of no racial discrimination by government that had made opposition to segregation irresistible." *Green* made "[t]he basic decision to move from prohibiting segregation to requiring integration, while claiming still to be only enforcing *Brown.*"[58]

Critics of *Green* assert that its integration goal went far beyond anything required by *Brown.* "The most careful reading of *Brown I* and *Brown II,*" writes Bernard Siegan, "does not reveal such a purpose."[59] Instead, opponents argue, the proper interpretation of *Brown* was that of Circuit Judge John J. Parker, who by the time of *Brown* had become one of the most respected federal judges in the country.

On remand of one of the cases decided in *Brown,* Judge Parker, writing for a three-judge district court, declared that *Brown* "has not decided that the states must mix persons of different races in the schools or must require them to attend schools or must deprive them of the right of choosing the schools they attend. What it has decided, and all that it has decided, is that a state may not deny to any person on account of race the right to attend any school that it maintains. . . . The Constitution, in other words, does not require integration. It merely forbids discrimination."[60]

The distinction between "Thou shall not segregate" and "Thou shall integrate" is of crucial importance.[61] Under the Parker interpretation, all that was required for compliance with *Brown* was to cease *governmental* action legally excluding black children from "white" public schools. But there was no duty to end existing dual school systems, provided only that they were no longer compelled by state law.

But the Parker view is inconsistent with *Brown*'s underlying premise—that blacks are to attend "public schools on a racially nondiscriminatory basis."[62] Achievement of that goal in a school system where there has been de jure segregation would be illusory if all that *Brown* required was the formal elimination from the statute book of laws compelling segregation. That was made clear by what happened in the South in the decade after *Brown*.

At the *Brown II* conference, Justice Black had predicted that there would be only "glacial movement" toward desegregation in the South.[63] As it turned out, this proved an understatement. In areas where segregation prevailed, *Brown* was met by obdurate resistance. The bitterness of the South's reaction to *Brown* is, of course, now a matter of history. The obloquy directed at the Warren Court, the hatred of the chief justice culminating in the "Impeach Earl Warren" campaign, and the increasingly violent resistance to the civil rights movement in the South all had their origins in the desegregation decision. The South resorted to every device, including pressure and intimidation, to block integration. As *The Oxford History of the American People* summarized it a decade after *Brown*, "In the lower South, the Supreme Court's decision was to all intents and purposes nullified and has remained so for ten years; John C. Calhoun would have been delighted!"[64] "All deliberate speed" may never have been intended to mean indefinite delay, yet that is just what it did mean in much of the South, at least until the Supreme Court itself felt compelled to act in the matter more than a decade after *Brown* itself.

There was no other way for the Court to correct the situation than by enunciating and enforcing the principle laid down in *Green* that school boards and ultimately the courts were "charged with the affirmative duty to take whatever steps might be necessary to convert to a unitary system" in which there would no longer be separate white and black schools. And the duty was to "come forward with a plan that promises realistically to work, and promises realistically to work *now*."[65]

In his third draft opinion in the *Swann* case, Chief Justice Burger sought to rely on the Parker statement of the governing principle in these cases. The draft went out of its way to assert, "The Constitution, of course, does not command integration; it forbids segregation." This restatement of Judge Parker's view was underscored by the further Burger draft statement, "The objective should be to achieve as nearly as possible that distribution of students and those patterns of assignments that would have normally existed had the school authorities not previously practiced discrimination."[66]

Once again, however, the other justices refused to accept the Burger attempt to narrow the effect of *Brown*. The Parker-like pastiche was particularly offensive to Justice Brennan, who thought that his *Green* opinion had relegated the Parker principle to a deserved oblivion. Brennan wrote to the chief justice strongly opposing the Burger statement that the Constitution does not command integration, but only forbids segregation. "I think," Brennan declared, "this would be a most unfortunate statement for us to make at this juncture in the struggle to gain compliance with *Brown*. That statement in almost *haec verba* was the rallying cry of the massive resistance movement in Virginia, and of die-hard segregationists for years after *Brown*. It calls to mind Judge Parker's opinion which caused so much trouble for so long a time. To revive it again would I think only rekindle vain hopes."[67]

More significant was the opposition of Justice Harlan, then the leading conservative on the Court. Harlan sent Burger a redraft of the most important part of the *Swann* opinion, which the chief justice essentially adopted. The Harlan redraft pointedly omitted the Parker-like declaration in the Burger draft; that sentence consequently does not appear in the final *Swann* opinion.

The Court's leading conservative, Harlan, and its leading liberal, Brennan, as well as the other justices, rejected the Parker-Burger notion that the Constitution only forbids legally required segregation and does not permit the courts to take whatever steps may be necessary to bring about a unitary school system. Nor is it accurate to assert, as Professor Graglia does, that "a requirement of school racial integration . . . clearly cannot be justified, as was attempted in . . . *Green*, on the basis of the principle that most easily justifies *Brown*'s prohibition of segregation— that all racial discrimination by government is prohibited."[68]

It is erroneous to assume that *Brown* simply meant that laws requiring segregation were to be inoperative. On the contrary, *Brown II* shows that the justices knew that equitable remedial power would have to be exercised to ensure that school segregation would be ended in practice as well as in the statute book. On January 15, 1954, Justice Frankfurter circulated a memorandum setting forth some of the "considerations [that] have arisen within me in regard to the fashioning of a decree" in *Brown*. In it he wrote, "A clear appreciation of what result is required is indispensable. The aim is summarized in the phrase 'integrated' schools." In seeking to achieve that aim, "the Court is, broadly speaking, promoting a process of social betterment."[69] The *Green* decision can best be understood as an attempt to give legal substance to the Frankfurter goal.

Critics of the Court's activism in *Green* forget that the justices had followed a virtual hands-off policy in school segregation cases for a decade after *Brown*. During that period, the Supreme Court left the enforcement problem to the lower courts. But it was becoming apparent that the war against school segregation was not being won, in large part because of the Supreme Court's post-*Brown* failure to assert an effective leadership role. In all too many areas, the schools still "operated, so far as actual racial integration was concerned, as though our *Brown* cases had never been decided."[70] If this situation was to be corrected, the "coercive assistance" of the Supreme Court itself "was imperatively called for."[71]

That the Court began to take an increasingly active role in the school cases may be explained by the justices' increasing exasperation at Southern refusals to implement *Brown*. As their irritation grew, so did their intervention. In an interview not long before his death, Justice Clark (who had participated in all the Warren Court cases before *Green*) noted that judicial power in the school cases "grew in small individual steps but 'like Topsy' with no grand design." The Court, Clark said, had tried "to give localities a chance to make a change in their own ways." When confronted in case after case with "wholesale obstruction," however, it had no choice but to broaden federal judicial supervision.[72]

The cases support the Clark summary. For a decade after *Brown*, the Court followed its hands-off policy, trusting to the school authorities and district courts to ensure elimination of school segregation. During the following five years, the justices moved from their immediate post-*Brown* inaction to an increasingly activist stance, culminating in *Green*, the key Warren Court case after *Brown* itself.

Yet *Green* was more than an assertion by the Court of an active role in the process of implementing *Brown*. *Green* altered the focus of inquiry in the school cases. In the process the Court changed the constitutional rule from the *Brown* prohibition against compelled segregation to an affirmative duty immediately to dismantle all dual school systems—a duty to be assumed by the federal courts where local authorities did not "come forward with a plan that . . . promises realistically to work *now.*"[73] As such, *Green* fixed the pattern for judicial enforcement in school cases and set the stage for the later decisions on the subject.

SWANN AND BUSING

Swann is, of course, the desegregation case that Professor Graglia singles out for his most severe criticism, terming it "the *Dred Scott* of the twentieth century." In *Swann*, the Court upheld the far-reaching desegregation order issued by the district court in the case, which included efforts to reach a white-black ratio of seventy-one percent to twenty-nine percent in the different schools, and provision for extensive busing to help attain that goal. The order required the busing of about ten thousand students solely for the purpose of desegregation—about one-fourth of the children attending schools in the district concerned.

The most important thing about the *Swann* decision was its recognition of broadside remedial power in desegregation cases. I have already dealt with this aspect of *Swann* and have shown that the *Swann* holding in this respect was wholly consistent with traditional notions of equitable remedial power. Those who argue the other way are really asserting that judicial remedial power is somehow less broad in this type of case than in what Chief Justice Burger's *Swann* draft termed "a classical equity case." Such an assertion is contrary to both logic and law. It was certainly rejected by the justices in *Swann*. As the *Swann* opinion put it, "[A] school desegregation case does not differ fundamentally from other cases involving the framing of equitable remedies to repair the denial of a constitutional right. The task is to correct, by a balancing of the individual and collective interests, the condition that offends the Constitution."[74]

Any other view would mean that the *Brown* decision would remain unenforceable. Covenants without the sword, says Thomas Hobbes, are but empty words. The same would be true of the *Brown* principle without equitable enforcement power. In his memo of January 15, 1954, Justice Frankfurter declared that it would be undesirable for the Court to limit itself to the *Brown* holding. As he saw it, "[O]ne can be confident in believing that a mere declaration of unconstitutionality will be the most prolific breeder of litigation and chaos. A mere declaration will not do."[75]

But neither would it do for the Court to issue the declaration and continue to leave enforcement to the lower courts without any guidance. That would have meant an indefinite period of what Justice Black called "glacial movement" toward desegregation. It should not be forgotten that, in these cases, the Court was acting to "change a deplorable situation into the ideal. . . . [W]e are asked in effect to transform state-wide school systems in nearly a score of States."[76] Certainly, as the Frank-furter memo put it, the "declaration of unconstitutionality is not a wand by which these transformations can be accomplished."[77] Only by the *Green-Swann* approach could the Court hope to bring about the needed change.

Critics of the *Swann* decision assert, however, that even under *Green* the Court went too far in upholding what Graglia calls "the almost totally irrational result of busing."[78] *Swann*'s "result would be . . . that parents who could not possibly be considered either as having violated any law or as having benefitted from a violation would have their children bused, even against their wishes, to attend schools outside their neighbor-hoods."[79]

It is, however, difficult to see why busing should be excluded from the range of remedial powers possessed by the courts in desegregation cases. The basic principle, as stressed, is the authority to take whatever mea-sures may be necessary to enforce *Brown*. Under *Green*,[80] the existence of dual schools became the key to judicial remedial power. Once the dual system was demonstrated, the only question was that of remedy—what measures to take that would eliminate the dual system. From the *Brown* invalidation of prohibitions against blacks attending white schools, the Court had moved to the *Green* affirmative duty to provide a unitary school system, with the federal judges having the ultimate responsibility for ensuring that the conversion from a dual system took place as soon as possible.

The clear implication was that the district courts should issue what-ever orders were necessary to bring about an integrated system, even if that required attention to administrative details normally within the school board's province. The *Green* opinion did not specify the remedial measures that might be ordered, though it did mention a modified "neighborhood school" concept as a possible remedy.[81] But that was only because the school district involved was a rural one with little residential

153

segregation. The same suggestion would prove inadequate in urban areas with entirely different residential patterns. In such areas, would neighborhood schools be sufficient to meet the constitutional standard or would more drastic remedies be appropriate? Could those remedies include busing between white and black areas if the district courts determined that it was needed to ensure meaningful integration?[82]

The answers are surely implied in the pre-*Swann* jurisprudence. *Green* imposes the duty to take whatever steps are necessary to convert to a unitary school system, including measures that promise realistically to work, and to work immediately. In the typical urban school district, pupil assignments to neighborhood schools would scarcely dismantle dual systems. Instead they would merely mirror existing residential patterns. If only transportation of children to schools outside their neighborhoods would hold any promise of realistically working to end dual systems, *Green* clearly implies that such transportation may be ordered. From this point of view Justice Brennan was correct when he wrote to Chief Justice Burger, in a memorandum on the *Swann* case, that "all that we are really required to do here is fill in the outline constructed by *Green*."[83] If judicial remedial authority includes the power to take any and all measures that may be deemed appropriate to attain the goal "of insuring the achievement of complete integration at the earliest practicable date,"[84] why should busing be excluded, even though, as in *Swann* itself, the district judge concludes that it is the only measure that promises to end the dual system?

BAKKE AND AFFIRMATIVE ACTION

It is scarcely surprising that jurists like Lino Graglia condemn affirmative action programs as "reverse discrimination" and hence inconsistent with the constitutional guaranty of equal protection. In an article published while the *Bakke* case,[85] the leading case on affirmative action, was pending before the Supreme Court, Graglia asked, "Should public institutions of higher education, as a matter of social policy, and may they, as a matter of constitutional law, grant preferences in admission of students on the basis of race or ethnic group? . . . May a person be denied admission to a public institution of higher education on the grounds that his government now prefers some races to others and that his is not one of the preferred races?"[86]

"To state the question in this form," Graglia went on, "is for most people, to make it virtually self-answering. The violation of a fundamental principle seemingly involved and the sense of gross injustice necessarily engendered seem so great that adoption or continuance of such a policy should not be contemplated except upon a clear showing of overwhelming benefits obtainable in no other way. No such showing has been or can be made by the proponents of racial preferences in higher education."[87]

Programs that grant racial preferences, in Graglia's view, violate "[t]he principle that no person should be disadvantaged by government because of race—a corollary of the basic democratic ideal of individual human worth, dignity, and responsibility"—a principle that "is perhaps as valuable and as close to an absolute as any principle we have."[88]

It must be admitted that affirmative action poses a dilemma not present in *Brown* and its immediate progeny. In the desegregation cases, the courts were confronted with school systems that violated the right guaranteed by the Equal Protection Clause. Judicial enforcement of that right did not deprive anyone else of the right to an equal education or any other legal right. In the words of one judge explaining the *Brown*-type case, "[P]roviding one child with a better, i.e., integrated, education did not operate to deprive another of an equal, integrated education. Benefit to one would not be at the expense of another."[89] Yet such a result is one of the inevitable consequences of an affirmative action program. As Graglia puts it, "The basic difficulty, of course, is that to grant preference to members of some racial or ethnic groups is to disadvantage members of other racial or ethnic groups."[90] Justice Marshall himself conceded this in a memorandum on the *Bakke* case: "[T]he decision in this case depends on whether you consider the action of the Regents as *admitting* certain students or as *excluding* certain other students."[91]

In *Bakke*, the real problem was that the special admissions program at issue there did provide both for admitting a specified number of minority students and for excluding those who might otherwise have filled their places. During the oral argument, Justice Marshall was to put his finger on the case's dilemma in this respect when he told Bakke's counsel,

"You are arguing about keeping somebody out and the other side is arguing about getting somebody in."[92] A decision upholding the program would keep Bakke and others like him out of medical school; a decision for Bakke would keep out the minority applicants who otherwise would be getting in under the special program.

In his memo, Justice Marshall also noted that the challenged program would be labeled according to whether the "getting in" or the "keeping out" was emphasized: "If you view the program as admitting qualified students who, because of this Nation's sorry history of racial discrimination, have academic records that prevent them from effectively competing for medical school, then this is affirmative action to remove the vestiges of slavery and state imposed segregation by root and branch. If you view the program as excluding students, it is a program of quotas which violates the principle that the Constitution is color-blind."[93]

To those who favor racial preferences in education and other fields, these measures are instruments of *affirmative action* designed to correct centuries of racial discrimination by positive measures aimed at moving minorities into the mainstream of the society. To opponents they are *reverse discrimination*, which, however benign its intentions, replaces discrimination against minorities with discrimination against whites who are themselves wholly innocent in the matter.

Opponents of "[t]he pernicious idea of racial preferences" argue that they infringe upon "the principle that *all* racial discrimination by government is evil." Instead it is replaced by "a principle permitting discrimination against whites but prohibiting it against nonwhites."[94] But the racial preference problem is not that simple. There are two situations in which racial preferences may be used and they are treated differently by the Supreme Court jurisprudence on the matter.

The first situation is the equivalent of de jure segregation in the school cases. Where such segregation exists, brought about by law or through the intentional acts of the school authorities, the full remedial power recognized in *Green* and *Swann* comes into play, including the authority to take whatever measures may be necessary to ensure the immediate transition from a dual to a unitary school system.[95] The same is not true where there is only de facto segregation,[96] "where racial imbalance exists in the schools but with no showing that this was brought about by discriminatory action of state authorities."[97]

A distinction similar to that drawn by the de jure-de facto line also exists in the nonschool cases. This is shown by a comparison between the *Bakke*[98] and *Fullilove*[99] cases. At issue in *Bakke*[100] was a special admissions program at the Davis medical school. Under it, sixteen of the one hundred places in the entering class were reserved for blacks and other minority applicants, who were judged under criteria considerably less demanding than those governing selection of students under the regular admissions program. Bakke was a white applicant who had been rejected by Davis, even though his admissions scores were higher than those of minority applicants accepted under the special program. The Court ruled that the special admissions program was invalid and that Bakke should be admitted to the medical school.

On the other hand, in *Fullilove v. Klutznick*,[101] the Court upheld a federal statute providing that at least ten percent of the grants for public works be spent for minority business enterprises (MBE), that is, businesses owned by members of specified minority groups. The key to *Fullilove* is that the program there had been set up by Congress after concluding that private and governmental discrimination had contributed to the negligible percentage of public contracts awarded minority contractors.

The distinction between *Bakke* and *Fullilove* can best be seen in the votes of Justice Powell, who provided the crucial fifth vote for invalidation of the *Bakke* special admissions program. How could Powell vote to uphold the MBE provision when his had been the decisive vote to invalidate the Davis program because it provided for a racial quota? "Like *Bakke*," a Powell memorandum on *Fullilove* conceded, "this is a quota system case." In his *Bakke* opinion, however, Powell noted a difference between the two: "In this case . . . there has been no determination by the legislature or a responsible administrative agency that the University engaged in a discriminatory practice requiring remedial efforts."[102]

The Powell memo pointed out that *Fullilove* "differs from *Bakke* in that the congressional record makes clear—at least for me—that Congress made appropriate findings of racial discrimination against minority contractors."[103]

More recently, the *Sheet Metal Workers* case[104] upheld employment plans that required fixed goals and numbers for hiring and promotion of blacks. At first glance, this also may seem inconsistent with the *Bakke* condemnation of the medical school program because it assigned a fixed number of seats to racial minorities. In *Sheet Metal*, however, as Justice Powell stated in a letter, the decision "is predicated primarily on the undisputed record of gross discrimination by the union over a period of at least two decades, and its intransigence in resisting every effort (including court orders) to implement appropriate remedies."[105] According to the opinions of both Justices Brennan and Powell, the finding that the union had committed egregious violations clearly established a governmental interest sufficient to justify the imposition of a racially classified remedy. The same result would undoubtedly have been reached in *Bakke* had a similar pattern of egregious discrimination by the medical school been proven.

It should be noted that though *Bakke* did find the special admissions program there invalid, the case also held that race was a factor that might be considered in an admissions policy without violating the Constitution. Under the *Bakke* decision, the medical school admissions program at issue was ruled violative of equal protection; but the decision specifically held that race might be considered as a factor in admissions programs. This has permitted the use of race in a flexible admissions policy designed to produce diversity in the student body, under which minority students may be admitted even though they may not fully measure up to the academic criteria used to judge the acceptance of white applicants.

From this point of view, *Bakke* has meant the continued validity of affirmative action programs. This has enabled universities and professional schools to go ahead with their programs designed to secure admissions of minority students. The justification for this result is the need for diversity in the student body—a need that supports consideration of race as a factor in admissions decisions.

Professor Graglia, however, rejects the "diversity" justification as an empty one. Graglia concedes, "All other things being equal, one might prefer racial or ethnic diversity to racial or ethnic homogeneity." He asserts, however, that "other things are not equal when diversity can be obtained only by denying persons advantages because of their race. In any event, we would have no *DeFunis*[106] or *Bakke* cases to discuss today if racial preferences were granted by institutions of higher education only on an all-other-things-being-equal basis, or even only within the normal range of administrative discretion in selecting students for admission."[107]

Yet that is precisely what we now have under the Supreme Court's *Bakke* decision. It permits admissions officers to consider race as a factor in their decisions. According to Justice Powell's key *Bakke* opinion, "[T]he State has a substantial interest that legitimately may be served by a properly devised admissions program involving the competitive consideration of race and ethnic origin."[108] This recognizes that universities may structure their admissions standards and procedures to consider race as a factor, provided they do not employ formal quotas of the type at issue in *Bakke* itself.

Despite the Graglia animadversion, race is legitimately one of the factors that may be considered in the effort to secure a diverse student body. As explained by one of the Court's leading conservatives, Justice O'Connor, "A state interest in the promotion of racial diversity has been found sufficiently 'compelling,' at least in the context of higher education, to support the use of racial considerations in furthering that interest."[109]

"YES, BUT"

New Right jurists such as Lino Graglia adopt a "Yes, but" posture toward the *Brown* case and its progeny. He concedes that it is hardly "possible to quarrel with the *Brown* decision," but interposes the caveat, "except on the ground that so important a social change should not have been made by unelected, lifetime appointees. The *Brown* case was less a traditional law suit than a call for a social revolution, and in a healthy democracy social revolutions are made by elected representatives authorized to effectuate their political views and accountable for the results."[110]

The whole point about *Brown*, however, was that the elimination of segregation could not realistically be left to elected representatives. Until the Court acted, government had done nothing to correct the almost patent violation of equal protection. Instead, both state and federal laws perpetuated the segregation that existed in much of the country, including the nation's capitol.

It was utterly quixotic to expect state governmental action to end segregation in those states where Jim Crow had become the norm. But Congress also failed to take action. Not only had Congress failed to outlaw segregation in the states, it had affirmatively provided for segregation in Washington, D.C. Chief Justice Fred M. Vinson emphasized this point in his presentation to the justices while presiding at the first conference held on the *Brown* case. Vinson stressed that segregation had never been questioned by Congress. "However [we] construe it," he said, "Congress did not pass a statute deterring and ordering no segregation." On the contrary, Congress itself had commanded segregation in the nation's capitol. "I don't see," Vinson affirmed, "how we can get away from the long-established acceptance in the District [of Columbia]. For 90 years, there have been segregated schools in this city." Vinson did admit that "it would be better if [Congress] would act."[111] But Congress had not done so and there was no indication that it would in the foreseeable future.

Chief Justice Warren approached the *Brown* issue from an entirely different point of view. Unlike his predecessor, Warren began his first *Brown* conference with a ringing declaration that segregation was unconstitutional. He stated the issue in moral terms: "[T]he more I've read and heard and thought, the more I've come to conclude that the basis of segregation and 'separate but equal' rests upon a concept of the inherent inferiority of the colored race."[112]

To jurists who felt this way, the claim of congressional acquiescence through inaction could scarcely justify the imprimatur of legality upon a patently immoral and unconstitutional practice. On the contrary, the years of legislative inaction coupled with the unlikelihood that Congress would attempt to correct the situation in the foreseeable future made it imperative for the Court to intervene. The alternative would leave untouched a practice that flagrantly violated both the Constitution and the ultimate human values involved. Chief Justice Warren and the other justices found such an alternative unpalatable. Since the other branches had defaulted in their responsibility, the courts had to ensure enforcement of the constitutional prohibition against racial discrimination.

Still, as seen earlier, Graglia and his New Right colleagues do not challenge the correctness of the *Brown* decision. Instead, they direct their censures at the *Brown* enforcement process, calling the use of far-ranging equity powers to eliminate segregation both unsupported by authority and unnecessary.[113] In *Brown II* and later cases, however, the Court was only exercising the traditional enforcement powers of courts of equity, which rested on the principle that the chancellor may order whatever may be deemed necessary to correct the wrong done in the given case.

As Justice Frankfurter put it, "[A] mere declaration of unconstitutionality" without provision for enforcement "will not do."[114] To deny the traditional enforcement powers of equity courts to courts enforcing *Brown* is, in practice, to make *Brown* itself a dead letter.

The same is true of those, like Professor Graglia, who deny the legitimacy of the post-*Brown* progeny—particularly *Green*[115] and *Swann*.[116] To Graglia, *Green* and *Swann* were usurpations of judicial power that worked a second judicial revolution "more drastic than that effected by *Brown*" and that turned *Brown* itself inside out, changing "the constitutional mandate from a prohibition to a requirement of racial discrimination in school assignment."[117]

What the Graglia censure ignores is that before *Green* and *Swann*, *Brown* itself had proved unenforceable. The massive resistance to *Brown* in Southern states would have continued to frustrate *Brown* enforcement had the Court not moved from *Brown* to *Green* and *Swann*. The facts cited in both *Green* and *Swann* demonstrate how little had been accomplished before the decisions in those two cases. Years after *Brown*, almost all the black children in the school districts concerned were attending all-black schools.

In some districts, indeed, the situation was even worse than before *Brown*. Prince Edward County, Virginia, for example, refused to levy any school taxes for the 1959–1960 school year, explaining that they were "confronted with a court decree which requires the admission of white and colored children to all the schools of the county without regard to race or color." As a result, the county's public schools did not reopen in the fall of 1959 and remained closed until the Supreme Court decided the case five years later. State and county tuition grants and tax credits were provided for whites attending "private" schools, which excluded blacks. A decade after *Brown*, then, one of the original *Brown* defendants saw its public schools shut down and only "private" white schools in operation. In Prince Edward County at least, the black schoolchildren were not only not better off after *Brown*, they were much worse; and the federal courts had been unable to help them during all that time.[118]

The situation in Prince Edward County was well described by the Court: "The case has been delayed since 1951 by resistance at the state and county level, by legislation, and by lawsuits. The original plaintiffs have doubtless all passed high school age. There has been entirely too much deliberation and not enough speed in enforcing the constitutional rights which we held in *Brown v. Board of Education, supra*, had been denied Prince Edward County Negro children."[119]

For the Court to keep hands-off in such a situation would have been to make the *Brown* principle one of morality only, not of law. That result was avoided precisely because the justices did intervene in cases like *Green* and *Swann*. And, the Graglia censure notwithstanding, the decisions in those cases were wholly consistent with the broad enforcement power recognized in *Brown II*. Only through that power, as exercised in *Green* and *Swann*, could the courts hope to ensure that there would be school systems "without a 'white' school and a 'Negro' school, but just schools."[120]

Even critics of the post-*Brown* cases should recognize that the Supreme Court decisions on the matter do form a logically consistent corpus. Where de jure segregation is found—that is, where it is either required by law or a product of purposeful intent—the decisions simply build on the prior case law. That is particularly true of *Green* and *Swann*, despite the Graglia-type criticism of those decisions. The courts have the duty to take action to correct a dual-school situation and their remedial power in this respect is as broad as the constitutional violation itself.[121] It includes the authority to order any "plan that promises realistically to work, and promises realistically to work *now*."[122] The courts may take any and all measures, including racial rezoning and extensive busing, that may be deemed appropriate to attain the desired goal.[123]

From this point of view, a case like *Swann* builds logically upon the prior cases, notably *Green*. As Justice Brennan put it in his memo on *Swann*, "[A]ll that we are really required to do here is fill in the outline constructed by *Green*." Yet *Swann* is the case that Professor Graglia likens with denunciatory fervor to the most discredited judicial decision in our history. If they note Graglia's censure at all, historians "may find hyperbole in the sanguinary simile."[124]

6

―――――――

PRICELESS RIGHTS
MADE WORTHLESS?

"THE FOURTEENTH AMENDMENT," says the famous Holmes protest, "does not enact Mr. Herbert Spencer's Social Statics."[1] Justice
Holmes was, however, alone in his *Lochner* dissent,[2] in which this statement was made. For, as seen in Chapter 3, *Lochner* was decided during
the "time when the Due Process Clause was used by this Court to strike
down laws which were thought unreasonable, that is, unwise or incompatible with some particular economic or social philosophy."[3]

By now, however, the Holmes approach to judicial review has long
been established doctrine. Under it, judges may no longer strike down
laws because they disagree with the economic theory on which the legislature had acted. According to the contemporary Supreme Court, economic "arguments are properly addressed to the legislature, not to us.
We . . . emphatically refuse to go back to the time when courts used the
Due Process Clause 'to strike down state laws, regulatory of business and
industrial conditions, because they may be unwise, improvident, or out
of harmony with a particular school of thought.'"[4] It is not for a court to
act because it disagrees with the economic theory behind a law: "Whether the legislature takes for its textbook Adam Smith, Herbert Spencer,
Lord Keynes, or some other is no concern of ours."[5]

This, however, is precisely what New Right jurists urge as the proper
concern of a reviewing court. According to them, the courts should judge
laws in light of the economic philosophy upon which they are based. If a
law is based upon what the court considers an incorrect economic theory,

the court should invalidate the law. Thus, as seen in Chapter 3, some neoconservatives assert that the *Lochner* decision was correct because the maximum-hours law at issue was based upon an unsound economic theory of regulation.

The difficulty is that such an approach would bring us back to the constitutional law at the turn of the century, when *Lochner* itself was decided. The primary criterion for those who see economics as the foundation of law is efficiency, and to them, efficiency is best promoted by the free operation of the market. Thus they are drawn inevitably to the *Lochner* rationale—that governmental interference with the market promotes inefficiency and must normally be considered arbitrary. "The best government is that which governs least"[6] has once more become the rallying cry; the welfare state is to be dismantled on economic (disguised as legal) grounds.

What Holmes said almost a century ago is directly relevant to the recent metamorphosis of the New Right jurist into homo economicus: "[P]eople who no longer hope to control the legislatures . . . look to the courts as expounders of the Constitutions, and . . . new principles have been discovered outside the bodies of those instruments, which may be generalized into acceptance of the economic doctrines which prevailed about fifty years ago."[7]

COST-BENEFIT ANALYSIS

In the field of public law, perhaps the most important practical effect of the advocacy of economics as the basis of law has been the increasing use of cost-benefit analysis (CBA). Not too long ago, CBA was simply another part of the arsenal of esoterica with which modern economics had armed itself. The layman was scarcely able to understand, much less appreciate, the abstruse discussions of the subject in texts by economists. But the underlying concept is as old as rational thought itself. Judge Posner states the concept in a deceptively simple way: "The weatherman has forecast rain and I must decide whether to take an umbrella with me when I leave the house. In making this decision I will consider (very rapidly, perhaps unconsciously) the probability that the forecast is correct, the discomfort of being rained on, the bother of carrying the umbrella, and the probability of losing it. This type of analysis which is called cost-benefit analysis by economists . . . is important in every department of thought and certainly in legal reasoning."[8]

The modern roots of CBA are to be found in the utilitarianism of Jeremy Bentham and John Stuart Mill. The "greatest happiness of the greatest number"[9] can scarcely be furthered by anything whose cost exceeds its benefit. Indeed, the Benthamite "felicific calculus"[10] of pain and pleasure was but a primitive way of stating the notion of costs versus benefits.

A decade after Bentham's death, Jules Dupuit, a French engineer, published *On the Measurement of the Utility of Public Works*,[11] which is considered the beginning of the literature on CBA.[12] In this country, cost-benefit analysis in public law is usually said to have started with the Flood Control Act of 1936, where Congress provided that federal projects should be undertaken "if the benefits to whomsoever they may accrue are in excess of the estimated costs."[13] This statute, the Supreme Court has stated, indicates an "intent on the face . . . that an agency engage in cost-benefit analysis."[14]

Such a provision was not long ago the rare exception in the federal statute book. More recently, however, it has been urged that CBA should be used widely as a basis for governmental action. According to the first chairman of President Reagan's Council of Economic Advisers, "The motive for incorporating benefit-cost analysis into public decision making is to lead to a more efficient allocation of governmental resources by subjecting the public sector to the same type of quantitative constraints as those in the private sector."[15]

The rationale for using CBA as a criterion by which to test governmental action is simple: Before taking action, such as building a highway or dam, government should try to figure out who will gain and who will lose from the action and by how much. Only if it looks as though the benefits to the winners are a lot more than the costs to those whose interests are hurt by the action, should it proceed.[16]

CBA AND ADMINISTRATIVE RULEMAKING

There are certain areas of public law where CBA can play a legitimate role. The most obvious is the field of administrative rulemaking covered by Executive Order 12,291, issued by President Reagan soon after he took office. Under the Reagan order, "Regulatory action shall not be undertaken unless the potential benefits to society for the regulation outweigh the potential costs to society."[17] In particular, the order provides detailed procedures for issuance of so-called major regulations by administrative agencies. All agencies are required to prepare regulatory impact analyses when they promulgate major rules.[18] They must analyze the costs and benefits of the proposed regulations, and they are required to "maximize the net benefits to society." If the least-cost alternative has not been selected, the agencies are required to explain why in the analysis.

Ultimately, the question of whether CBA should be used in the administrative rulemaking process is one for Congress to decide. In the Flood Control Act of 1936, Congress expressly provided for CBA.[19] There are comparable provisions in more recent regulatory statutes. A notable example is the Consumer Products Safety Act. It authorizes the Consumer Products Safety Commission to promulgate safety standards, provided that "[a]ny requirement of such a standard shall be reasonably necessary to prevent or reduce an unreasonable risk of injury associated with such product."[20] According to the Supreme Court, Congress used the "unreasonable risk" phrase, as shown by the House committee statement, "to signify a generalized balancing of costs and benefits."[21] Thus, in exercising the statutory power, the CPSC will "have to determine whether the benefits expected from the standard bear a reasonable relationship to the costs imposed by the standard."[22]

The most important opinion on rulemaking under a statute providing for CBA was written by Justice Scalia when he was a circuit judge. At issue was the automobile bumper standard issued by the National Highway Traffic Safety Administration (NHTSA). Under the relevant statute[23] the agency was required to promulgate a bumper standard that "shall seek to obtain the maximum feasible reduction of costs to the public and to the consumer." To do this NHTSA was to take into account "the cost of implementing the standard and the benefits attainable as the result of implementation of the standard," as well as the "effect of implementation of the standard on the cost of insurance and prospective legal fees and costs," and "savings in terms of consumer time and inconvenience."

According to Judge Scalia, these provisions imposed a "statutorily required cost-benefit analysis" on NHTSA. "The agency was to identify the costs and benefits of alternative standards, measure them, and select the standard which displays the greatest net benefit."[24]

The issue before the agency centered on the degree of protectiveness to be required of auto bumpers. More particularly, should bumpers be required to withstand a 2.5 mile per hour crash or a 5.0 MPH crash? The 5.0 MPH bumper would, of course, be able to withstand more severe impacts than the 2.5 MPH bumper. But would the benefits in this respect outweigh the costs involved in the heavier bumper?[25]

The CBA involved in answering this question is, of course, "more easily said than done, since . . . the process was as much one of prediction as of analysis."[26] But that does not mean that CBA is not of value in such a case. On the contrary, NHTSA's action in promulgating the bumper standard shows how useful CBA itself can be in the rulemaking process. The agency found that the heavier bumper system entailed greater costs in both the extra expense of the heavier bumper and the lower fuel efficiency owing to the weight increase. In addition, the increased price of the heavier bumper imposed additional finance costs on the consumer. NHTSA quantified the sum of these costs to produce a cost advantage of $54 to $131 for the 2.5 MPH system.

On the benefit side of the scale, NHTSA used crash data to assume that the 2.5 MPH bumper was only sixty-three to sixty-seven percent as effective as the 5.0 MPH bumper.[27] This was counterbalanced by the fact that only a minute fraction of auto accidents are caused by defective protection afforded by bumper systems.[28] The agency stated that the assumptions "were based on engineering judgment of the agency's experts." Judge Scalia wrote that the court had "no reason to disbelieve that statement, and engineering judgment is assuredly the sort of expertise that NHTSA preeminently possesses."[29]

NHTSA's ultimate conclusion was that CBA favored the 2.5 bumper standard. The slightly greater effectiveness of the heavier bumper was more than outweighed by the cost advantage of the 2.5 system. NHTSA worked out the difference in this respect between the two systems (as well as for combinations of the two types of bumpers) in specific monetary terms. These were, to be sure, only educated guesses. But the statutory direction to use CBA still plays a vital part in the rulemaking process of an agency such as NHTSA. Without it, the agency might well have required the 5.0 bumper, relying on the fact that it was somewhat more protective and that demanding it would be consistent with the agency's responsibility to protect auto safety. With CBA, the agency must determine whether the heavier bumper benefits consumers on balance, when the slight gain through accident reduction is more than offset by the greater costs of such a bumper. In rulemaking, at least, CBA may definitely enhance the rationality of the administrative process.[30]

Judge Scalia went further and indicated that use of CBA lends added weight to administrative action when it is challenged in the courts. The judicial posture of deference to the administrator, says Scalia, requires the court not to substitute its judgment for that of the agency: "This is especially true when the agency is called upon to weigh the costs and benefits of alternative policies, since '[s]uch cost-benefit analyses epitomize the types of decisions that are most appropriately entrusted to the expertise of an agency. . . .'"[31]

THE *TEXTILE MANUFACTURERS* CASE

Congress may, of course, enact cost-oblivious statutes, which do not permit CBA. This has been particularly true under statutes providing for protection of public health. Thus, in enacting the provision for national ambient air standards in the Clean Air Act,[32] Congress decided that the public has the right to the prescribed levels of air quality, regardless of what CBA might indicate in the matter.

A statute that does not go quite that far is the Occupational Safety and Health Act.[33] Under it, the Occupational Safety and Health Administration (OSHA) is given power to promulgate safety and health standards to protect workers. Section 3(8) of the act defines an "occupational safety and health standard" as a standard that is "reasonably necessary and appropriate to provide safe and healthful employment." Where toxic materials or harmful physical agents are concerned, a standard must also comply with section 6(b)(5), which directs the agency to "set the standard which most adequately assures, to the extent feasible, on the basis of the best available evidence, that no employee will suffer material impairment of health or functional capacity." In promulgating a standard limiting worker exposure to cotton dust, OSHA took the position that no safe exposure level could be determined and that section 6(b)(5) required it to set an exposure limit at the lowest technologically feasible level that would not impair the viability of industries regulated. The administrative view was that the very notion of CBA was inconsistent with the aim of the act to provide the safest possible workplace for employees. OSHA asserted that, in a case where the harmful agent regulated was a carcinogen, the risks could not be reliably quantified and that there was no acceptable way to put a dollar value on them even if they could be.

The OSHA position was tested in *American Textile Manufacturers Institute v. Donovan*.[34] After finding that inhalation of cotton dust was the primary cause of byssinosis ("brown lung" disease), OSHA issued its cotton-dust standard, which established mandatory permissible exposure limits. The standard stated that it was based on an interpretation of the act that required adoption of the most stringent standard to protect against material health impairment, bounded only by technological and economic feasibility. An action challenging the standard claimed that the act required OSHA to determine that the costs of the standard bore a reasonable relationship to its benefits. The court of appeals rejected the claim and the Supreme Court affirmed.

The opinion of the Court rejecting CBA was simple—if not simplistic—in its approach. Justice Brennan stressed the section 6(b)(5) provision that OSHA "shall set the standard which most adequately assures, *to the extent feasible*, on the basis of the best available evidence, that no employee will suffer material impairment of health or functional capacity."[35] The key phrase, said Justice Brennan, was that italicized— "to the extent feasible." Using standard dictionaries, Brennan concluded that section 6(b)(5) directed OSHA to promulgate the standard that most adequately assured that no employee would suffer material health impairment—"limited only by the extent to which this is 'capable of being done.'"[36]

In light of its ordinary meaning, the word "feasible" could not be construed to articulate congressional intent to require CBA: "Cost-benefit analysis . . . is not required by the statute because feasibility analysis is." As the Court saw it, "Congress itself defined the basic relationship between costs and benefits, by placing the 'benefit' of worker health above all other considerations save those making attainment of this 'benefit' unachievable. Any standard based on a balancing of costs and benefits by [OSHA] . . . strikes a different balance than that struck by Congress."[37]

It is, however, erroneous to conclude that the *Textile Manufacturers* decision sounded the knell for CBA or the Reagan order based upon it. In fact, the decision leaves it up to the different agencies to decide whether, and to what extent, to use such analyses. From this point of view, the Court, like the Congress, declined to make the crucial policy decision itself. Congress, says Justice Rehnquist in his *Textile Manufacturers* dissent, declined to make the decision to require or prohibit CBA. Instead, it passed and left the choice to OSHA.[38] The same is true of the *Textile Manufacturers* decision. It leaves OSHA free to choose whether to require the most technically sophisticated equipment possible for worker safety or to set limits on cost by using CBA. The Court, no less than Congress, passed on the decisive policy choice.

Hence, *Textile Manufacturers* means only that the Court will not impose requirements on rule making in addition to those demanded by Congress. The agency is free to interpret its enabling legislation along CBA lines. If it does so, as the Rehnquist dissent indicates, the Court will defer to its judgment that the statute permits the agency to undertake CBA.

NEED FOR REGULATORY CBA

CBA, as indicated, was originally a tool of economics. More recently, the CBA approach has been used in the law; even with the *Textile Manufacturers* decision, there is still wide scope for CBA in our public law. Nor is its use as a criterion for governmental action one that will be disputed in many fields. Thus, before undertaking a public works project such as a highway or a dam, the agency concerned should try to determine who will gain and who will lose from the action and by how much. Only if the projected benefits are greater than the costs should the agency proceed with the scheme. That is, if nothing else, simple common sense applied to public action. "For which of you, intending to build a tower, sitteth not down first, and counteth the cost."[39]

Even though more controversial there, CBA can also play a proper part in administrative regulatory action. When the Reagan executive order requiring CBA before major rules are promulgated was issued, a

New York Times editorial commented that that, too, was "timely common sense."[40] When an administrative regulation can have such drastic impact, it is only proper that the agency concerned should consider the costs as well as the benefits and not issue the regulation "unless the potential benefits to society for the regulation outweigh the potential costs to society."[41]

The appropriateness of CBA in regulatory administration is particularly apparent in the newer area of so-called social regulation.[42] Traditional regulatory agencies, patterned on the archetype of the Interstate Commerce Commission,[43] have regulated specific industries. An agency such as the ICC, concerned with the totality of its regulated industry, has always concentrated primarily on economic factors. When it fixes rates, issues licenses, or imposes regulatory requirements, it must inevitably consider the costs its action imposes on the industry. Thus, the ICC has to pay attention to the effects of orders fixing rates and entry for truckers under its statutory mission to ensure a trucking business that provides adequate and economical transportation services to the public.[44] If the costs imposed by ICC action are disproportionate to the benefits secured, the statutory goal will not be met.

In addition, the private adversaries in the traditional administrative process are even more intimately concerned with costs. Whether the theory of "capture" of the ICC-type agency by its industry[45] is valid or not, it is certainly true that the agency's primary "constituency" is the industry being regulated. An agency that ignores the costs it imposes on its constituency does so at its peril. The regulated industry has sufficient influence, on Capitol Hill and elsewhere, to ensure that its dominant concerns will normally be met by the agency concerned.

During the past two decades, however, a new generation of administrative agencies has been created. These agencies have been a direct product of the increased concern with consumer and environmental protection that has so changed our public law in recent years. The leading agencies among this newer breed are the Environmental Protection Agency, the Occupational Safety and Health Administration, and the Consumer Products Safety Commission.

The jurisdiction of these agencies is not limited to a single industry. Instead, it cuts across the economic system. The newer agency also operates in a narrower sphere than the traditional regulatory agency. It is

171

not concerned with the totality of an industry, but only with the segment of its operations that comes within its bailiwick. Thus, the EPA, like the ICC, may be concerned with trucking, but its interest is only in the effect of trucking operations on the environment.[46]

The new breed of EPA-type agency was established to promote social, rather than economic, goals. The traditional theory of regulation has been geared to a world where the regulators, as well as their constituency, are concerned almost entirely with business factors, such as prices and costs. The EPA-type agency is normally oblivious to these factors. That is also true of its constituency, which is not a particular industry but the public interest groups supporting its efforts. Both the agency and its constituency tend to condemn as callous any consideration of cost, or other economic factors, in decisions on product, personnel, or environmental safety.[47]

CBA is particularly appropriate in the EPA-type agency engaged in social regulation. However desirable the goals pursued by such an agency, their attainment should be subject to a balancing of costs versus benefits. Not only that, the agency should be required, as the Reagan executive order demands, to issue a statement explaining its CBA, describing both potential benefits and potential costs and then its determination of potential net benefits.[48] Without such a CBA requirement the EPA-type agency can act to achieve its regulatory goals without any consideration of the costs involved, wholly ignoring the economic impact of its actions.

That this is not mere speculation is shown by what actually happened in the *Textile Manufacturers*[49] case. OSHA there issued its cotton-dust standard without any CBA and the Court held that CBA was not required by the governing statute. On the merits of the standard, the Court deferred to the agency determination on the limitation to be imposed on cotton dust, holding that it could not reverse the court of appeals conclusion that it was supported by substantial evidence. The outside observer is, however, bound to be disturbed by the flimsy nature of the evidence supporting the OSHA standard and the estimates upon which it was based.[50]

In determining the feasibility of its standard, OSHA did give some consideration to the cost to the industry of implementing the new requirement. OSHA had before it two financial analyses. The first was prepared by Research Triangle Institute under an OSHA contract. Despite the fact that the study was by a group under contract to OSHA, its cost estimates were rejected by OSHA. The other study was prepared by industry representatives. But its estimates assumed a less stringent standard than that issued. OSHA concluded that this was an overestimate of the costs of the less stringent standard the study was assuming. Then the agency decided that it would be treated as a reliable estimate for the more costly standard finally promulgated.[51] As Justice Stewart, dissenting, noted, OSHA "never rationally explain[ed] how it came to this happy conclusion." Analysis of the record leads to the inevitable conclusion that the agency's estimate was sheer guesswork—"unsupported speculation," as Justice Stewart termed it.[52]

The dominant theme of the *Textile Manufacturers* opinion is deference toward administrative expertise, even though close analysis of the record shows that the OSHA conclusions were based on "unsupported speculation." Perhaps, as some claim, agencies "express an intuition of experience which outruns analysis and sums up many unnamed and tangled impressions; impressions which may lie beneath consciousness without losing their worth."[53] One would have hoped, however, that the highest Court would require more than the mystique of administrative devotees to support so far-reaching a regulatory standard.

OSHA's cotton-dust standard suffered from what Harold Laski once termed the limitations of the expert[54]—in this case, zeal in promoting the agency's own administrative policy regardless of the cost to other, broader interests. OSHA imposed its standard without comparing costs in relation to benefits, finding only that compliance with the standard would not threaten the economic viability of the industry and hence was economically feasible. In considering costs, OSHA assumed that they would be borne by employers, indicating that the protections imposed were to be without cost to the employee.[55]

The notion that the cost of the OSHA standard was to be imposed only on employers is, however, illusory. Employers may pay the compliance costs initially. That, however, is not the end of the matter. The cost will ultimately be passed on to consumers. The higher prices will lead them to consume less cotton products, leading to industry contraction and to worker layoffs. Then, too, at future bargaining sessions with labor, management will be unable to grant increased wages and benefits without further industry contraction and layoffs.[56] OSHA's desire to have compliance with its standard at no cost to employees thus turns out to be administrative pursuit of a will-o'-the-wisp.

JUDGE POSNER AND CBA

It is one thing to use CBA for public works projects or even for administrative rule making. It is quite another to make it a general touchstone in our public law. Yet that is what has been advocated by New Right jurists who have urged economic analysis as the foundation of jurisprudence.

We can take as the focus of our discussion here the view expressed by Professor (now Judge) Richard A. Posner on the exclusionary rule (which bars admission of illegally seized evidence in a criminal case) under the Fourth Amendment. In articles in 1981 and 1982[57] as well as in his *Economic Analysis of Law*,[58] Posner applied his economic analysis to the Fourth Amendment and ended up with a CBA approach to the exclusionary rule.

Judge Posner analyzes the Fourth Amendment in terms of the economic approach taken throughout his work. To him, the key criterion in law, as in economics, is "efficiency." A legal rule does not promote efficiency if its costs are excessive in relation to its benefits. So far as the Fourth Amendment is concerned, this means that the concept of "reasonableness," which governs legality under the amendment, must be analyzed in cost-benefit terms. Thus Posner interprets a leading case[59] as holding "that wiretapping was a form of seizure within the meaning of the Fourth Amendment and hence unlawful if unreasonable (which means . . . if the costs exceed the benefits)."[60]

In his analysis of the Fourth Amendment, Judge Posner uses what he calls the Hand Formula.[61] This is the negligence formula stated by Judge Learned Hand in a 1947 case.[62] As explained by Posner in a 1982 opinion, "Judge Hand, designating by 'B' the burden of the precautions necessary to avert an accident, by 'L' the magnitude of the loss if the accident occurred, and by 'P' the probability that if the precautions were not taken the accident would occur, reasoned that a shipowner or other alleged tortfeasor was negligent if $B < PL$, that is, if the burden of precautions was less than the harm if the accident occurred discounted (i.e., multiplied) by the probability that it would occur. The higher P and L are, and the lower B is, the likelier is a finding of negligence."[63]

Posner applies the Hand Formula to the Fourth Amendment as follows:

> A search (or seizure) is reasonable if the cost of the search in impaired privacy (B) is less than the probability (P) that without the search the target of the search cannot be convicted, multiplied by the social loss (L) of not convicting him. P has two components: the probability that the search will turn up something of value to the police (probable cause); and the probability that that something is essential to conviction. The value of the search is therefore less if the same evidence could be obtained without a search (so presumably at a lower B). The more intrusive the search, the more essential the evidence sought must be (P) or the graver the crime being investigated must be (L) in order to justify the higher B imposed.[64]

What the Hand Formula comes down to here is a "balancing approach" comparable to that used in negligence cases. Here, as in tort law generally, says Judge Posner, "reasonable" (that is, the test under the Fourth Amendment) "is at least a rough synonym for 'cost-justified.'" Thus, to Posner, "A reasonable search is a cost-justified search." This is, of course, to use a CBA approach to Fourth Amendment cases: "[O]nly if the costs of a particular method of search are disproportionate to the benefits in more effective law enforcement is a search unreasonable."[65]

The same CBA approach is used by Posner to judge the validity of the exclusionary rule. Under the Posner analysis, the rule is found wanting when weighed in the CBA balance. To Posner, the exclusionary rule "is a classic example of overdeterrence. The cost to society of doing without the evidence may greatly exceed the social costs of the search."[66]

This result is reached by Posner through application of the Hand Formula. "Suppose," he states, "that B, the cost to the defendant of the search in terms of damage to property or seizure of lawful private communications is $1,000; P, the probability that he could not be convicted without this search, was 1 percent at the time of the search; and L, the social cost (in reduced deterrence and prevention of crime) of not convicting him is $50,000."[67] Such a search would be illegal under the Hand formula. Suppose, however, that "the evidence obtained in the search is essential to conviction."[68] In that case, under the Posner analysis, "even though the social cost of the search is only $1,000, the exclusionary rule will impose a punishment cost of $50,000 on the society."[69]

Hence, to Judge Posner, the exclusionary rule clearly fails the CBA test: "[T]he private (and social) cost imposed on the government may greatly exceed the social cost of the [police] misconduct."[70]

THE COURT, THE EXCLUSIONARY RULE, AND CBA

In a 1981 article urging the CBA approach just summarized, Professor Posner conceded that his approach was contrary to that followed by the Supreme Court up to that time. He noted, indeed, that the Court had recently rejected a "multifactor balancing test" as the criterion in determining Fourth Amendment issues.[71]

Yet it was essentially the Posner CBA approach that the Court adopted in its decisions narrowing the exclusionary rule during the 1983 term. In *United States v. Leon*,[72] the justices read in a good-faith exception to the rule, holding that where the police acted in good-faith reliance upon a defective warrant, the evidence seized under the warrant should not be excluded. The *Leon* Court used CBA to buttress its conclusion that a good-faith exception to the exclusionary rule was warranted. In its opinion the Court stated, "Whether the exclusionary sanction is appropriately imposed in a particular case . . . must be resolved by weighing the costs and benefits of preventing the use of [the illegally obtained] evidence."[73]

It was, however, in the companion case of *Immigration and Naturalization Service v. Lopez-Mendoza*[74] that the Court elevated the Posner analysis to the status of accepted doctrine.[75] *Lopez-Mendoza* arose out of a deportation proceeding. The alien had objected to evidence introduced at the deportation hearing, contending that it should have been suppressed as the fruit of an unlawful arrest. The INS held that the evidence was admissible because application of the exclusionary rule to deportation proceedings was inappropriate. The court of appeals reversed, ruling that the evidence was the fruit of an unlawful arrest and that it must be suppressed under the exclusionary rule.

The *Lopez-Mendoza* conference was closely divided. The crucial question was, of course, that stated at the outset by Chief Justice Burger:

"Should the exclusionary rule be extended to civil deportation proceedings?" Burger answered in the negative, saying, "I reject the argument that this is more like a criminal case, despite the hardship incident to deportation."

All the justices at the *Lopez-Mendoza* conference assumed that CBA was appropriate to determine whether the exclusionary rule should be applied in a given case. Even Justice Brennan, who led the argument in favor of affirmance, did not dispute the application of CBA to decide the issue. Brennan's use of CBA, however, differed from that by the majority. "I would conclude," Brennan told the conference, "that the balance of costs and benefits . . . tips decisively in favor of applying the Rule to deportation hearings. I would therefore affirm the judgment of the Ninth Circuit."[76]

Brennan gave three reasons to support his conclusion that CBA tipped the balance in favor of the exclusionary rule: "*First*, here . . . there is a direct connection between the conduct of INS agents and the application of the Exclusionary Rule in deportation proceedings. . . . *Second*, the fact that the INS is a single, integrated federal agency actually weighs in favor of applying the Rule here." That was true "because here we can be especially confident that applying the Rule will yield substantial benefits in terms of deterring unconstitutional law-enforcement activity." Finally, Brennan stressed the fact that "despite Andy Frey's[77] protestations, the evidence that we have suggests that the Exclusionary Rule has been thought for many, many years to apply in deportation proceedings. . . . Consequently, we have direct evidence of the kind that we rarely have in this area that a law-enforcement regime which applies the Exclusionary Rule is able to function smoothly and without substantial problems."

Justice Brennan was supported by Justices White, Marshall, and Stevens. The others, however, voted to reverse. "This for me is civil," said Justice Blackmun, "and I won't extend [this] judge-made rule to it." Blackmun stated the CBA conclusion of the conference majority: "The societal costs greatly exceed the benefits here."

The *Lopez-Mendoza* decision, like the conference vote, reversed by a bare majority. The O'Connor opinion of the Court followed a CBA approach that weighed the benefits secured from the exclusionary rule in the deportation case against the costs of applying the rule in such a case.

The deterrent value of the exclusionary rule was seen to be its primary benefit. O'Connor found the benefit to be significantly reduced in the deportation case. She then concluded that the social costs of applying the exclusionary rule in deportation proceedings "are both unusual and significant."[78] These costs, particularly in terms of delay and the increased burden on the agency, outweigh the benefits in the O'Connor calculus. Justice Byron R. White, who delivered the principal dissent, did not disagree with the cost-benefit approach. White simply appraised the costs and benefits differently, concluding that the Court had unduly minimized the benefits and exaggerated the costs associated with applying the exclusionary rule in this context.

CBA AND CONSTITUTIONAL RIGHTS

Before the Supreme Court decision in *Lopez-Mendoza*, the cases had held that the exclusionary rule is also a due process requirement in an administrative hearing. The principle that the exclusionary rule is applicable to administrative as well as criminal proceedings had been all but uniformly applied to a wide range of agency proceedings, running the gamut from Federal Trade Commission hearings to deportation cases.[79] The cases had assumed the *Mapp v. Ohio*[80] thesis that the exclusionary rule is included in the requirements of due process and that hence it is binding in administrative as well as criminal proceedings. They had asked only whether the exclusionary rule had been violated in the particular case.

This is, of course, the question that must normally be asked in cases involving alleged violations of constitutional rights: Has a right guaranteed by the Constitution been violated in the given case?

Under *Lopez-Mendoza*, an affirmative answer is not enough to lead to a decision in favor of the individual. Instead, CBA must be applied to determine whether the right itself is guaranteed in the particular proceeding. If the CBA balance tilts against the right in the given case, the government will be upheld even though it has violated the right concerned.

From this point of view, *Lopez-Mendoza* marks a culmination in the application of CBA to legal issues. It is one thing for CBA to be used by administrative agencies before they issue substantive regulations. Rule making inevitably has economic impact and it is normally desirable for agencies to use a tool originally developed by economists. It is quite another to hold that CBA should be applied to the denial of procedural rights in an administrative hearing—even where the right is so fundamental as that embodied in the exclusionary rule. The *Leon* case[81] indicates that the cost-benefit calculus is also one that should be used in other areas of public law, including those involving the rights of criminal defendants. The opinion in *Leon* was delivered by Justice White, illustrating that his disagreement with the *Lopez-Mendoza* majority was not in their use of the cost-benefit approach, but in his different appraisal of the balancing of costs and benefits at stake.

The disagreement between Justice White and the *Lopez-Mendoza* majority may, however, show the dangers involved in using CBA as a general lodestar in public law. CBA has about it a delusive aura of scientific objectivity that may be justified in the field of economics in which it began and has often been used. As a public-law tool, however, it is as subjective as the Benthamite "felicific calculus"[82] that was its primitive progenitor. Just as each utilitarian would apply the "greatest happiness of the greatest number"[83] principle according to his own subjective judgment of the pains and pleasures involved, so each judge employing CBA will use his own individual calculus in weighing the procedural rights at issue.

Advocates of CBA in the law assert that it involves only one uncontroversial test: If a legal rule helps more than it hurts, it should be put into effect.[84] So viewed, CBA appears as simple common sense. But its use in public law "can have a narcotic effect. It creates an illusion of technical precision and ineluctability."[85] In reality, as the difference between Justice White and the *Lopez-Mendoza* majority shows, CBA in practice depends upon the individual value judgments of the particular judge. What appears as objective analysis is really Benthamism in a modern dress, and with a subjective vengeance.

CBA in constitutional law reduces our basic rights to the level of the counting house. Those rights were placed in the organic charter "as fundamental choices of principle, not as instrumental calculations of utility or as pseudo-scientific calibrations of social cost against social benefit—calculations and calibrations whose essence is to deny the decision maker's personal responsibility for choosing."[86] Under a decision like that in *Lopez-Mendoza*, it has been said, "the Supreme Court, long our nation's principal expositor of the Constitution, is coming increasingly to resemble a judicial Office of Management and Budget, straining constitutional discourse through a managerial sieve in which the 'costs' (usually tangible and visible) are supposedly 'balanced' against the 'benefits' (usually ephemeral and diffuse) of treating constitutional premises seriously."[87]

Even more disturbing is the inevitable result where CBA becomes the measuring rod for the protection of constitutional rights. When we deal with a constitutional right such as that protected by the exclusionary rule, it is much easier to quantify costs than benefits. It is, indeed, all but impossible to measure most constitutional rights in monetary terms, though it is not difficult to do so as far as the costs of protecting those rights in given cases are concerned. How much is freedom from illegally seized evidence worth?

Judge Posner answers this question in a manner that gives a new perspective to the noted Wilde aphorism on price and value. He uses the following illustration to show the effect of the exclusionary rule: "[S]uppose that evidence that is indispensable to convicting a criminal is seized as an incident to some illegal search. Further suppose that the illegal search imposes a cost of $100 on the person searched in terms of lost time spent cleaning up after the searching officers, but that the loss to society from not being able to convict him can be valued at $10,000."[88] In such a case, says Posner, the social cost imposed on government plainly exceeds the benefit of having the illegal evidence excluded.

For Judge Posner, the violation of the Fourth Amendment right is measured only in terms of the bare economic loss to the victim—the one-hundred-dollar cost of the "lost time spent cleaning up after the searching officers." Inevitably, the dollar cost of that "lost time" will not be high. And what about the case where the police search neither destroys anything nor leaves any untidy mess to be cleaned up later?[89]

The truth is that it is all but impossible to quantify constitutional rights such as the freedom from illegal searches and seizures in dollars-and-cents terms. The Posner valuation, couched solely in economic analysis, seems almost ludicrous—that is, until we try to assign a monetary value to the right ourselves.

One of the most difficult problems arising from the widespread use of CBA in regulatory administration has been the need to estimate the worth of an individual. What is the dollar value of a human life? Different agencies have come up with different figures, ranging from as low as $70,000 to as high as $132,000,000.[90] Certainly, as one study recognizes, "There remain substantial limitations of current methodology to incorporate all the variables that affect societal valuations of human life."[91] The same is at least as true of estimates of the pecuniary worth of a constitutional right, unless we use the crabbed economic-analysis approach of Judge Posner.

In cases such as *Lopez-Mendoza*, it is much easier to measure the costs than the benefits. Since the constitutional right cannot really be quantified in monetary terms, the cost-benefit approach will always tend to a weighing of the balance on the cost side of the scale. The result, in the *Lopez-Mendoza*-type case, is that the law is "drawn into a curious world where the 'costs' of excluding illegally obtained evidence loom to exaggerated heights and where the 'benefits' of such exclusion are made to disappear with a mere wave of the hand."[92]

A system that values basic rights in more than dollars-and-cents terms should hesitate before following an approach according to which, *priceless* may too often mean *worthless*.[93]

POSNERIAN ECONOMIC ANALYSIS

"The application of economics to an ever-increasing range of legal fields, including [that] at once so fundamental and apparently noneconomic as . . . constitutional law" is, according to Judge Posner, "the most important development in legal thought in the last quarter century."[94] Posner himself has, of course, been the leader in the movement to subject the law to the criterion of economic analysis. Its greatest success thus far has been the increasing resort to CBA both in administrative agencies, particularly under President Reagan's executive order,[95] and in the courts, in cases such as *Leon* and *Lopez-Mendoza*.[96]

But CBA illustrates only a part of the potential inherent in the Posner approach. Applied throughout our public law, Judge Posner's use of economic analysis could make for what he called in another connection a "seismic constitutional change."[97] More than that, it would take our

181

public law back to the day when the judges read their own economic beliefs into the Constitution and rendered governmental efforts contrary to those beliefs ineffective.

For Judge Posner, the goal of law, as of economics, is efficiency. As he once defined it, "Efficiency is a technical term: it means exploiting economic resources in such a way that human satisfaction as measured by aggregate consumer willingness to pay for goods and services is maximized."[98] "Man," says Posner, "is a rational maximizer of his ends in life."[99] Hence efficiency, to him, is conceived of in terms of wealth maximization, which he sees as the norm in the law as in the economic system itself.[100]

The Posner concept of efficiency as wealth maximization is based on the existence of the market. As he puts it, "[R]esources tend to gravitate toward their most valuable uses if voluntary exchange—a market—is permitted."[101] Indeed, in the words of one critic, "the picture of American society presented by Posner . . . has created one grand system—the market, and those market-supportive aspects of law (notably 'common,' judge-made law)—which is almost flawless in achieving human happiness."[102]

It is, however, a short step from the Posner conception to that which dominated our public law not too long ago. If efficiency and wealth maximization are to be the legal lodestar and if their attainment depends upon the market, then any interference with the free operation of the market is to be condemned. When Posner concludes that when judges make law, the rules of law laid down by them will be consistent with the dictates of efficiency,[103] he is really positing judge-made jurisprudence consistent with the free operation of the market and hostile to any action that hampers its untrammeled operation.

It thus turns out that the Posnerian economic analysis of law furnishes support to the New Right positions in public law discussed in the prior chapters. Judge Posner recognizes this himself, at least to some extent. A "common criticism of the 'new' law and economics . . . ," Posner notes, "is that it manifests a conservative political bias. We shall see that its practitioners have found, for example, that capital punishment has a deterrent effect, legislation designed to protect consumers frequently ends up hurting them, no-fault automobile insurance is probably inefficient, and securities regulation may be a waste of time. Findings such as these indeed provide ammunition to the supporters of capital punishment and the opponents of the other policies mentioned"[104]—all policies opposed by New Right jurists.

To consider the market as the be all and end all of law, as it is in classical economics, is to reach legal results that most jurists would consider singular. Thus Professor Richard Epstein, now the leading New Right academic jurist, defends *Hammer v. Dagenhart*,[105] which most commentators today place with the *Lochner* case[106] on the list of discredited Supreme Court decisions. The Court in *Hammer* struck down a federal law that forbade the shipment in interstate commerce of goods manufactured in any plant that used child labor. In doing so, the Court relied upon a narrow conception of the congressional commerce power that has since been repudiated.[107]

Professor Epstein concludes that *Hammer* was correct in its interpretation of the Commerce Clause. But he does not stop there. Instead, he takes what he terms a "skeptical view of the substantive issues in *Hammer*."[108] By this he means the substantive power of government to enact child labor laws themselves. On that issue, Epstein attacks what he admits "was a powerful consensus in the Progressive movement that these statutes were absolutely necessary to counteract the evils of an unrestrained laissez-faire economic system which tolerated, and indeed encouraged, child labor."[109]

The *Hammer* Court, Professor Epstein concedes, "made no substantive attack on the child labor laws—rather, [it] sympathized with them." Epstein, however, rejects the notion that the child labor laws were "highly desirable social legislation." Instead, he writes, *Hammer* itself "takes on a different complexion, . . . if one looks with even modest suspicion on child labor statutes, as I do, and thinks that as a general rule the only proper grounds for government intervention in family relations are abuse or neglect."[110]

To support his antipathy toward child labor laws, Epstein refers to a well-known novel of half a century ago. "Any reader of Laura Ingalls Wilder's *Farmer Boy*,"[111] he states, "knows that child labor was not a creature of the industrial revolution." As Epstein sees it, "The children in the factories were certainly not as well off as we would like, but they were probably better off than they would have been back on the farm, or than if they had been left in the city without any opportunity to sell their labor. Their families had voted to leave the farm or the old country with their feet, as a matter of life and death." From this point of view, the laws limiting child labor "may well have been misguided initiatives that inflicted harm upon the very persons they were ostensibly intended to benefit."[112]

To Professor Epstein, then, "there is no obvious reason" to start "with the assumption that child labor laws are intrinsically good." On the contrary, "Even if the police power is thought to be extensive enough to 'protect' children from their parents as a constitutional matter . . . , there is a clear risk that the proper limits of the police power will be exceeded when legislation is used by interest groups that do not rely upon child labor to undercut rivals who do. Stated otherwise, child labor legislation could well be misguided paternalism or interest-group politics."[113]

For most of us, of course, the theme was set in the Holmes *Hammer* dissent: "[I]f there is any matter upon which civilized countries have agreed . . . it is the evil of premature and excessive child labor."[114] But the Epstein view on child labor laws is far from an aberration among New Right advocates of the Posner-type economic analysis of law, including the law of the Constitution. Thus, Judge Posner himself states that the law was "on solid economic ground when it refused to enforce agreements to join unions, enjoined picketing . . . and enforced yellow dog contracts." Posner also asserts that a statute like the Occupational Safety and Health Act is not necessary, since, without the law, "The employer has a selfish interest in providing the optimal . . . level of worker health and safety." Indeed, "Legislation prescribing the health and safety conditions of employment may raise the level of health and safety beyond the level desired by the employees and the employers and then both groups will be harmed."[115]

The Posnerian economic analysis of law, grounded as it is upon the efficiency furthered by the market, inevitably looks with a hostile eye upon governmental acts that interfere with the free operation of the market. We are thus, as indicated in Chapter 3, brought back to the public law at the turn of the century, when cases like *Lochner* set the pattern for judicial reception of laws that attempted to curb the excesses and abuses of a completely unrestrained market.

According to Judge Posner, under decisions like *Lochner*, "Classical economic theory was . . . elevated to the status of constitutional principle." But "the idea that voluntary transactions almost always promote welfare, and regulations that inhibit such transactions almost always reduce it" is not only the "staple of classical [economic] theory."[116] It is also the foundation of both the Posnerian economic analysis of law and the New Right jurisprudence discussed in prior chapters. Judge Posner rejects the common notion that the *Lochner*-type "liberty of contract decisions reflected a weak grasp of economics."[117] On the contrary, it is the Brandeis dissenting criticism of the *Lochner* era's economic approach that is the object of Posner's censure.[118]

JUDGES AS ECONOMISTS

From a broader point of view, the Posner economic approach to public law is subject to the same objection as the New Right attempt to revive the preferential treatment of economic rights discussed in Chapter 3. It leads the judge deciding a constitutional case to act on the basis of the economic theory that he deems correct. The judge qua economist will inevitably write his own economic views into the Constitution, and, as Holmes put it in an already-quoted passage, all too often on the basis "of the economic doctrines which prevailed about fifty years ago."[119] Thus, once again the courts will substitute their economic beliefs for the judgment of legislative bodies.[120] In practice, under the Posner-type approach to the subject, they will again take for their theories those of Adam Smith and even Herbert Spencer, rejecting those of Lord Keynes, which in many cases the legislature may have followed.[121]

The judge as Posner-type economist in operation is well illustrated by *Hall v. Santa Barbara*,[122] discussed in Chapter 4.[123] The ninth circuit there struck down a rent control ordinance applicable to mobile home parks. The decision was based on the Takings Clause. The rent control regulation was ruled a taking: "[T]his oversteps the boundaries of mere regulation and shades into permanent occupation of the property for which compensation is due."[124]

The *Hall* opinion of Judge Kozinski relies upon Professor Epstein's approach to the Takings Clause. But it is also sprinkled with citations to the writings of economists. Analysis of the court's decision shows that it is based upon the judges' economic evaluation of the rent control at issue. In particular, Judge Kozinski notes the claim that the rent control here had resulted in a substantial increase in the market price of mobile homes subject to the ordinance. He asserts that "this may well hinder rather than assist lower-income families seeking access to rental units in mobile park homes,"[125] and holds that, on remand, this issue must be considered and addressed on the basis of a complete record by the district court.

But the *Hall* opinion goes further and questions the economic basis of rent control as such. "We also note," states the court, "what appears to be a growing consensus that 'rent control causes a reduction in the quality of the existing rental housing stock and discourages investment in new rental property,' actually exacerbating the problems it is intended to ameliorate." Texts and articles by economists are cited to support this statement, including a survey that reported that "fewer than 2 percent of United States economists surveyed at random generally disagreed with the proposition that '[a] ceiling on rents reduces the quantity and quality of housing available.'" Judge Kozinski then concludes, "The rationality of rent control *vel non* may have to be reassessed in light of this growing body of thought on the subject."[126]

Judge Posner himself expressed similar skepticism about regulation of the landlord-tenant relation in *Chicago Board of Realtors v. Chicago*.[127] At issue was a Chicago ordinance giving tenants certain legal rights. In particular, it required landlords to pay interest on security deposits and hold those deposits in Illinois banks, authorized rent withholding for landlord lease violations, and prohibited charges of more than ten dollars a month for late payment of rent. The seventh circuit upheld the ordinance against Contract Clause and Due Process attacks.

Judge Posner (joined by Judge Easterbrook, another leading New Right academic appointed by President Reagan to the bench) concurred in the decision and wrote an opinion that stressed "the strong case that can be made for the unreasonableness of the ordinance."[128] The Posner opinion, though in form a concurrence, was actually the majority opinion, since it was supported by two of the members of the three-judge panel.

Judge Posner's opinion questions the ordinance through use of the economic analysis that permeates his work. According to him, forbidding landlords to charge interest at market rates on late payment of rent is "hardly . . . calculated to improve the health, safety, and welfare of Chicagoans or to improve the quality of the housing stock. But it may have the opposite effect." The rule will make housing more costly. "Landlords will try to offset the higher cost (in time value of money, less predictable cash flow, and, probably, higher rate of default) by raising rents. To the extent they succeed, tenants will be worse off, or at least no better off." If landlords do not succeed in efforts to offset the effects of the ordinance, "the cost of rental housing will be higher to landlords and therefore less will be supplied—more of the existing stock than would otherwise be the case will be converted to condominia and cooperatives and less rental housing will be built."[129]

The other ordinance provisions are similarly subjected to the Posner test and found wanting. Speaking of the security deposit requirements, Judge Posner asserts, "Their only apparent rationale is to transfer wealth from landlords and out-of-state banks to tenants and local banks—making this an unedifying example of class legislation and economic protectionism rolled into one." And any benefits from the rent-withholding provision "are likely to be offset by the higher costs to landlords, resulting in higher rents and less rental housing."[130]

Judge Posner concludes that the Chicago ordinance is not, despite its ostensible intent, in the interest of poor tenants. Rather, "As is frequently the case with legislation ostensibly designed to promote the welfare of the poor, the principal beneficiaries will be middle-class people"—"the most influential group in the city's population." Hence, according to Posner, "[T]he politics of the ordinance are plain enough, . . . and they have nothing to do with either improving the allocation of resources to housing or bringing about a more equal distribution of income and wealth."[131]

But Judge Posner does not stop with his expression of skepticism toward the Chicago ordinance at issue in the case. Instead, he follows up his questioning of the ordinance with an attack upon the economic theory behind rent control in general. "A growing body of empirical literature," Posner writes, "deals with the effects of governmental regulation of the market for rental housing." This literature is significant "in showing that the market for rental housing behaves as economic theory predicts: if price is artificially depressed, or the costs of landlords artificially increased, supply falls and many tenants, usually the poorer and the newer

187

tenants, are hurt." To support this statement, Posner cites two studies of rent control by economists, and then asserts, citing another article on economists' views, "The single proposition in economics from which there is the least dissent among American economists is that 'a ceiling on rents reduces the quantity and quality of housing available.'"[132]

The Posner analysis here could apply equally to other regulatory laws, since they, too, involve what Posnerian economics would consider undesirable interferences with the operation of the market. The implications of the Posner approach are thus far-reaching. Indeed, pushed to the *Chicago Board of Realtors* extreme, classical economics in its Posnerian garb may also have the potential to undermine the juristic foundation of the welfare state.

If we have learned anything in the public law of this century, however, it is that judges should not substitute their economic judgments for those of the legislature. What Justice Holmes told his fellow justices is still as valid as it ever was—that the Constitution was not "intended to give us *carte blanche* to embody our economic . . . beliefs in its prohibitions."[133] "Otherwise," as Holmes put it in his first Supreme Court opinion, "a constitution, instead of embodying only relatively fundamental rules of right, . . . would become the partisan of a particular set of . . . economical opinions, which by no means are held *semper ubique et ab omnibus*."[134]

The Posnerian economic analysis of law may have a legitimate role in such fields of private law as torts and contracts. In public-law cases, however, it remains out of place. The economic theory behind a law should continue to be primarily a question for the legislator, not the judge. Provided that they have a rational basis, it is the judge's duty to enforce even "laws that I believe to embody economic mistakes."[135]

"Judges," reads another famous Holmes passage, "are apt to be Naif, simpleminded men."[136] This is particularly true when they use their conceptions of economics as their legal compasses. With the revival of classical economics and the recent attempt to elevate the market to the constitutional plane, there is danger that the Constitution will once again be treated as a legal sanction of the survival of the fittest.

That danger will be avoided only if the courts reject the view that their notions of economics should override the economic theory upon which the legislature acts. Today, as in Holmes's day, it is for the judge to say that even though "speaking as a political economist, I should agree in condemning the law, still I should not be willing or think myself authorized to overturn legislation on that ground, unless I thought that an honest difference of opinion was impossible, or pretty nearly so."[137]

7

TURNING BACK
THE ADMINISTRATIVE
LAW CLOCK

HE YEAR 1987 was not only the bicentennial of the first constitution that attempted to establish a government on the principle of the
separation of powers. That same year also marked the centennial of
another event that greatly altered the system of separated powers—the
birth of the modern administrative agency in the Interstate Commerce
Act of 1887.[1] Since that time, the independent regulatory agencies have
become an essential part of modern government.

Because of the independent agencies, "the Presidency is not the
sole power, as the radical right wishfully preaches these days."[2] Yet
here, too, as this quote from Anthony Lewis indicates, eminent New
Right jurists disagree with the way in which our system has developed.
They protest the "erosions of presidential power" caused by the creation
of independent agencies[3] and would return to the days before the Interstate Commerce Commission, when all officers carrying out the laws
were agents of the president. In the process these jurists strike at the
very heart of the administrative state and its ability to exercise the
functions that public opinion has required it to assume. Before examin-
ing the attacks levied against the independent agencies, however, I shall
begin with a look at the creation of the archetype agency—the ICC
itself.

THE ARCHETYPE AGENCY

Nothing is more striking to a European traveler in the United States, wrote Alexis de Tocqueville, "than the absence of what we term the government, or the administration. Written laws exist in America, and one sees the daily execution of them; but although everything moves regularly, the mover can nowhere be discerned."[4]

The century and a half that has elapsed since Tocqueville wrote has seen many important changes in the American scene, but none perhaps more profound than in the area of administration. The French visitor of the 1830s could note the absence of administrative authority; the present-day observer must, on the contrary, immediately note the all-pervasive fact of governmental regulatory power. Since Tocqueville's day we have become a much-governed nation. Indeed, it is now almost trite to point out how the operations of the federal government have come to regulate the lives and fortunes of our citizenry from the cradle to the grave.

The starting point for the contemporary administrative state was the establishment of the Interstate Commerce Commission. "One might," said Henry Adams, "search the whole list of Congress, Judiciary, and Executive during the twenty-five years 1870 to 1895, and find little but damaged reputation. The period was poor in purpose and barren in results."[5] One important result of the period, however, the consequences of which a contemporary skeptic could not possibly estimate, was the rise of the modern administrative agency. The basic institutions of American law—executives, legislatures, and courts—had been fixed in form and function at the outset of the nation's history. The one important exception was the administrative agency, which first took form during the last half of the nineteenth century.

The history of the Interstate Commerce Commission, the first of the modern administrative agencies, presents in capsule form the difference between the beneficent aims of legal Darwinism and its rigor in actual practice. It was quixotic to assume that laissez faire would prove adequate to restrain the abuses that developed in the railroad industry of the time. Stimulated by a policy of benevolent promotion and subsidization on the part of both the states and the federal government, the industry expanded rapidly, especially during the post–Civil War period of industrial growth. Governmental generosity, unaccompanied by effective restrictions, inevitably generated serious abuses.[6] Freedom from public interference led to highly speculative railroad building, irresponsible financial manipulation, destructive competitive warfare resulting in monopolies, fluctuating and discriminating rates—and the inevitable public reaction.

"The first puff of the engine on the iron road announced a revolution in the law."[7] More than that, it announced the inadequacy of laissez faire and legal Darwinism in a burgeoning industrial economy. Adam Smith's "invisible hand" was not merely invisible but nonexistent to the farmer dependent on the railroad to move his crops. Freedom of contract was merely a euphemism to those who were, practically speaking, at the mercy of the railroads. Anyone with a grievance against the railroads was described as standing "alone, weak and poor and ignorant though he may be, with a ten-dollar case or a one-hundred dollar case. He must make his own case against a wealthy corporation."[8] As stated in a congressional debate on the remedies then afforded by the law, "Pygmies do not invite giants to combat."[9]

The resentment of farmers led to the Granger movement, which swept the Midwest in the early 1870s. The Grangers became a powerful political force, seeking to correct railroad abuses by state regulation. They secured laws in Illinois, Wisconsin, Minnesota, and Iowa regulating railroads, including limitations on railroad rates. These laws were upheld in the landmark *Granger Cases* (1877),[10] where the Court recognized the essential public power to regulate "businesses affected with a public interest," such as railroads. Even during the apotheosis of Spencerian doctrine, this ruling remained as a potential restraint upon abusive business activity.

The *Granger Cases* had sustained state regulation, yet the railroad problem transcended state boundaries; by its very nature it was an interstate problem and called for federal control. Nevertheless, the chances of passing congressional legislation appeared remote—railroad regulation had been before both Houses for almost two decades, but little had been done. Then the Supreme Court, by its *Wabash* decision in 1886,[11] injected a categorical congressional imperative.[12] *Wabash* denied state power to regulate railroad transportation when its origin or

192

destination went beyond state boundaries, even to regulate that part of the transportation that was entirely within the state. Since some three-fourths of the country's railroad tonnage was interstate in character, Congress was obliged to act under its commerce power if railroads were to be regulated at all. Within a few months of the *Wabash* decision, the Interstate Commerce Act of 1887 was enacted.

The 1887 act accomplished two main goals: (1) it prohibited certain railroad practices deemed objectionable, such as rate discrimination, rebating, and the charging of unjust and unreasonable rates; and (2) it set up the Interstate Commerce Commission to aid in the enforcement of these prohibitions.

A look back at the 1887 act, however, is proof that "more important than the immediate powers that in 1887 were vested in the Interstate Commerce Commission was the creation of the Commission itself."[13] For the first time, Congress had set up an independent regulatory agency, which was to serve as the model for later, similar bodies. Testifying before Congress in 1885, Charles Francis Adams had stated that "Congress would provide for a commission of men who were at once honest, intelligent and experienced, whose business it should be to observe this question very much as a physician would observe the progress of disease."[14] Now, with the 1887 act, the instrument of administrative regulation had been created. What was of basic significance was the deliberate organization of a governmental unit (located outside the traditional departments) whose single concern was the regulation of a vital national industry.[15]

During the next century the ICC was the model for a multitude of similar administrative agencies. The need for governmental specialization to deal with specific problems of economic regulation was met in the same way that it had been in 1887. A whole host of administrative agencies patterned upon the ICC was set up, particularly during the New Deal period. As Justice Rehnquist has written, "The term 'alphabet soup' gained currency in the early days of the New Deal as a description of the proliferation of new agencies." But the creation of ICC-type agencies did not stop with the New Deal. In a 1979 administrative law case Rehnquist writes, "The terminology required to describe the present controversy suggests that the 'alphabet soup' of the New Deal era was, by comparison, a clear broth."[16]

193

AGENCY INDEPENDENCE

As instituted by the 1887 act, the ICC "was something new in the American system of government: a strange amalgam of executive, legislative, and judicial powers, combining functions of all three branches."[17] As such, the commission may appear inconsistent with the separation of powers. As an opponent put it during the congressional debate on the matter, "I believe that it is absolutely unconstitutional and void, because to my mind it is a blending of the legislative, the judicial, and perhaps, the executive powers of the Government in the same law."[18] The overwhelming consensus in the Congress, however, rejected this constitutional attack,[19] agreeing, in the words of one supporter of the bill, that the "question . . . is not one of power, but one of expediency."[20] The law on the matter has agreed with the bill's supporters, and more recently the Supreme Court has held specifically that the combination in one agency of executive, legislative, and judicial powers does not violate the Constitution.[21]

Another aspect of the ICC-type agency that may seem incompatible with the tripartite structure of government established by the Constitution is its independence. The ICC and its progeny were not set up within any of the three branches; instead, they were created as independent bodies, structurally outside the traditional departments. This led an important study to characterize the ICC-type agencies as "in reality miniature independent governments set up to deal with the railroad problem, the banking problem, or the radio problem. They constitute a headless 'fourth branch' of the Government, a haphazard deposit of irresponsible agencies and uncoordinated powers."[22]

There is no doubt that the independent ICC-type agency is a hybrid body, set up to perform functions that at first glance appear incompatible. In the first place, these agencies are vested with positive duties of implementing their regulatory laws, both by the exercise of the power to make rules and regulations and by administering the statutory provisions. Especially significant is the affirmative duty imposed upon the commissions to ensure that the terms of their regulatory statutes are in fact complied with and to ferret out violators. These are basically executive functions that might, with complete propriety, be conferred directly on the executive branch.

Why not then place these functions within the structure of the executive branch, subject to the hierarchical control of the president? Such a solution is precluded by the fact that these agencies, in addition to their executive functions, are vested with the duty of deciding cases in which alleged violators of the legislation are proceeded against. This latter duty is basically judicial in nature—that of trying defendants brought before the bar of justice. Under American conceptions, a function of this type is deemed to be best exercised in an atmosphere of independence.

The judicial nature of much of the ICC-type agencies' work is the principal factor preventing them from being placed under direct executive control. But there are other reasons as well that have led Congress to opt for the independence of these agencies. These may be summarized as follows:

1. The example of the ICC. The success and prestige in its earlier years of the first important regulatory agency persuaded Congress to set up other commissions patterned after it. This is clear from the legislative history of most of the independent agencies. The witnesses and committee reports constantly refer to the ICC as a model.

2. The need to secure impartiality in administration. Because of the vast powers vested in these agencies and the tremendous pressures to which they may be subject, it has been felt essential that they be insulated from partisan influence or control. As the Senate Committee on Interstate Commerce stated in its report on the Radio Act of 1927, "The exercise of this power is fraught with such great possibilities that it should not be entrusted to any one man nor to any administrative department of the Government. This regulatory power should be as free from political influence or arbitrary control as possible."[23] Independence and security of tenure of the commissioners were intended to ensure such freedom.

3. The need for continuity of policy. For those industries regulated to plan effectively, the regulatory agency must achieve a basic stability in methods and policy. With an independent commission whose members held office for substantial and overlapping terms, continuity of policy and stability of administrative method could be built up.

195

4. The need to assemble a body of experts competent to deal with highly complicated and technical problems. Independence has been deemed to enhance the professional attractions of the agency, enabling both the heads and the staff to secure expertise needed for effective regulation. In the words of one of the greatest modern commissioners, Joseph Eastman of the Interstate Commerce Commission, "To be successful, [agency officials] must be masters of their own souls, and known to be such."[24]

THE *HUMPHREY* CASE

When Franklin D. Roosevelt became president in 1933, the independent regulatory agencies were manned by commissioners appointed by his Republican predecessors and hence generally unsympathetic to the New Deal policies. The new president found this situation intolerable. Where possible, he sought to induce incumbent commissioners to resign. When the president failed to secure voluntary resignations, he did not hesitate to use more drastic methods. Thus, an important factor that led Roosevelt to support the Communications Act of 1934 was that it abolished the Federal Radio Commission outright and permitted the president to appoint all the members of the Federal Communications Commission that was set up in its place.

In the case of the Federal Trade Commission, Roosevelt resorted directly to the presidential power of removal. William M. Humphrey, a member of the commission, was a Hoover Republican who strenuously resisted all Roosevelt's efforts to reorganize the FTC as a New Deal agency. The president sent Humphrey a letter stating that he was being removed from office as of October 7, 1933, on the ground "that the aims and purposes of this Administration with respect to the work of the Commission can be carried out most effectively with personnel of my own selection." The Federal Trade Commission Act provides that members of the FTC are to hold office for terms of seven years and that "any commissioner may be removed by the President for inefficiency, neglect of duty, or malfeasance in office."

By the middle of 1934, President Roosevelt had appointed his own men to all five positions on the FTC. A year later, however, he learned from the Supreme Court that his removal of Mr. Humphrey had been illegal.

The Court, in a case brought by Humphrey challenging the legality of his ouster, held that the president's wide removal power over officers appointed by him in the ordinary executive departments did not extend to members of a regulatory commission such as the FTC. The President's removal power was instead limited to removal for the causes specified in the statute.

Pointing to the judicial-type functions of the FTC, Justice George Sutherland, who delivered the *Humphrey* opinion, asserted that freedom from presidential control was vital to their successful execution. "The authority of Congress," he declared, "in creating quasi-legislative or quasi-judicial agencies, to require them to act independently of executive control cannot well be doubted; and that authority includes, as an appropriate incident, power to fix the period during which they shall continue in office, and to forbid their removal except for cause in the meantime."[25]

That the regulatory agencies may be largely independent of the president is a direct result of the *Humphrey* case. The key to independence is security of tenure. For, in the apt words of the *Humphrey* opinion itself, "it is quite evident that one who holds his office only during the pleasure of another cannot be depended upon to maintain an attitude of independence against the latter's will."[26] That the members of an agency such as the FTC do not hold their offices only for the duration of the president's pleasure permits them to maintain an attitude of independence against the presidential will. In its 1958 *Wiener* decision,[27] which reaffirms the principle of security of tenure, the Court stated that Congress did not wish to have hanging over commissioners the Damocles' sword of removal by presidential fiat.

PRESIDENTIAL REMOVAL POWER

Presidential control of the executive branch depends, in the last resort, upon the removal power. If the chief executive can remove from office at will, it is impossible for the holders of such offices effectively to resist his will. The removal power is thus the sanction provided by the Constitution to enable the president to control the executive branch in all its official actions.

The key pre-*Humphrey* case on presidential removal power was *Myers v. United States*.[28] That case arose out of the removal from office of a first-class postmaster at the specific direction of President Coolidge. The removal was contested on the ground that it was contrary to a statute providing that postmasters "may be removed by the President with the advice and consent of the Senate." The Court upheld the order of removal and ruled that the statute was an invalid attempt to restrict the president's removal power.

The *Myers* opinion was delivered by Chief Justice Taft, himself wholly cognizant of the relationship between the removal power and responsible administration. The very purpose of the framers, declared the chief justice, was to create a strong executive and thus avoid the humiliating weakness of the Congress during the Revolution and under the Articles of Confederation. But one who had served as chief executive well knew that without the removal power, the intent of the framers could hardly achieve practical reality. In Taft's phrase, as the president's "selection of administrative officers is essential to the execution of the laws by him, so must be his power of removing those for whom he cannot continue to be responsible."[29]

Under *Myers*, the removal power is an inherent incident of the constitutional delegation of executive power. Article II, states Taft, "grants to the President the executive power of the government—i.e., the general administrative control of those executing the laws, including the power of appointment and removal of executive officers—a conclusion confirmed by his obligation to take care that the laws be faithfully executed." The power to remove officers "is an incident of the power to appoint them, and is in its nature an executive power."[30]

Under *Humphrey*, however, the same is not true of the presidential power to remove the members of independent agencies such as the ICC and the FTC. As recently explained by Chief Justice Rehnquist, "In *Humphrey's Executor*, we found it 'plain' that the Constitution did not give the President 'unlimitable power of removal' over the officers of independent agencies. Were the President to have the power to remove FTC commissioners at will, the 'coercive influence' of the removal power would 'threate[n] the independence of [the] commission.'"[31]

The *Humphrey* doctrine makes it possible for Congress to vest significant powers in independent agencies outside the ordinary departments
that are not subject to the hierarchical control of the president. The key
to practical implementation of the legislative power in this respect is the
fact that the members of those agencies may not be removed from office
at the will of the president. Without such security of tenure, the independent status that Congress intended for such agencies would remain
an empty form. More than that, the exercise of adjudicatory functions
with that "cold neutrality of an impartial judge" of which Burke speaks is
impossible where the adjudicator himself lacks security of tenure.
Humphrey makes it possible for commissioners to resist White House
pressures to an extent that could hardly be expected in officials of the
executive branch.

INDEPENDENT AGENCIES AND THE NEW RIGHT

Humphrey was decided over half a century ago. The decision there, it
was thought, had settled the constitutionality of the independent ICC-
type agencies and their insulation from unlimited presidential removal
power. Now, however, both *Humphrey* and its position as the charter for
agency independence have been subjected to challenge by New Right
jurists. Just before his Supreme Court appointment, Justice Scalia asserted, "It has in any event always been difficult to reconcile *Humphrey's
Executor's* 'headless fourth branch' with a constitutional text and tradition establishing three branches of government."[32]

This Scalia statement was based on the assumption that "the rationale . . . of *Humphrey's Executor* requires, that the presidential removal
for cause permitted under the statute upheld there did not include removal because of the appointee's failure to accept presidential instructions regarding matters of policy or statutory application delegated to
him by Congress."[33] This rationale has, of course, been the foundation
for agency independence, since it denies presidential power to remove
agency members for failure to follow White House instructions.

But Judge Scalia went even further and questioned the very concept of
agency independence underlined by *Humphrey* as one "stamped with
some of the political science preconceptions characteristic of its era and
not of the present day." According to Scalia, "It is not as obvious today

199

as it seemed in the 1930s that there can be such things as genuinely 'independent' regulatory agencies, bodies of impartial experts whose . . . decisions . . . so clearly involve scientific judgment rather than political choice that it is even theoretically desirable to insulate them from the democratic process."[34]

During the Reagan presidency, leading members of the administration carried the Scalia animadversion to its logical extreme. In a widely reported speech, Attorney General Meese challenged the very foundation of the ICC-type agency, asserting that its independence from presidential control was contrary to the Constitution. Indeed, according to Meese, the entire system of independent agencies is of questionable constitutionality. "It should be up to the President to enforce the law," Meese declared. "Federal agencies performing executive functions are themselves properly agents of the executive. They are not 'quasi' this or 'independent' that. In the tripartite scheme of government, a body with enforcement powers is part of the executive branch of government." Meese urged that "we should abandon the idea that there are such things as 'quasi-legislative' or 'quasi-judicial' functions that can be properly delegated to independent agencies."[35]

The implications of the Meese argument are extensive. They were pointed out by Judge Posner in a case in which the constitutionality of the FTC was challenged: "[Plaintiff] is asking us to adopt a principle that would make every independent federal administrative agency unconstitutional; for the logic of its argument is not limited to the Federal Trade Commission but extends to the Interstate Commerce Commission, the Federal Communications Commission, the Federal Reserve Board, and the other well known, long established federal agencies whose members the President selects but cannot remove (before their terms expire) without cause. [Plaintiff] thus is asking us to decree a fundamental change in the structure of American government."[36]

Such a "seismic constitutional change"[37] would be the result if the independent agencies were ruled unconstitutional. In our present system, says Senator William Proxmire,

the independent agencies have provided a very useful balance wheel for the immense power concentrated in the executive branch. . . . All of this would be lost if the courts decide, as Messrs. Meese and Miller[38] have argued, that the executive branch and the executive branch alone has the exclusive and total right to enforce every law and regulation of this vast and complex American economy. Suppose the view of Attorney General Meese prevails. Then what? Then Mr. Meese and his Department of Justice will have the power, and the only power, to enforce the law in this vast, rambling complex Federal Government. Would anyone except the administration really want that?[39]

Not surprisingly, the courts have thus far rejected the claim that *Humphrey* was wrong and that the independent agencies are consequently unconstitutional. The most important decision directly in point thus far has been by the ninth circuit, which relied on the *Humphrey* case to reject the constitutional challenge.[40] *Humphrey*, said the court, has never been limited or overruled. On the contrary, the decision in *Bowsher v. Synar*,[41] (to be discussed in the next section) only confirms its continuing vitality. A concurring opinion rejected the notion that Article II confers upon the president exclusive power to execute *all* of the laws. In our system the powers assigned to the three branches "are not 'hermetically' sealed from each other" and grants of powers to administrative agencies have been validated by the courts. "Certainly the modern proliferation of administrative agencies has severely strained the Framers' pristine notion of separation of powers. . . . Nevertheless, I doubt the wisdom of invalidating a statutory mechanism which Congress, in supervising the various fields over which it enjoys constitutional reign, has seen fit to create frequently in order to administer complex and sweeping legislative ends."[42]

BOWSHER V. SYNAR CONFERENCE

In *Bowsher v. Synar*,[43] Solicitor General Charles Fried argued that "'executive' powers . . . may only be exercised by officers removable at will by the President."[44] Despite the implications of this argument for the independent agencies, during the *Bowsher* oral argument the solicitor general told the justices that the proponents of the constitutionality of the challenged Gramm-Rudman Act were trying to "scare" them with the argument that upholding the lower court on the constitutional issue would endanger the independent agencies such as the Federal Trade

Commission and the Federal Reserve Board. At this, Justice O'Connor interposed, "They scared me with it."[45]

The other justices must have felt the same fear, for they went out of their way in *Bowsher* to indicate that their decision did not apply to the independent agencies. Yet, though the opinion of the Court did reject the claim that the ICC-type agency is unconstitutional, its reasoning may well lend support to such a claim.

In *Bowsher* itself the Court dealt with the assignment to the comptroller general of certain functions under the 1985 Gramm-Rudman Act. The comptroller general is appointed by the president but may be removed from office by a joint resolution of Congress. Gramm-Rudman was a drastic attempt by Congress to eliminate the now-endemic federal deficit. The act set a maximum deficit amount for federal spending for each of the fiscal years 1986 through 1991. If, in any fiscal year, the budget deficit exceeded the prescribed maximum by more than a specified sum, the act required across-the-board cuts in federal spending to reach the targeted deficit level. These reductions were to be accomplished under the act's "reporting provisions," which required the directors of the Office of Management and Budget and the Congressional Budget Office to submit their deficit estimates and program-by-program reduction calculations to the comptroller general, who, after reviewing the directors' joint report, then was to report his conclusions to the president. The president then had to issue a "sequestration" order mandating the spending reductions specified by the comptroller general, and the sequestration order became effective unless, within a specified time, Congress legislated reductions to obviate the need for the sequestration order.

At the postargument conference, all except Justices White and Blackmun were for invalidating the challenged statute. Chief Justice Burger remarked, "Comptrollers have always thought they were Congressional aides and not independent." Burger then stressed the powers vested in the comptroller general. "The 1985 Act," he said, "pointedly refused to give the President the powers vested here in the Comptroller General. He's required to decide and issue reports to the President that bind the latter. The implementing responsibility is in the Comptroller General."

Burger referred to the *Myers* and *Humphrey* cases.[46] "*Myers*," the chief justice told the others, "said the power of removal was crucial to the

Presidency. But that power as to the Comptroller General rests with Congress without any meaningful review anywhere." Burger concluded by asserting, "*Humphrey* did not overrule *Myers.*"

The implication in Chief Justice Burger's conference statement is that presidential removal power was a constitutional sine qua non for all officers executing laws. The further implication is that that was also true for the ICC and FTC-type independent agency—which cast doubt on those agencies' constitutionality, as well as on the *Humphrey* case, which had upheld their validity.

Justice Brennan, who spoke next, rejected the Burger implication. As the justice put it in his conference statement, "[T]his case raises only the concern with keeping basic governmental powers distinctly separate. That is, what is problematic about Gramm-Rudman is that it involves a blending of legislative and executive functions." Justice Brennan also discussed removal power. "[T]he power to remove," he said, "is the power to *control*. Therefore, to the extent that Congress asserts power to remove an executive officer, Congress asserts a power to control that officer's execution. The Constitution does not permit Congress to do that."

Brennan interpreted *Myers* and *Humphrey* so as not to cast any doubt on the latter's continuing validity. "I note," he stated, "that the law in *Myers* was unconstitutional for just this reason—Congress required the President to obtain approval from the Senate before allowing removal. I note also that, under this analysis, the law in *Humphrey's* was *not* unconstitutional. In *Humphrey's*, Congress did not attempt to retain power to participate in the removal process; rather, Congress simply qualified the President's removal power. Thus, while *Humphrey's* did implicate the question whether the Constitution requires an absolutely unitary executive, it did not implicate separation of powers properly understood. Therefore, striking down Gramm-Rudman because Congress has retained the power to remove in no way draws *Humphrey's* into question."

Justice Brennan ended his conference statement by urging the Court specifically to reject the anti-*Humphrey* implications of the *Bowsher* case. "I would," the justice declared, "make very clear that *Humphrey's* is still good law. The notion that Congress can limit the President's power to remove as long as Congress does not itself participate in the removal process is no longer open to question. Indeed, the First Congress limited the President's power to remove the Comptroller two weeks after it made the famous 'Decision of 1789.' In addition, the ICC and FTC long ante-dated the New Deal. . . . Moreover, a very large part of Government has been developed in reliance on *Humphrey's*, and so the force of *stare decisis* is very powerful."

It was important, Brennan stressed, that *Humphrey* be confirmed, since the opinion of Judge Scalia in the lower court[47] had cast doubt on *Humphrey* as a precedent. "It [is] important," Brennan told the confer-ence, "to reaffirm *Humphrey's* . . . because the District Court opinion includes a lot of dictum which questions the continuing validity of *Humphrey's*. This dictum is wrong and unwarranted, and we should make this very clear."[48]

The other majority justices agreed that, as Justice O'Connor told the conference, "[t]he Act violates basic separation of powers concerns." The reason, Justice Powell summarized it at the conference, was that "the delegation was to execute a substantial portion of law and Congress reserved the power to remove." This was to be the essential holding of the *Bowsher* decision.

The conference majority also agreed with the Brennan view on *Humphrey* and the independent agencies. In a June 2, 1986, "Dear Chief" letter, Justice O'Connor summarized the conference accord on the matter: "My review of the Conference notes indicates that, with the possible exception of Bill Rehnquist, those who voted to affirm hoped to make sure that the opinion not cast doubt on the constitutionality of independent agencies."

Despite this consensus, when Chief Justice Burger circulated his seventeen-printed-page May 31, 1986, draft *Bowsher* opinion, it became apparent that he had not felt bound by the conference majority. Instead, the Burger draft expressed an expansive view of presidential power that did bring into question the constitutionality of the independent agencies.

BOWSHER V. SYNAR: BURGER DRAFT

In a 1986 talk, Justice Blackmun said that in classifying justices he had always put Chief Justice Burger and Justice Rehnquist "on the right."[49] Next to Rehnquist, the chief justice was the most conservative member of the Burger Court. He was, however, far from extreme in his views and could scarcely be classified as a New Right jurist. On the issue of presidential power, however, the Burger position was much closer to that expressed by members of the Reagan administration such as Attorney General Meese. In the 1974 *Nixon* case, the chief justice wrote a draft opinion of the Court that was far more receptive to the claims of presidential power than the opinion ultimately delivered. The other justices were unwilling to accept the *Nixon* draft because they felt that it tilted the balance unduly in favor of the president. Only after Burger abandoned his original approach and eliminated the analysis favorable to the president was he able to secure a Court for his opinion.[50]

Now, in *Bowsher v. Synar*, Burger again circulated a draft[51] that was based on a broader conception of presidential power than the justices were willing to endorse, one that would have accepted the New Right claim that the independent agencies are unconstitutional. The key portion of the *Bowsher* draft in this respect was Part III, which began with a general discussion of separation of powers. The draft stated the truism that "[t]he Constitution does not contemplate that the President alone will 'faithfully execute' the laws." The president is given the power to appoint officers to carry out executive functions. Control over them, the draft went on, is maintained by the removal power: "[T]he draftsmen of the Constitution recognized that a President could not fulfill his Constitutional duties without the power to remove any of his officers who failed to execute his policies faithfully. The commissions issued to many of the major executive officers have recited that the holder serves 'during the pleasure of the President.'"

The draft then discussed the *Myers* case, where, as Burger summarized it, "this Court emphatically reaffirmed the sole power of a President to remove his officers even though their initial appointment was subject to the approval of the Senate." *Myers* was quoted to emphasize that the Constitution "grants to the President the executive power of the Government, i.e., the general administrative control of those executing the laws, including the power of appointment and removal of executive officers—a conclusion confirmed by his obligation to take care that the laws be faithfully executed."

The Burger draft referred to the *Humphrey* case only to assert that the holding there "is wholly consistent with the Court's holding in *Myers*, and the *Humphrey's Executors* Court took pains to distinguish the *Myers* decision." The draft did not mention the *Humphrey* holding limiting presidential removal power or the Court's emphasis there on the independence of the ICC and FTC-type agency. Instead, Burger quoted *Humphrey* on the need to maintain the independence of the three branches, including the *Humphrey* Court's assertion "The sound application of a principle that makes one master in his own house precludes him from imposing his control in the house of another who is master there."[52]

In addition, the Burger draft noted that a more recent case had "reaffirmed the teaching of *Myers* that the President has 'supervisory and policy responsibilities of the utmost discretion and sensitivity . . . and management of the Executive Branch—a task for which 'imperative' reasons requir[e] an unrestricted [presidential] power to remove the most important of his subordinates. . . .'"

The Burger conclusion was that "from 1789 to the present, it has been recognized that the President's authority to direct his subordinates is enforced through the power of removal." That power, the draft asserted, is the key to the effective management of modern government: "Given the vast growth of government, the authority of the President today to remove an officer of the Executive Branch appointed by him is even more crucial to the management of the government and execution of the law than it was at the inception of the government when that authority was defined by the first Congress in 1789."

Next in the Burger draft came a paean to presidential removal power: "A modern President must depend upon literally thousands of subordinates to give effect to the President's policies with fidelity. A subordinate of the Executive Branch who fails because of incompetence or want of experience—or is in disagreement with a President's policy—must be subject to replacement promptly if a President's policies are to be given effect. In no other way can the affairs of a complex, modern government of divided power be conducted."

Part III of the draft ended by asserting that "because the power of removal over Executive Branch officers resides in the President, Congress may not retain the sole power of removal of an officer charged with the execution of the laws." To permit Congress to retain that power would be "precisely the type of aggrandizement by one branch of Government that our Constitutional scheme was designed to prevent."

The rest of the Burger draft found that the comptroller general was entrusted with executive powers by the challenged statute and that "these functions of the Comptroller General constitute the performance of duties explicitly conferred by the Constitution on the President to execute laws enacted by Congress." The ultimate conclusion, in Part VII of the draft, was "that the powers vested in the Comptroller General under §261 violate the command of the Constitution that the President 'shall take Care that the Laws be faithfully executed.'"

BOWSHER V. SYNAR: OBJECTIONS TO DRAFT

The Burger *Bowsher* draft stated a far more expansive view of presidential power than the other justices were willing to accept. Even more clearly than at the conference, the chief justice was stating that the president possessed complete removal power over all officers charged with carrying out laws. As the draft put it, "Exercising judgment concerning facts that affect the application of the law is precisely the type of action performed by the President through officers appointed by him charged with implementing a statute." Once again, the implication was that the ICC and FTC-type independent agencies were unconstitutional, since they were not subject to the president's unlimited removal power, even though they were plainly "charged with implementing a statute."

All of the members of the *Bowsher* majority except Justice Rehnquist objected to Part III of the Burger draft. The first to do so was Justice Stevens. In a June 2, 1986, letter to the chief justice, Stevens wrote, "I think your opinion casts substantial doubt on the legal status of independent agencies and that it would be a serious mistake for the Court to adopt this approach."

Justice Thurgood Marshall sent a June 2 "Dear Chief" letter seconding the Stevens letter. Marshall declared, "Your current draft's focus on the need for the President to be 'master in his own house' raises a host of important issues—including the propriety of independent agencies—that we do not have to consider at this time."

Justice O'Connor also circulated a June 2 letter. Reference has already been made to the statement in her letter that the majority had hoped to make it clear that the decision should not bring the constitutionality of the independent agencies into question. "I fear," O'Connor wrote, "that the opinion as now written, especially Part III, does just that. For example, the draft discusses *Myers* extensively, and suggests that it stands for the general proposition that the power to appoint carries with it the general power to remove. Yet, with the exception of quoting some general language about separation of powers, the draft disregards *Humphrey's Executor* almost entirely. As I read *Humphrey's*, it limits *Myers* considerably by suggesting that Congress can impose significant limitations on the President's removal power over executive officers *even if* they perform 'executive functions.'"

As the O'Connor letter saw it, the draft was wrong in suggesting "that the constitutional infirmity of the Act lies in the fact that the President does not have the power to remove the Comptroller General. In my view, precisely the obverse is the problem: The infirmity lies in the fact the *Congress* does have the power to remove, not in the fact that the *President* does not."

The next day, June 3, Justice Powell wrote to the chief justice, "I share generally the views expressed by other Justices who have written you." Powell informed Burger, "I could not join an opinion that casts substantial doubt on the constitutionality of the independent agencies, and do not think the vote at Conference supports such a view."

The chief justice also received a longer June 3 letter from Justice Brennan. "I agree," Brennan's letter began, "with what has been said by Sandra, John and Thurgood that the reasoning of the opinion in this case must be that Congress cannot retain the power to remove an officer charged with executing the law, and that the opinion should not rely on the rationale that the President must have power to remove such officers. Moreover, I think it very important that the opinion explain the basis and importance of this distinction, since it is only by doing so that we shall make clear that we are not questioning the viability of independent agencies."

The Brennan letter stated that there was a difference between "qualifying the President's power to remove" and retention of the removal power itself by Congress. "*Myers* and *Humphrey's Executors*," Brennan wrote, "can be understood in light of this distinction. In *Myers* Congress retained power to participate in the removal of an officer performing executive functions. This gave Congress direct control over an officer executing the law and thus violated the fundamental precept that Congress not control execution in addition to legislation. In *Humphrey's Executors*, on the other hand, Congress did not itself participate in the removal process, but simply limited the President's power to remove at will. In upholding the provisions for removal of FTC Commissioners, *Humphrey's Executors* made clear that the dictum in *Myers* suggesting that the President's removal power must remain unfettered was incorrect."

Brennan's letter then pointed out his difficulty with the Burger draft's treatment of *Myers* and *Humphrey*: "My concern is that by not making the distinction between *Myers* and *Humphrey's Executors* express, the opinion will give credence to the view—strongly suggested by the District Court—that *Humphrey's Executors* was wrong and that the *Myers* dictum was correct. I think that the opinion in this case must expressly draw the distinction between Congress having the power to remove and the President not having that power, and must clearly explain that our decision is based solely on the fact that Congress has removal power (and thus control over) the officer charged with executing the Budget Deficit Act."

Justice Brennan concluded with the point he had emphasized at the conference—the need to "make very clear that *Humphrey's* is still good law." "I think," Brennan wrote,

> that the opinion also should reaffirm the holding in *Humphrey's Executors* that Congress can create independent agencies (*i.e.*, agencies staffed by officers not removable at the President's pleasure). The District Court opinion includes a lot of dictum that questions the continuing validity of *Humphrey's Executors*. This dictum is simply wrong. The notion that Congress can to some extent limit the President's power to remove as long as Congress does not itself participate in the removal process is no longer open to question. Indeed, the First Congress limited the President's power to remove the Comptroller two weeks after the so-called "Decision of 1789." In addition, the ICC, the United States Shipping Board (now the Federal Maritime Commission), the FTC, and perhaps other independent agencies, were created by the Congress long before our decision in *Humphrey's Executors*. Finally, even were there some reason to doubt the strength of the conclusion in *Humphrey's Executors*, a very large part of Government has been developed in reliance on that decision, and so the force of *stare decisis* is very powerful.

On June 4, Burger sent around a "MEMORANDUM TO THE CONFERENCE" that indicated he did not think the objections to his draft opinion were really important: "After reviewing carefully the various comments and

209

memos, I conclude the essence of the problem is whether we skin the tiger from the neck to the tail or vice versa. Either way suits me, and the printer is now turning the tiger around. The hide, however, will look the same—at least as I see it."

Despite his memo's flippancy, Burger did circulate a second draft on June 5 that substantially changed the Part III passages to which objection had been taken. The revised Part III was essentially similar to the version contained in the final *Bowsher* opinion. But it did contain the statement that the *Humphrey* "Court characterized the Federal Trade Commissioner as an officer who 'occupies no place in the executive power vested by the Constitution in the President,' but acts only 'in the discharge and effectuation of . . . quasi-legislative or quasi-judicial powers, or as an [officer of an] agency of the legislative or judicial departments of the government.'"

This statement led to a June 6 letter from Justice Brennan. It informed the chief justice, "Your second draft does indeed accommodate many of my concerns. However, I still have problems with sections of the opinion that, I am afraid, still may cast doubt upon the continuing viability of many—if not all—independent administrative agencies. I refer in particular to . . . the description of agency functions as 'quasi-legislative' or 'quasi-judicial' in contradistinction to 'executive' functions that only the President or officers removable at his pleasure may perform."

Brennan wrote, "My concern is that reintroducing such notions as whether some function is 'quasi-legislative' or 'quasi-judicial' will encourage claims that all sorts of independent agency activity is neither, and that it must therefore be under the President's control. In other words, I am afraid that reintroducing this analysis will cast doubt upon the legality of much of the work of independent administrative agencies despite disclaimers that the question is presented. This problem can easily be avoided simply by not using this terminology in the discussion."

The Brennan letter suggested that "rather than quoting the language from *Humphrey's Executors*, I would simply describe the result in that case." Thus, Brennan suggested deleting the *Humphrey* quote to which he objected "and substituting something like the following":

The Court upheld the statute, holding that "illimitable power of removal is not possessed by the President" with respect to certain kinds of administrative bodies that, like the FTC, were "created by Congress to carry into effect legislative policies" embodied in statutory enactments. 295 U.S., at 628–629. The Court distinguished *Myers*, reaffirming its holding that congressional participation in the removal process of executive officers is unconstitutional, but "disapprov[ing]" expressions in that opinion "beyond the point involved." *Id.* at 626.

Burger included most of this suggested passage in his final opinion.

With this change, the Burger opinion was acceptable to the majority justices (except for Justices Stevens and Marshall, who concurred only in the judgment). The consensus was that stated by Justice Powell, in a June 12 letter joining Burger's opinion, "I certainly do not want to undercut the type of independence the great administrative agencies have enjoyed, and I do not think your opinion—as now drafted—does this."

THE *BOWSHER* DECISION AND IMPLICATIONS

The *Bowsher* decision held that the role of the comptroller general in the deficit reduction process violated the separation of powers. As the decision was explained by Chief Justice Burger in a June 10, 1986, letter to Justice Stevens,

> [T]he central point is that the Comptroller General is removable by Congress, and therefore may not be entrusted with executive powers. Part III states: "In light of these precedents, we conclude that Congress cannot reserve for itself the power of removal of an officer charged with the execution of the laws except by impeachment." Part IV states: "Against this background, we see no escape from the conclusion that, because Congress has retained removal authority over the Comptroller General, he is not an officer of the Executive Branch." Part V states: "It is apparent then, that Congress has placed executive powers in the hands of an officer who is subject to removal by Congress. . . . The Constitution does not permit breaching the boundaries of separated powers in this fashion."

But *Bowsher* has implications as well for the constitutionality of independent agencies. As seen, most of the majority justices wanted the opinion to indicate that their decision did not apply to the independent agencies. Because of the objections to his first draft, Chief Justice Burger added a footnote that specifically distinguishes the ICC and FTC-type agencies from the comptroller general. According to it, "Appellants . . . are wide of the mark in arguing that an affirmance in this case requires casting doubt on the status of 'independent' agencies because no issues involving such agencies are presented here." That is true because "statutes establishing independent agencies typically specify either that the agency members are removable by the President for specified causes . . . or else do not specify a removal procedure." There is "no independent agency whose members are removable by the Congress for certain causes short of impeachable offenses, as is the Comptroller General."[53]

The key to constitutionality for the independent agencies is thus the absence of congressional power over the removal of their members. The fact that presidential removal power is limited to removal for cause is not enough to support a challenge to their validity; that this makes them independent of presidential control does not cast doubt upon their constitutionality.

In a June 6, 1986, letter to Justice Brennan, Chief Justice Burger referred to the *Bowsher* footnote and stated, "I think I've made it clear we are casting no doubt on the SEC, FTC, EPA, etc." Burger thus intended his footnote to inter the doctrine of the unconstitutionality of the independent agencies urged by Attorney General Meese. Unfortunately, however, there is language in the chief justice's opinion that supports a contrary view. In many ways, the reasoning in the opinion is inconsistent with the majority's attempt to seal the Pandora's box of independent-agency unconstitutionality. If the power delegated to the comptroller general had been exercised directly by Congress through provision in the statute for the mandatory budget cuts, no one would doubt that the power in question was "legislative" in nature. But the Court holds that it is not the same when exercised by the comptroller general. Why? The answer seems to be that the power has not been exercised by the legislature itself. The implication, then, since the power is plainly not "judicial," is that any power giving effect to a statute that is not exercised by the legislature or the courts must be "executive."

This approach may be criticized as a lapse into the faulty logic of the familiar parlor game: "It is not animal. It is not vegetable. Therefore, it must be mineral." More important, however, is its implication for the independent agencies. If the carrying out of a law by someone other than the legislature or the courts must be "executive," why is that not true of the powers delegated to the independent agencies? Yet if that is the case, how can those powers be exercised by agencies that are independent of the president?

REHNQUIST AND REMOVAL POWER

It is somewhat ironic that this last question has been answered for the Court by Chief Justice Rehnquist in a manner wholly inconsistent with the New Right challenge to the constitutionality of independent agencies.

Before Justice Scalia's appointment, it was Rehnquist who was considered the most conservative justice—"The Court's Mr. Right," as he was dubbed in a *Newsweek* article.[54] As chief justice, however, Rehnquist has taken a more restrained approach to presidential removal power than his predecessor. In *Bowsher v. Synar*,[55] Chief Justice Burger had indicated in his draft opinion that the president possessed unlimited removal power over all officers carrying out laws. This implied that the independent agencies were unconstitutional. In his *Bowsher* opinion of the Court, too, despite his express disclaimer, Burger cast doubt on the constitutionality of independent agencies. In *Morrison v. Olson*,[56] on the other hand, Chief Justice Rehnquist went to the opposite extreme and cast doubt on presidential removal power over executive agencies themselves. In doing so, he indicated that the limitations upon presidential removal power over the ICC and FTC-type independent agencies are, as the *Humphrey* case[57] held, not subject to constitutional challenge.

At issue in *Morrison v. Olson* was a law that provided for the appointment of an "independent counsel" to investigate and, if appropriate, prosecute high-ranking government officials for criminal violations. The attorney general, upon receipt of information that he determines is "sufficient to constitute grounds to investigate whether any person [covered by the statute] may have violated any Federal criminal law," is required to conduct an investigation. If the attorney general then determines that there are "reasonable grounds to believe that further investigation or prosecution is warranted," he is to apply to a special court for the appointment of an independent counsel, who is granted all the powers of a federal prosecutor.

Under the statute, an independent counsel "may be removed from office, other than by impeachment and conviction, only by the personal action of the Attorney General and only for good cause, physical disability, mental incapacity, or any other condition that substantially impairs the performance of such independent counsel's duties." There is provision for judicial review of any such removal action.

In the *Morrison* case, an independent counsel had been appointed to investigate allegations against Department of Justice officials. She caused a grand jury to issue and serve subpoenas on the officials. They moved to quash, claiming that the independent-counsel law was unconstitutional. Their principal objection was that the statute violated separation-of-powers principles by impermissibly interfering with the functions of the executive branch.

The Court held that the statutory provision restricting the attorney general's power to remove the independent counsel only for "good cause" did not impermissibly interfere with the president's exercise of his constitutionally appointed functions. The key point was that here, as contrasted with *Bowsher*, Congress had not attempted to gain a role in the removal of executive officials. Instead, the act put the removal power squarely in the hands of the executive branch. Nor did the statute's imposition of a "good cause" standard for removal unduly trammel on executive authority. The congressional determination to limit the attorney general's removal power was essential, in Congress's view, to establish the necessary independence of the office of independent counsel.

Hence, the Court concluded, the statute did not violate the separation of powers, since it did not impermissibly undermine the powers of the executive branch, or disrupt the proper balance between the different branches by preventing the executive branch from accomplishing its constitutionally assigned functions. Even though counsel is "independent" and free from executive branch supervision to a greater extent than other federal prosecutors, the statute gives the executive branch sufficient control over the independent counsel to ensure that the president is able to perform his constitutionally assigned duties.

The chief justice's opinion states that *Bowsher* turned upon the retention of the removal power there by Congress itself. Since that was not the case under the independent counsel statute, it was not subject to the same separation of powers objection.

But then the Rehnquist opinion goes on to indicate that the same was also true in *Myers v. United States*,[58] which, as I have shown, has been the leading case on presidential power to remove executive officers. Rehnquist writes that in *Myers*, too, "the essence of the decision . . . was the judgment that the Constitution prevents Congress from draw[ing] to itself . . . the power to remove or the right to participate in the exercise of that power. To do this would be to go beyond the words and implications of the [Appointments Clause] and to infringe the constitutional principle of the separation of governmental powers.'" In *Morrison*, there was no attempt by Congress to gain a role in the removal of executive officials. On the contrary, says Rehnquist, the independent counsel statute "puts the removal power squarely in the hands of the Executive Branch; an independent counsel may be removed from office, 'only by the personal action of the Attorney General, and only for good cause.'"[59]

Yet, as Justice Scalia points out in his *Morrison* dissent, "This is somewhat like referring to shackles as an effective means of locomotion. As we recognized in *Humphrey's Executor v. United States* . . . indeed, what *Humphrey's Executor* was all about—limiting removal power to 'good cause' is an impediment to, not an effective grant of, presidential control." In *Humphrey*, limiting the president's removal power over FTC members to removal only for cause was upheld because the commission exercises adjudicatory functions, which "require[s] absolute freedom from Executive interferences." Now, "What we in *Humphrey's Executor* found to be a means of eliminating presidential control, the Court today considers the 'most importan[t]' means of assuring presidential control."[60]

The *Myers* case itself has been the juristic foundation of the president's position as chief executive. The president has the authority to control the operation of the executive branch because of his unfettered power of instant dismissal. In this respect, might makes right within the executive. What the president commands will be done by executive officials—at least if they wish to retain their appointments.

In *Morrison*, the Court in effect overrules the essential *Myers* holding that Congress may not limit the president's removal power over executive officers. The distinction between *Myers* and *Humphrey* had always been considered that between "purely executive" officers (where the Constitution vested the president with unfettered removal power) and officers exercising "quasi-legislative" and "quasi-judicial" powers (where Congress could limit presidential power to removal for cause). In the *Morrison* opinion, this settled distinction is abandoned: "[O]ur present considered view is that the determination of whether the Constitution allows Congress to impose a 'good cause'-type restriction on the President's power to remove an official cannot be made to turn on whether or not that official is classified as 'purely executive.'" Instead, the test is not "the functions served by the officials at issue": "[T]he real question is whether the removal restrictions are of such a nature that they impede the President's ability to perform his constitutional duty, and the functions of the officials in question must be analyzed in that light."[61]

The *Morrison* Court finds that the "good cause" provision does not unduly limit the removal power: "[W]e cannot say that the imposition of a 'good cause' standard for removal by itself unduly trammels on executive authority." It does not impermissibly burden the president's power to control the independent counsel, as an executive official. "Rather, because the independent counsel may be terminated for 'good cause,' the Executive, through the Attorney General, retains ample authority to assure that the counsel is competently performing her statutory responsibilities in a manner that comports with the provisions of the Act."[62]

Unless the Court is suggesting that despite the "good cause" restriction, the president's removal power in practice is not limited, this statement is contrary to both language and law. If the "good cause" language was not intended to limit the removal power, why was it put in the statute? And if it is a significant limitation, it is contrary to *Myers*, so far as "purely executive" officers are concerned. Under the *Morrison* opinion, congressional power to impose a "good cause" limitation no longer turns on whether the officer involved is exercising "executive" as opposed to "quasi-legislative" and "quasi-judicial" functions. In this respect, the *Morrison* opinion is a standing invitation to Congress to impose "good cause" limitations upon the president's power to remove "purely executive" officers.

If this analysis is correct, *Morrison's* ultimate effect may be a weakening of the president's position as administrative chief of the government. Under *Myers*, Article II "grants to the President the executive power of the government—i.e., the general administrative control of those executing the laws, including the power of appointment and removal of executive officers—a conclusion confirmed by his obligation to take care that the laws be faithfully executed."[63] Under the Rehnquist *Morrison* opinion, presidential control may be limited by "good cause" provisions even where only "purely executive" officers are concerned.

Whatever may be the effect of *Morrison v. Olson* upon the executive branch, however, it contains the complete legal answer to the New Right claim that the independent agencies are unconstitutional because their members are not subject to unlimited presidential removal power. The answer gains added significance because it was given by the present chief justice, himself one of the most conservative justices to sit on the highest bench.

Under *Morrison*, statutes limiting the president's removal power to removal only for cause are clearly valid. *Morrison* states expressly, "[W]e cannot say that the imposition of a 'good cause' standard for removal by itself unduly trammels on executive authority."[64] One may question the applicability of this statement to the executive branch itself. But there are no such doubts as far as the independent agencies are concerned. With regard to them, *Morrison* only confirms the *Humphrey* holding that presidential removal power over the ICC and FTC-type agencies may constitutionally be restricted to removal only for cause.

Morrison thus relegates to legal limbo the New Right claim that the ICC and FTC-type independent agencies are unconstitutional because their members do not serve at the president's pleasure. That they are not subject to unrestricted removal power enables these agencies to be independent. Because of that independence, the White House has never been able to control the ICC and FTC-type agencies the way it has been able to dictate policies and practices in the executive departments.

"HAREM" DECISION PROCESS?

The lack of accountability to the White House enables the FTC and ICC-type commissions to make their own decisions, which may be subject to judicial review but are not subject to legal control by the president.

Their independent position is sharply different from that of the executive departments, which are under plenary presidential control.

In 1981, President Reagan issued Executive Order 12,291.[65] It provided detailed procedures for issuance of so-called major regulations by executive branch agencies. The Reagan order was limited to agencies in the executive branch. Presidential power in this respect does not extend to the independent ICC and FTC-type commissions. Executive Order 12,291 recognized this, as indeed it had to under the *Humphrey* case. For comparable requirements to be imposed upon the independent commissions, Congress would have to demand them by statute.

There is, of course, a basic difference between constitutionality and desirability. The challengers of independent agencies are wrong, not only on the legal question of constitutionality, but on the policy question as well. Whatever the chief justice may have said in *Morrison* on the relation of removal restrictions to the functions performed by the officials at issue, it cannot be denied that independence is desirable in the ICC and FTC-type agencies precisely because of the functions performed by them.

The line between *Myers* and *Humphrey*[66] was based on the distinction between purely executive officers and those vested with significant nonexecutive functions—particularly those that *Humphrey* characterized as "quasi-judicial" functions.[67] As Justice Frankfurter once explained it, *Humphrey* "drew a sharp line of cleavage between officials who were part of the Executive establishment and were thus removable by virtue of the President's constitutional powers, and those who are members of a body 'to exercise its judgment without the leave or hindrance of any other official or any department of the government,' as to whom a power of removal exists only if Congress may fairly be said to have conferred it."[68]

The key to the distinction is the nature of the functions exercised by the officer concerned. In Frankfurter's own words, "This sharp differentiation derives from the difference in functions between those who are part of the Executive establishment and those whose tasks require absolute freedom from Executive interferences."[69] The *Myers* holding of illimitable removal power applied to purely executive officers, engaged in carrying out the president's own charge to execute the laws. But Congress can limit the removal power over agencies like the ICC and FTC because they are vested with important duties that are judicial in nature.

Most of these agencies exercise other functions as well, but their common characteristic is the power to decide cases involving private rights and obligations. The exercise of such a power is, without a doubt, best exercised in an atmosphere of independence rather than as part and parcel of the very process of execution of the laws, exposed to all of the pressures that play upon the political branches. That is why agencies exercising adjudicatory authority like the ICC and the FTC have been set up by Congress as independent commissions, not located within any of the ordinary executive departments. The object of the laws thus setting up these agencies is to give to the citizen a guaranty that his case will be decided by them in independence of the political executive. It is as legitimate to give effect to that guaranty as it is to safeguard the tenure of a judge from executive interference.

Those who preach the need for presidential control over all federal agencies, including the now-independent ICC and FTC-type commissions, are really urging the subjection of those agencies' work to the political process that dominates White House decision making. I had a rare opportunity to learn what that means some years ago when I served as chief counsel of a congressional committee investigating the independent agencies.[70] One of those agencies was the Civil Aeronautics Board, which had regulatory jurisdiction over civil aviation until 1985.[71] The CAB then had the authority to grant or deny licenses to airlines to fly specified routes. Where foreign air routes were concerned, however, the governing statute provided that the CAB's action in granting or denying "any certificate authorizing an air carrier to engage in overseas or foreign air transportation . . . shall be subject to the approval of the President."

In these cases involving foreign routes, Congress refused to give the CAB the complete regulatory authority that it had in purely domestic cases. Instead, it made the president an express participant in the regulatory process. The board's foreign-route decisions under the statute had to run the gantlet of presidential approval before they attained full legal effect. In the words of a 1948 Supreme Court opinion, in these cases "Congress has completely inverted the usual administrative process. Instead of acting independently of executive control, the agency is then subordinated to it."[72]

The president's control was complete over CAB foreign route decisions. He consistently asserted a full reviewing power on the merits and reversed the board on matters such as the economic fitness of the carrier to serve the public interest, competitive factors, and the like—on all of which the CAB had been set up as the regulatory expert. The result was, as the Supreme Court put it, that presidential control "is not limited to a negative but is a positive and detailed control over the Board's decisions, unparalleled in the history of American administrative bodies."[73]

In the foreign-route cases the competing applicants for an overseas air route presented all their evidence and arguments at a lengthy CAB hearing presided over by an examiner. Then there was a full appeal to the board from the examiner's decision. But my investigation at the time showed that while the CAB decision ended the public proceedings, it only began the real jockeying for position by the parties, for they knew that the final decision would be made by the president, who was in no way bound by the board's action.

The competing airlines therefore applied every pressure available to them in the Bureau of the Budget[74] (to which foreign-route proceedings were first referred after the CAB decisions) and the White House itself. The parties fully realized that though in form the final decision would be the president's, the actual work in the case would be done by the White House staff. Thus it was vital to get one's arguments to the key staff people, and if it could be done ex parte, so much the better. A former solicitor of the Department of Commerce well described the White House in these cases as a "harem" in which each airline had its favorites, all of them endeavoring to reach the ears of the decision makers.

In other words, everything that Congress had intended to avoid by the creation of the independent agencies characterized the White House process of decision in these foreign-air-route cases. I asked the CAB chairman at a public hearing whether he thought it would be proper for an airline to make private arguments to the Bureau of the Budget and the White House after the board's decision. "I do not think it would. No," answered the CAB head.[75] Behind-the-scenes pressures and arguments were, nonetheless, a well-nigh inevitable concomitant of White House review in foreign-route cases. Where decisions meant so much to the contesting parties, it would have been too much to expect them not to use all the political influence and other resources they could muster. Nor would it have been realistic to expect the president's office (swayed as it normally is by such influences) to operate in a nonpolitical vacuum only in these cases.

Would it really be desirable to have all agency decisions subject to the same type of "harem" decision process? Inevitably, this would be the result of subjecting the now-independent agencies to presidential control. Perhaps it would make for a tidier governmental structure if all officials carrying out the laws were located within the executive branch, subject to the president's hierarchical control. From this point of view, the independent agency may be an anomaly in a government set up under the separation of powers.

Montesquieuan tidiness is not, however, the only consideration to take into account. The ICC-type agency has been one of the great American contributions to political science precisely because it permits regulatory decisions to be made independently of the political process. To be sure, the commissions have not always realized the goal of freedom from political and other pressures. But they at least have the capability of attaining it. There is no such possibility in agencies controlled by the White House.

Referring to the present system of independent agencies, Senator Proxmire asks, "What has been the result?" His answer: "The Government regulates and administers many phases of American life without relying on the centralized, exclusive, total power of a single administration. Agencies like the Federal Reserve Board and the Securities and Exchange Commission are held in very high regard by the Congress, the public and the regulated industry. Why? Because, by and large, they have been insulated from political pressure."[76]

All these advantages would be lost if the administrative law clock were turned back to the days before the ICC. All federal agencies would then be subject to the White House, which would mean unrestricted scope for political pressures and influence in administrative adjudication. Such would be the results in a system in which all decision making were under presidential control. "Would anyone except the [Reagan] administration really want that?"[77]

8

NEW RIGHT
ON THE BENCH

D URING HIS TENURE, President Reagan was able to recast the
makeup of the federal bench. The president appointed 368 judges;[1]
when he left office, more than half of the federal judiciary were Reagan
nominees. Not unnaturally, Reagan tried to choose judges who shared
his own views. Almost all the Reagan appointees were conservatives who
shared the president's widely expressed desire to tilt the federal bench to
the right. They concurred with Chief Justice Rehnquist when he said
that, when he was appointed, "the boat was kind of heeling over in one
direction. Interpreting my oath as I saw it, I felt that my job was . . . to
kind of lean the other way."[2]

It is true that President Reagan was not able to win confirmation for
some of his most controversial judicial nominees. The Senate vote
against Judge Robert H. Bork's elevation to the Supreme Court is, of
course, the outstanding example. Equally significant, however, was the
inability of the Reagan administration to secure federal appellate judgeships for Bernard H. Siegan and Lino A. Graglia, whose views were
discussed in Chapters 3 and 5. One can only speculate on what it would
have meant to our public law if those men had been able to use the
federal appellate bench to translate their extreme positions into constitutional doctrine.

It is, however, erroneous to assume that the failure to obtain the
Siegan and Graglia judgeships meant that the Reagan administration was
unable to elevate prominent New Right jurists to the federal bench. On

the contrary, some of the leading jurists whose work I have discussed were appointed to federal appellate judgeships during the Reagan years. They include Antonin Scalia, Richard Posner (perhaps the foremost academic theorist of New Right jurisprudence before his judicial appointment), and Alex Kozinski.

During his confirmation hearings, Professor Siegan told the Senate Judiciary Committee that, as a U.S. court of appeals judge, he would follow established constitutional jurisprudence and not try to write his professorial positions into the law of the land.[3] The failure of the Siegan nomination made it impossible to learn how far he would have been faithful to this promise. The same has not been true of the New Right jurists whom Reagan did succeed in appointing to the bench. This chapter will be devoted to the abovementioned Reagan appointees and the question of how far their judicial practice has been influenced by their New Right jurisprudence. Do their decisions mark the judicial shift to the right that their legal philosophy espouses? Or are their decisions really not much different from those of their colleagues who take a different juristic approach?

SCALIA'S RIGID CONSTITUTION

In many ways, Justice Antonin Scalia is not a typical New Right jurist. Scalia disagrees with the view of Professors Siegan and Epstein (discussed in Chapters 3 and 4) that the courts should assume an expanded review power, comparable to the kind exercised during the *Lochner* era,[4] to protect property rights. To Scalia, "The Supreme Court decisions rejecting substantive due process in the economic field are clear, unequivocal and current . . . [and] in my view the position the Supreme Court has arrived at is good."[5] Scalia favors judicial restraint in reviewing economic legislation,[6] though for reasons that differ from those motivating the makers of the "constitutional revolution" of half a century ago, which relegated the *Lochner* approach to the limbo of discarded doctrine.

At the same time, on the Supreme Court itself, Justice Scalia has been, in the words of an English commentator, "the court's most conservative member,"[7] displacing Chief Justice Rehnquist as the Court's Mr. Right. In certain respects, indeed, Scalia's conservative views have coincided with those expressed by New Right jurists. Thus, as seen in Chapter 4, the justice has moved in the direction of Professor Epstein's expansive interpretation of the Takings Clause. He has also taken a rigid approach to the constitutional division of powers, which tends to magnify presidential power—a goal that, as Anthony Lewis tells us, is widely espoused by "the radical right."[8]

Mention has been made of Justice Scalia's opinion in *Pennell v. San Jose,*[9] where a rent control ordinance was challenged. The ordinance permitted various factors to be considered in deciding whether a proposed rent increase was reasonable, including "the hardship to a tenant." Landlords attacked the ordinance as facially invalid in violation of the Takings Clause. In dealing with the challenge, Chief Justice Rehnquist and Justice Scalia took different approaches.

Speaking for the Court, the chief justice found that the Takings Clause claim was premature, since there was no indication that the "hardship" provision at issue had ever been relied upon to reduce a rent below what it would otherwise have been. This was to take a view of the case consistent with the general conservative approach to constitutional adjudication. To a true conservative, what Judge Posner terms "rededication by federal judges to the principles of judicial self-restraint" requires prudential self-restraint.[10] This means, as then-Justice Rehnquist stated in an important case, "The constitutional power of federal courts cannot be defined, and indeed has no substance, without reference to the necessity 'to adjudge the legal rights of litigants in actual controversies.' . . . The power to declare the rights of individuals . . . 'is legitimate only in the last resort, and as a necessity in the determination of real, earnest and vital controversy.'"[11] According to the Rehnquist opinion of the Court, the Takings Clause claim was not ripe for review before application of the hardship provision in a specific case and the Court should refrain from deciding the claim until that occurred. Hence the *Pennell* decision did not deal with the merits of the takings issue.

Justice Scalia, in dissent, disagreed that the takings claim was premature. To him, the ordinance was subject to facial attack: it would in all its applications work a taking, since providing financial assistance to impecunious renters is not a state interest that can legitimately be furthered by regulating the use of property. Scalia points out that the ordinance does not require specification of how much reduction in rent is attributable to each of the various factors that may be taken into account. Consequently, no landlord may be able to meet the requirement of showing in a particular case how the hardship factor figures in the rent determination. This, says Scalia, makes review necessary, in order not "to shield alleged constitutional injustice from judicial scrutiny."[12]

Yet the traditional conservative approach to Article III's "case" and "controversy" requirement is to refuse to weaken it merely because otherwise there would be no review. The basic concept here is that the "courts are not charged with general guardianship against all potential mischief in the complicated tasks of government."[13] If the case is not "ripe for determination,"[14] the judge should leave it untouched, even if it means that there will be no review over the challenged act.

One may ask whether, in *Pennell*, Justice Scalia did not allow his view on the merits to outweigh the conservative's normal tendency to construe the "case" and "controversy" requirement strictly. As seen in Chapter 4, Scalia's *Pennell* dissent strongly condemned the rent control ordinance's hardship provision as a violation of the Takings Clause. To Scalia, the provision had no relation to the purpose of rent control. Instead, it effected a wealth transfer "privately funded by those landlords who happen to have 'hardship' tenants."[15]

The Scalia objection here could apply to comparable regulatory measures. In particular, minimum wage requirements have the same effect as that noted in the Scalia dissent, so far as they exceed "the fair value of the services rendered"[16] by given employees. Are we then to condemn minimum wage laws because they run counter to the justice's theory of the proper relation between economic regulation and wealth transfers? To do so would return our law to the now-discredited decision in the *Adkins* case,[17] which struck down wage legislation on just such a theory.

The Scalia tenure on the bench has been marked not only by opinions such as that in *Pennell v. San Jose*, but also by a rigid approach to the Constitution reminiscent of the public law of an earlier day. More specifically, the justice has taken a formalistic approach to the separation of powers that tends to exalt presidential power at the expense of the other branches of government. Thus Scalia gives a judicial perspective to the Anthony Lewis comment that "the radical right wistfully preaches these days [that] the Presidency is . . . the sole power." To Scalia, as to former Attorney General Meese, the president must be the hierarchical superior of all officers and agencies charged with carrying out the laws.

Scalia gave expression to his separation-of-powers view in three important opinions: *Synar v. United States*[18] (the lower court case in *Bowsher v. Synar*,[19] where the Gramm-Rudman Act was invalidated), *Morrison v. Olson*[20] (where the independent counsel law was upheld), and *Mistretta v. United States*[21] (where the law authorizing a commission to issue sentencing guidelines was sustained). The *Synar* opinion in the three-judge district court is labeled "PER CURIAM," but it is an open secret that it was written by then-Judge Scalia, a member of the lower-court panel. At any rate, it is wholly consistent with the Scalia approach to the separation of powers.

The Gramm-Rudman Act, it will be recalled,[22] vested functions that both the lower court and Supreme Court found to be "executive" in the comptroller general, an officer removable only by Congress. In his *Synar* opinion, Judge Scalia indicated "that the Constitution implicitly confers upon the President power to remove civil officers whom he appoints, at least those who exercise executive power."[23] The implication is that legislative restrictions upon presidential removal power over officers carrying out the law are invalid. The further implication is that the *Humphrey* case,[24] which upheld restrictions on the president's power to remove members of the FTC-type independent agencies, was incorrectly decided. "It has . . . ," the Scalia opinion asserts, "always been difficult to reconcile *Humphrey's Executor's* 'headless fourth branch' with a constitutional text and tradition establishing three branches of government."[25]

Justice Brennan was clearly correct when he asserted at the *Bowsher v. Synar* conference that the Scalia opinion in the lower court had cast doubt on *Humphrey* as a precedent. "It [is] important," Brennan told the conference, "to reaffirm *Humphrey's* . . . because the District Court opinion includes a lot of dictum which questions the continuing validity of *Humphrey's*. This dictum is wrong and unwarranted, and we should make this very clear."[26]

Despite Brennan's call at the conference for the Court to "make very clear that *Humphrey's* is still good law," since congressional authority to "limit the President's power to remove as long as Congress does not itself participate in the removal process is no longer open to question," the *Bowsher* draft opinion of Chief Justice Burger took essentially the same position as the Scalia opinion. As seen in our previous discussion of the case, the Burger draft expressed an expansive view of presidential power that did bring into question the constitutionality of the independent agencies.[27] According to the draft, "Exercising judgment concerning facts that affect the application of the law is precisely the type of action performed by the President through officers appointed by him charged with implementing a statute." As in the Scalia opinion, the implication was that the FTC-type independent agencies were unconstitutional, since they were not subject to the president's unlimited removal power, even though they were plainly "charged with implementing a statute."

Once again Justice Brennan expressed disagreement with the Scalia *Synar* opinion. In a letter[28] Brennan expressed concern that Burger's draft "will give credence to the view—strongly suggested by the District Court—that *Humphrey's Executors* was wrong and that the *Myers* dictum was correct." The Court's opinion, Brennan wrote, "should reaffirm the holding in *Humphrey's Executors* that Congress can create independent agencies (*i.e.*, agencies staffed by officers not removable at the President's pleasure)."

Almost all the majority justices expressed support for the Brennan position. The chief justice gave way and the *Bowsher* opinion of the Court does expressly repudiate the Scalia view on *Humphrey* and the independent agencies.[29] But that did not prevent Justice Scalia from taking a similar rigid position in *Morrison v. Olson*[30]—the Rehnquist Court's first important separation-of-powers case. The Court there rejected the claim that the separation of powers was violated by the law providing for independent counsels appointed by a special court to investigate and prosecute high-ranking officials. Justice Scalia delivered a lone dissent that asserted that the law effected an "important change in the equilibrium of power" because it "deprives the President of exclusive control over [a] quintessentially executive activity."[31]

To Justice Scalia, the functions performed by the independent counsel were plainly executive. To him the statute was invalid because "those functions have been given to a person whose actions are not fully within the supervision and control of the President." To have an independent official who can investigate and prosecute is, Scalia asserts, a patent violation of Article II. "We should say here that the President's constitutionally assigned duties include *complete* control over investigation and prosecution of violations of the law, and that the inexorable command of Article II is clear and definite: the executive power must be vested in the President of the United States."[32]

The Scalia *Morrison* dissent is contrary both to the express language of the Appointments Clause of Article II (which specifically provides for appointment of inferior officers by "the Courts of Law") and the *Humphrey* case[33] (which holds that Congress may limit presidential removal power over independent agencies such as the FTC). As seen, Justice Scalia himself has cast doubt upon *Humphrey*. But, as Justice Brennan put it in his *Bowsher* conference statement, the Scalia dictum to that effect "is wrong and unwarranted."

In his dissent in the *Mistretta* case, Justice Scalia deprecates "the regrettable tendency of our recent separation-of-powers jurisprudence . . . to treat the Constitution as though it were no more than a generalized prescription that the functions of the Branches should not be commingled too much."[34] To Scalia, the separation of powers embodied in the U.S. Constitution is the strict separation provided for in the Massachusetts Constitution of 1780, which declared expressly: "[T]he legislative department shall never exercise the executive and judicial powers, or either of them; the executive shall never exercise the legislative and judicial powers, or either of them; the judicial shall never exercise the legislative and executive powers, or either of them"[35]

When Madison proposed the amendments that became the federal Bill of Rights, he included a provision similar to that in the Massachusetts Constitution: "The powers delegated by this constitution are appropriated to the departments to which they are respectively distributed; so that the legislative department shall never exercise the powers vested in the executive or judicial nor the executive exercise the powers vested in the legislative or judicial, nor the judicial exercise the powers vested in the legislative or executive departments."[36] But this proposed amendment was rejected by the Senate[37] and never became part of the U.S. Constitution.

Despite this, Justice Scalia interprets the Constitution as though it does contain Madison's proposed amendment.[38] Rejection of that amendment indicates that "the Framers did not require—and indeed rejected—the notion that the three Branches must be entirely separate and distinct."[39] It is because of this that our public law has taken as gospel the famous Cardozo warning that "[t]he Separation of powers is not a doctrinaire concept to be made use of with pedantic rigor."[40] To be sure, if we think of the separation of powers as dividing the branches of government into watertight compartments,[41] we would probably have to conclude that independence from presidential power for any officer carrying out the law is automatically invalid. In actuality, such a rigorous application of the constitutional doctrine is neither desirable nor feasible; the only absolute separation that has ever been possible was proposed in the theoretical writings of Montesquieu, who looked across at foggy England from his sunny Gascon vineyards, and, we now know, completely misconstrued what he saw.

As far as the *Morrison* case is concerned, there is at least as much reason for having an independent counsel to investigate and prosecute high-ranking officers as there is for having FTC-type independent agencies. As Chief Justice Rehnquist stated in *Morrison*, "Congress of course was concerned when it created the office of independent counsel with the conflicts of interest that could arise in situations when the Executive Branch is called upon to investigate its own high-ranking officers."[42] That concern is as legitimate as the concern for judicial-type independence for the FTC-type agencies exercising adjudicatory authority. Congress can remove those agencies from presidential control because it is desirable that adjudicatory functions be exercised in an atmosphere of independence, free from the political and other pressures that are endemic in the White House. Why is the same not true for counsel investigating and prosecuting alleged crimes by the president or his close associates?

Judge Scalia's rigid separation-of-powers approach can also be seen in another recent case involving the delegation of adjudicatory authority. The opinion there reaffirmed that the power to decide cases involving public rights may be delegated to administrative agencies. The Court expressly stated its rejection of the view that "a matter of public rights must at a minimum arise 'between the government and others.'" Instead, "the Federal Government need not be a party for a case to revolve around 'public rights.'"[43]

This statement was too much for Justice Scalia. He went out of his way, in a concurrence, to assert, "In my view a matter of 'public rights,' whose adjudication Congress may assign to tribunals lacking the essential characteristics of Article III courts, 'must at a minimum arise between the government and others.'" According to Scalia, only cases in which the government is a party may be assigned to agencies: "The notion that the power to adjudicate a legal controversy between two private parties may be assigned to a non-Article III, yet federal, tribunal is entirely inconsistent with the origins of the public rights doctrine," under which administrative agencies may be given power to decide cases involving public rights. The "public rights" doctrine applies only to "rights *of the public*—that is, rights pertaining to claims brought by or against the United States."[44] Only cases that arise between the government and others may, in the Scalia approach, be assigned to administrative agencies for adjudication.

The crippling effect of the Scalia view on delegation of adjudicatory authority, if it should ever be elevated to the level of accepted doctrine, soon becomes clear. It would mean a quantum change in the whole system of administrative adjudication. It would mean that workers' compensation involves an unconstitutional delegation of judicial power—though workers' compensation cases have been delegated to agencies for almost a century, with the delegation receiving the Supreme Court imprimatur in *Crowell v. Benson*.[45]

More than that, Justice Scalia's approach would invalidate the long-established reparations power of agencies such as the ICC (also almost a century old) and the CFTC (specifically confirmed by the Court in 1986),[46] as well as the back-pay power of the NLRB and the compensation power of human-rights agencies. Scalia himself has complained about the overload of the federal courts, urging that "a substantial amount of business [should] be diverted from the regular federal courts, [so that] the latter would have a chance of remaining in the future what they have been in the past."[47] It is doubtful that Justice Scalia's judicial confreres (both federal and state) would appreciate a doctrine on adjudication that would add so greatly to the judicial workload. Workers' compensation cases alone would all but swamp judicial dockets if they had to be transferred from agencies to Article III courts and their state counterparts.

POSNER—JUDEX ECONOMICUS?[48]

Richard A. Posner is without a doubt the foremost exponent of New Right jurisprudence on the bench, as before his judicial appointment he was the leading academic advocate of the views urged by what have been termed "the conservative legal economists."[49] It is Posner's economic analysis of law[50] that has served as the foundation for much of New Right jurisprudence. His work has, indeed, been the catalyst that sparked the movement to apply economics to law, which has shifted the jurisprudential center of gravity away from the liberal jurists who had previously been the focus of legal thought.

Has the judicial work of Judge Posner really been influenced by the jurisprudence of Professor Posner? Do the Posner opinions demonstrate an economic approach to law all that different from the more traditional legal approach of most of his colleagues? More specifically, has the free-market bias on which the Posner "efficiency" criterion is based[51] led to decisions significantly to the right of those rendered by other judges?

On the bench, Judge Posner has continued the hyperactive production schedule that characterized his prior work as an academic author. From his 1982 appointment to the end of 1988, he wrote over six hundred opinions—certainly one of the most prolific outputs by a federal judge. Posner's output is so vast that a detailed analysis would prove inordinately cumbersome. Instead, I shall try to gauge the Posner judicial posture by focusing upon some of the important themes running through his opinions.

As seen in Chapter 6, the primary Posner criterion, for law as for economics, is efficiency.[52] As far as the courts themselves are concerned, Posner has written that efficiency is promoted by judicial self-restraint: "Greater self-restraint would seem a natural prescription for a court system suffering from acute overload." Posner further writes, "I am mainly interested in what I shall call 'separation-of-powers judicial self-restraint,' or less clumsily 'structural restraint.' By these terms, . . . I mean the judge's trying to limit his court's power over other government institutions. If he is a federal judge he will want federal courts to pay greater deference to decisions of Congress, of the federal administrative agencies, of the executive branch."[53]

The notion of deference to the executive and administrative agencies fits in with the Posner concept of efficiency: avoiding repetition of the work done by the administrative expert leaves the courts freer to devote more of their time to the other cases in the ever-burgeoning judicial caseload. Judicial resources would thus be husbanded, as the judges defer to nonjudicial agencies for dispute resolution. Thus, says Posner about the decisions of National Labor Relations Board administrative law judges, "to [those] decisions the principles of administrative review require the courts of appeals to give as much and maybe more deference than to decisions of federal district judges."[54]

Labor Law and Antitrust   On the bench, however, Judge Posner has not consistently followed the deference approach that he claims, in his writings, would further his primary goal of efficiency. Indeed, an analysis of the Posner opinions in labor law cases involving review of decisions of the NLRB shows that those decisions were affirmed in six cases[55] and reversed in eleven.[56] A reversal rate of almost two-thirds is far more than would result from a judge who followed Posner's ostensible deference doctrine. Even the affirmances, it should be noted, are at times grudging. "More important than verbal niceties in the standard of review," declares one Posner affirming opinion, "is judicial impatience with the Board's well-attested manipulativeness in the interpretation of the statutory test for 'supervisor.'"[57]

Particularly significant is what is revealed by a closer look at the Posner opinions reversing NLRB decisions. All but one of the eleven opinions in this category are reversals that resulted in loss of the case by a worker or union. "In these cases," writes a commentator, "we find Posner violating his preference for judicial self-restraint, overturning [administrative] decisions . . . , almost always to the detriment of labor."[58]

That this comment is accurate can be seen from analysis of some of the Posner opinions reversing the NLRB. To be sure, Judge Posner begins those opinions with a formal statement of obeisance to the board. But he goes on to say that this does not give the agency carte blanche to make irrational findings, and that the finding at issue in the case was unreasonable.[59] Thus, in a 1986 case, the NLRB dealt with an employer's announcement to its employees (then subject to a unionization effort) that it considered employee names, addresses, and wages to be confidential and that an employee could be disciplined for divulging that information. The board found the statement indicated that any disclosure of such information was subject to discipline, regardless of how the employee obtained the information.

The Posner opinion reversed the NLRB on the ground that the inference drawn from the employer's statement was completely irrational—the board had acted in "a fantastic fashion."[60] Neither the lurid language nor his formal incantation of the rule of limited review of inferences[61] masks the fact that Judge Posner simply disagreed with an inference that most observers would find, at the least, reasonable.

The Posner tendency in these cases to engage in what has been called his "*post hoc* redeciding of factual questions"[62] is also apparent in his other opinions reversing the NLRB. In *Continental Web Press v. NLRB,*[63] Judge Posner rejected the board's certification of a union for the pressmen of a printing company. The company's production process consisted of two stages. First, "preparatory employees" made plates; then the pressmen ran the plates in the presses (located in another part of the plant). The pressmen had a different supervisor, apprenticeship program, hours of work, and working conditions. The board had found the pressmen to be an appropriate bargaining unit. The Posner opinion rejected this finding, saying, "[W]e find it difficult to understand why there should be separate units for pressmen and preparatory employees."

In these cases, however, as Posner himself acknowledges, "the Board need only choose an appropriate unit—its choice need not be the most appropriate unit." According to Posner, "The greatest conflicts of interest among workers are over wages, fringe benefits and working conditions. But there do not seem to be any significant differences between the preparatory employees and the pressmen in Continental Web's plant along any of these dimensions."[64] Yet these matters are surely questions of fact for the NLRB to decide on the basis of the testimony at the agency hearing.[65]

An even more blatant disregard of the deference due to administrative findings of fact may be seen in a 1983 Posner opinion. The NLRB had issued a bargaining order to remedy a restaurant's unfair labor practices. The one that Judge Posner termed as presenting "the most interesting and difficult question"[66] arose out of a speech made by the restaurant's owner to its employees. The owner asserted, "Unions do not work in restaurants. . . . If the Union exists at Shenanigans, Shenanigans will fail. . . . The cancer will eat us up, and we will fall by the wayside. And if you walk into this place five years down the road, if there is a Union in here, then I guarantee you it won't be a restaurant."

The NLRB had ruled that this speech was a coercive threat to close down the restaurant. To Judge Posner, however, the speech was only a fair statement of what would happen if the union won. The Posner opinion analyzes the impact of unionization in a highly competitive market and concludes, "It is well known that union wage demands sometimes result in plant closings. For example, some of the shift of industry in recent decades from North to South is apparently a consequence of the much lower rate of unionization in the South compared to the North." Hence, Posner decides that the speech was not coercive, since it only "offered a competent if extremely informal analysis of likely economic consequences of unionization in a highly competitive market in which most companies are not unionized—the restaurant market in Decatur."[67]

Yet the finding of coercion appears to be the very type of finding of fact that the administrative agency as arbiter of fact is best qualified to make. In this case, it is hard to see why the NLRB finding of coercion was not a reasonable one.[68] Indeed, as one commentator puts it, "If an employer's description of a union as 'cancer' is not sufficient in this connection to substantiate the Board's findings that it was threatening to the workers, it is difficult to imagine what could be."[69] Most disturbing of all is the Posner reliance upon his own controversial economic analysis of the consequences of unionization to reject the finding by the administrative trier of fact. Leaving aside any question of the result reached by Judge Posner, his approach was not the proper one when he sat on review of a decision made by an administrative agency.

The reversals in the abovementioned cases were really based on the Posner attitude toward the National Labor Relations Act and the NLRB's action in certifying bargaining units. Judge Posner has shared the general deprecating attitude of New Right jurists toward the federal labor law. He writes, "The main purpose of a union, most economists have long believed, is to limit the supply of labor so that the employer cannot use competition among laborers to control the price of labor." Hence, the judge concludes, "The common law was thus on solid economic ground

when it refused to enforce agreements to join unions, enjoined picketing . . . and enforced yellow dog contracts."[70] Regarding yellow dog
contracts, Posner writes that the worker probably would demand compensation for giving up his right to join a union[71]—a questionable assertion in view of the economic inequality between employer and employee
when such contracts were enforceable.[72] On the other hand, if the worker
"was not compensated generously, this was not a social loss, since any
compensation for not combining with other workers to create a labor
monopoly is itself a form of monopoly gain."[73]

To Judge Posner, the federal labor law is a law that supports "workers
combining with other workers to create a labor monopoly." As Posner
sees it, "[U]nions are basically worker cartels and . . . the National
Labor Relations Act basically encourages union formation." This leads
the judge to conclude, "The NLRA is a kind of reverse Sherman Act,
designed to encourage cartelization of labor markets."[74]

Judge Posner is also critical of the NLRB posture in certification
cases. He writes that the board generally acts as it did in the *Continental
Web* case.[75] "Consistently with the law's policy of promoting worker
cartels, the Board generally certifies the smallest rather than largest
possible unit." This, says Posner, is beneficial primarily to workers in
the smaller units: "Transaction costs among workers are lower the fewer
the workers and the more harmonious their interests . . . while the benefits of unionization are greater the smaller the unit is relative to the total
employment of the firm."[76] But the benefits are not shared by employers.
"It is costly for an employer to have to negotiate separately with a number
of different unions."[77]

The tilt in favor of workers here is only an illustration supporting the
Posner general conclusion on the federal labor statute: "In sum, the Act
does not go as far as it could go to promote cartelization of the labor
supply, but it is not neutral; if the law were neutral, unions would be less
common and less effective than they are."[78]

Judge Posner's skeptical attitude toward the National Labor Relations
Act is a prime factor in his decisions overruling the NLRB. His analysis
of the statute as a law that distorts the neutral balance of the market to
one favoring employees has, without a doubt, led him to his reversals
that work to the systematic disadvantage of labor.[79] The same has been
true in other areas of Posner's judicial work. There, too, the Posner

economic approach has led to decisions that, because of his market predilection, have tended to coincide with the positions taken by New Right jurists.

For example, Judge Posner's opinions reflect his minimalist view of antitrust law,[80] under which all antitrust laws other than section 1 of the Sherman Act should be repealed and the antitrust laws themselves should be interpreted to proscribe only inefficient conduct.[81] An analysis of the Posner antitrust opinions[82] shows that in the seventeen antitrust cases in which the judge wrote opinions on the merits, only one was decided in favor of the antitrust plaintiff.[83] Posner's negative attitude toward the antitrust laws has led him to interpret them restrictively, so as to place heavy burdens on plaintiffs who rely on statutes that interfere so directly with the efficiency produced by free operation of the market.[84]

Procedural Due Process   Judge Posner's restrictive attitude is also evident in his opinions on protection of constitutional rights. The Posner analysis of those rights is bound to give a higher value to economic rights, which can be more readily quantified than personal rights of the type discussed in Chapter 6. That Posner as a judge follows the narrow approach to the latter rights may be seen from his opinions involving procedural due process claims by public employees.

As a starting point, it should be noted by way of comparison that Judge Posner has been willing to adopt an expansive view of similar procedural due process claims where the economic rights of those engaged in business were violated. Thus, in a pathbreaking opinion, Posner held that a liquor license was "property" within the meaning of the Due Process Clause. Hence it might not be taken away without notice and hearing. The same was true in a case of nonrenewal of a short-term liquor license; there, too, the licensee was protected by procedural due process. The prevailing rule had previously been that a liquor license was a mere "privilege" that might be taken away summarily.[85] In the first federal appellate case so holding, Judge Posner rejected the old rule and held firmly that the liquor license was "property" in the due process sense.[86]

In the cases involving due process claims by public employees, on the other hand, Judge Posner starts with the same skeptical attitude that he has in labor and antitrust cases. He notes the rule laid down by the

Supreme Court that "holds that teachers and other public employees with tenure contracts . . . have a property right in their jobs so that if they are fired without a hearing their constitutional rights have been violated."[87] Posner questions the basis of the rule. He writes, "The use of the term 'property right' in these cases is not conventional. Tenure is a contract right, not a property right." In addition, Posner states,

> it is odd that courts should think these employees in need of federal constitutional protections. If a public employee who has tenure is fired, he can sue the state under state contract law. . . . And since the right that is enforced in a suit under the Fifth or Fourteenth Amendments to enforce a tenure contract is a product of that contract, and since remedies for breach can be viewed as an implied term of the contract, it is not clear what property right the employee has been deprived of if he receives the remedies to which he is contractually entitled, even if they do not include a hearing that meets federal due process standards.[88]

Despite his doubts, Judge Posner has had to follow the Supreme Court rule in cases where it has been clearly applicable. Where a public employee had tenure, the Posner opinion held that she might not be discharged without a hearing.[89] Where the facts of the case give him leeway, however, the Posner tendency is to decide against the public employee.[90] In one case, he did this on the ground stated above—that the employee has an adequate remedy in a contract action. "Such a suit would be process—in fact more elaborate process than the plaintiffs would have received had the defendants given them an administrative hearing."[91]

Judge Posner has also questioned the Supreme Court's holding that a public employee is deprived of a "liberty" interest protected by procedural due process when government, in declining to retain him in employment, "imposed on him a stigma . . . that foreclosed his freedom to take advantage of other employment opportunities."[92] According to a Posner opinion, "The public employees's constitutional right not to be fired on 'stigmatizing' grounds is one of the more mysterious innovations in modern constitutional law. Reputation is not 'property' or 'liberty' within the meaning of the due process clauses." To Posner, then, "It seems odd that merely because a defamatory statement (not a deprivation of liberty) is coupled with firing an employee-at-will (not a deprivation of property), the public official is guilty of a federal tort. It sounds like the legal equivalent of $0 + 0 = 1$."[93]

In the "stigma" case, too, Posner reverts to his view that the public employee's case can be taken care of by a suit in a state court—this time by a tort action. "One might have thought that the only significance of the firing would be to make it easier for the victim to prove damages in a suit in state court for defamation, assuming he wasn't promptly hired in an equally good job."[94]

The Posner opinion in question states that his "stigma" theory "is not important to the present case."[95] But it is the background for his holding that even where an official has been fired by the governor in a stigmatizing manner, no constitutional right has been violated, because the governor has reasonably relied upon a court of appeals decision holding that there was no right to notice and hearing in a similar case.[96] Yet the Supreme Court had held only a few years earlier that the right to notice and hearing existed even though the right was unknown at the time the public employee was discharged. This was true because the decision holding that there was a procedural due process right in such a case[97] was not handed down until several months after the discharge.[98]

Facts and Shadows   Even more disturbing than his actual decisions is the Posner tendency to articulate his economic theories in his opinions, despite their lack of direct relevance to the facts of the cases concerned. Thus in two antitrust cases Judge Posner's opinions contain long and irrelevant discussions of the relationship between antitrust and patent law[99] and the nature of the tie-in and price-fixing aspects of antitrust law.[100] In each case, a member of the court refused to concur in the Posner economic theorizing. As one of them put it, "Unfortunately, I cannot concur in much of the discussion contained in the majority opinion . . . because I believe it is dicta—dicta that might tend to influence and prejudice decisions in cases yet unborn but which may come to this court for review."[101]

At times, Judge Posner's opinions rely upon his economic approach to question long-established legal principles. I have already discussed the Posner opinion casting doubt on rent control.[102] Another example occurred in a case involving a claim by psychologists that their exclusion from membership on hospital medical staffs by a state agency denied them due process and equal protection. The Posner opinion denying relief pointed out that the "federal courts long ago, and whether rightly or wrongly, got out of the business of second-guessing state decisions on occupational licensure." But then the opinion went on to indicate doubts about the federal court posture in this respect and, more broadly, about occupational licensing in general.

"Granted," writes Judge Posner, "there is now a large body of scholarly literature which questions the wisdom of occupational licensure and might question the wisdom of Illinois' excluding psychologists from hospital medical staffs. The scholars have found that governmental restrictions on the professions create barriers to entry, reduce competition, and raise professional incomes, without bringing about compensating increases in the quality of professional services."[103]

"However," the Posner opinion notes, "neither this literature, nor the broader literature (of which it is a part) that is skeptical of regulation, . . . has yet persuaded the courts to reconsider their hands-off policy toward economic regulation challenged under the Constitution." Hence, in this case in which exclusion from professional opportunities was challenged, the court would continue to follow the rule of extreme deference in cases involving licensing—"whatever we might personally think of the Court's Manichaean conception of 'personal' versus 'economic' rights."[104]

The Posner questioning of licensing was a gratuitous expression of his own economic views on the matter. Even if, as his opinion concludes, it did not change the result in the given case, it still has disquieting implications. In refusing to join Judge Posner's economic theorizing in a case, one of his colleagues asserted that "we should confine our discussion to the legal principles applicable to the case at hand. Shadows cast beyond the facts of a particular case tend to confuse the trial judges and haunt our own appellate court."[105]

But the Posner dicta are more than mere "shadows cast beyond the facts." They are indications of what the judge might do if he were not merely a lower court judge, bound by adherence to current Supreme Court jurisprudence. If he were elevated to the Court for which his name has often been suggested in recent years, Justice Posner would be confined by no such compunction. He would then be free to give full rein to his economic approach to law. The "shadows" in his court of appeals opinions could become the basis for a quantum transformation of our public law.

KOZINSKI: NEW RIGHT CLONE?

Justice Scalia and Judge Posner are the "stars" among the judges selected by President Reagan. There are, however, other Reagan appointees who may not be as well known, but who also illustrate the tendency to mirror their New Right jurisprudence in their public law opinions. Representative of them is Alex Kozinski, who was chosen by President Reagan as a judge on the U.S. Court of Appeals for the Ninth Circuit.

It was Judge Kozinski who made the statement quoted at the beginning of this book on the emergence of New Right jurisprudence as "a new school of thought."[106] Kozinski fully shares the juristic tenets of the new school and its call for "a constitutional ethos of economic liberty."[107] Thus, he strongly disagrees with Justice Brennan's statement that "[t]he modern activist state is a concomitant of the complexity of modern society; it is inevitably with us."[108]

To Judge Kozinski, this Brennan statement "is the cause for the greatest alarm." In Kozinski's view, "Rather than accepting 'the modern activist state' as a given and quibbling over how much 'human dignity' we can squeeze out of the remaining portions of the Constitution, we might question whether we have not taken a wrong turn somewhere and yielded to the state too much power over our lives."[109]

In particular, Judge Kozinski shares the censure by New Right jurists such as Professors Siegan and Epstein of "the deconstitutionalization of economic rights" that they claim has occurred during this century. Kozinski asserts that "the substitute for precisely defined property rights is an increase in the scope and power of government." The consequence is a drastic increase in regulation, with a proliferation of regulatory agencies. Indeed, declares Kozinski, "It sometimes seems like the only free competition left in our economy is between government agencies as to which can grab the most power." Kozinski, with other New Right jurists, questions the desirability of most regulation, which he sees as entailing the costs of decreased regulatory efficiency, market disruptions, and even the loss of civil liberties.[110]

If Kozinski had expressed his opinions as an academic theorist, one might agree or disagree, but few would question the propriety of a professor stating even the most extreme views as grist for the academic mills. But Kozinski was a federal appellate judge when he gave voice to these views, and he has put them into practice in his work on the bench.

The most striking example of this translation of theory into action is the Kozinski opinion in *Hall v. Santa Barbara*.[111] In that case, the court struck down a rent control ordinance applicable to mobile home parks as a violation of the Takings Clause. In the course of his opinion, Judge Kozinski went out of his way to question the economic soundness of rent control in general. Citing works by economists and a survey of their views, Kozinski indicated support for the notion that rent control's effect is that of "exacerbating the problems it is intended to ameliorate" and actually "reduces the quantity and quality of housing available." The growing body of professional opinion in this respect, the judge concluded, indicates that the "rationality [and hence the constitutionality] of rent control . . . may have to be reassessed."[112]

The Kozinski dictum questioning the constitutionality of rent control is at least as disturbing as Judge Posner's dictum to the same effect,[113] as well as the Posner animadversion, also by way of obiter, against occupational licensing.[114] Both rent control and licensing may have deficiencies in practice, but their constitutionality has long been settled in the law. To cast shadows on their legality beyond the facts of the particular case can only bring doubts into a heretofore settled legal area. To do so on the basis of controversial economic analysis is to revive the *Lochner* approach to judicial review.[115]

The Posner and Kozinski-type dicta are, however, more than shadows casting doubt on settled doctrine. They indicate the future path of our public law if jurists like their authors are appointed to the highest bench, where they will no longer be restricted by the constraints imposed by Supreme Court jurisprudence upon lower court judges.

On the bench, Judge Kozinski has adopted a separation-of-powers approach as rigid as that followed by Justice Scalia.[116] The key Kozinski separation-of-powers opinion was rendered in *Gubiensio-Ortiz v. Kanahele*.[117] At issue there were mandatory guidelines promulgated by the U.S. Sentencing Commission, which was set up by Congress to issue guidelines controlling federal judges in their imposition of sentences in criminal cases. The commission was composed of seven members appointed by the president, three of whom were to be sitting federal judges, chosen from a list of six submitted by the judicial conference.

The Kozinski opinion of the court held that the provision for judges to serve as members of the commission violated the separation of powers because federal judges might not constitutionally perform the rule-making functions Congress had assigned to them. The Kozinski reasoning on this point is of the simplistic kind followed by those who advocate an inflexible separation-of-powers interpretation: The Constitution gives federal judges only "the judicial Power" and restricts its exercise to "cases" and "controversies." Therefore judges may not exercise nonjudicial duties. Here the rule-making powers of the sentencing commission are nonjudicial in nature. Hence they may not constitutionally be performed by federal judges. QED!

Such an approach, as a leading case on the rule-making power of the courts points out, "stems from an oversimplification of the doctrine of the separation of powers."[118] Our Constitution is as much one of blended powers as it is of separation between the branches. Thus, "adjudication is not exclusively a judicial function,"[119] nor is rule making exclusively an executive or administrative one. Since the Middle Ages, the English courts have issued rules for controlling practice and procedure.[120] In this country, too, the Supreme Court provided for rules governing practice as early as 1792.[121] Since that time, the Supreme Court, under congressional delegations, has issued rules governing civil and criminal procedure, bankruptcy, and evidence.[122]

According to Judge Kozinski, however, these rules were different from the sentencing guidelines, which were "substantive regulations" and "[i]t has never before been thought appropriate to grant judges the power to issue substantive rules." It is difficult to accept the force of the Kozinski distinction in this respect between procedure rules and the sentencing guidelines. The Kozinski opinion concedes "that federal judges have occasionally been granted authority over matters that are not strictly cases or controversies." But, writes Kozinski, these are "carefully circumscribed exceptions," which "generally involve matters directly affecting the efficient performance of judicial functions."[123] Even if that is true, why do sentencing guidelines not come within this principle? Few matters impair "the efficient performance" of the federal courts more than the exercise of uncontrolled discretion in sentencing by district judges.

The decision on the law giving the Supreme Court power to promulgate procedure rules is directly in point.[124] The rule at issue in the case was one authorizing the district courts to order a plaintiff suing for personal injuries to take a physical examination. Before that rule, such a plaintiff had a right not to be compelled to submit to such an examination.[125] Indeed, according to Justice Frankfurter, that right "rested on considerations akin to what is familiarly known in the English law as the liberties of the subject." To Frankfurter, the power to make such "a drastic change in public policy in a matter deeply touching the sensibilities of people or even their prejudices as to privacy"[126] might not be made under the general delegation of the power to make procedure rules.

The Court, however, upheld both the delegation and the rule at issue. "The test," stated the opinion, "must be whether a rule really regulates procedure,—the judicial process for enforcing rights and duties recognized by substantive law and for justly administering remedy and redress for disregard or infraction of them."[127] According to the Court, the procedure rules, including the rule at issue, plainly met this test.

It is hard to see why the same is not true of the sentencing guidelines. They, too, enforce "rights and duties recognized by substantive [criminal] law" and provide "for justly administering remedy and redress" for violations.

At any rate, the Supreme Court has now definitively decided the matter in *Mistretta v. United States*.[128] The Court there, with only Justice Scalia dissenting, categorically rejected the Kozinski approach when it upheld the law establishing the U.S. Sentencing Commission. The highest Court found "that the role of the Commission in promulgating guidelines for the exercise of that judicial function bears considerable similarity to the role of this Court in establishing rules of procedure under the various enabling acts." Both the sentencing guidelines and the procedure rules are "court rules" which the judiciary may be authorized to issue. "In other words, the Commission's functions, like this Court's function in promulgating procedural rules, are clearly attendant to a central element of the historically acknowledged mission of the Judicial Branch."[129]

The Court's rejection of the rigid Kozinski approach is warranted by the latter's undesirable consequences. Chief Justice Vanderbilt once explained why there has been a trend in the direction of judicial rule-making power: "Rules of court are made by experts who are familiar with the specific problems to be solved and the various ways of solving them." Since the judges participate in their making, this also makes for a further benefit: "Rules of court, moreover, have the great advantage that not only are they made by experts, but they are interpreted and applied by Judges who are sympathetic with them."[130] Under the Kozinski approach, this would not be true of rules governing sentencing, which could not be made by "an independent body within the judicial branch staffed in part by federal judges who have expertise in matters involving criminal punishment."[131]

The Kozinski approach also means that any body given authority to issue sentencing guidelines will be chosen solely by the president, who will not have to select any independent judges as members. This would, of course, make for an increase in presidential power.

"ASHCANS OF THE LEGISLATIVE PROCESS"?

A similar consequence would follow if the approach of some New Right jurists to statutory interpretation were followed. Urged primarily by Justice Scalia and Judge Kozinski, their position might well result in increased deference to the executive.

It has long been accepted in our law that the courts will make use of legislative history in cases involving statutory interpretation. Thus, judges will rely on statements made from the floor, as well as on committee reports and hearings, to help determine the meaning of a law.[132] While still a circuit judge, Justice Scalia questioned this widespread judicial reliance on legislative history. In *Hirschey v. FERC*,[133] the decision rested upon a statement in a House committee report dealing with amendments to a statute. The report noted that there was a split in the circuits on the meaning of the statute and stated that it rejected the interpretation taken by one circuit court. Scalia objected to the reliance on the committee report.

Perhaps, wrote Scalia, in a concurring opinion, the report's "datum should be accorded the weight of an equivalently unreasoned law review article." But the report should not be relied upon as the basis of the court's decision. "I frankly doubt," declared Scalia, "that it is ever reasonable to assume that the details, as opposed to the broad outlines of purpose, set forth in a committee report come to the attention of, much less are approved by, the house which enacts the committee's bill. And I think it time for courts to become concerned about the fact that routine deference to the detail of committee reports, and the predictable expansion in that detail which routine deference has produced, are converting a system of judicial construction into a system of committee-staff prescription."[134]

In a later statement on the subject, Judge Scalia noted that, despite this criticism in his opinion, "[a]s an intermediate federal judge, I can hardly ignore legislative history when I know it will be used by the Supreme Court." Scalia urged, however, that the courts "at least be more selective in the sorts of legislative history we employ." Scalia said that in evaluating historical evidence he would rank amendments defeated on the floor first in importance, and next "extended floor debate." On the other hand, "At the bottom of the list I would place—what hitherto seems to have been placed at the top: the committee report."[135]

The Scalia view on the matter has been supported by Judge Kozinski. He strongly seconds Scalia's warning against relying on detailed discussions in legislative reports. Kozinski, too, asserts that the courts place far too much reliance on legislative history: "Once you start focusing on legislative history then you really cut the court loose because you never really have absolutely clear legislative history on one side. So then where are you?"[136] As Kozinski sees it, "The fact of the matter is that legislative history can be cited to support almost any proposition, and frequently is. The propensity of judges to look past the statutory language is well known to legislators. It creates strong incentives for manipulating legislative history to achieve through the courts results not achievable during the enactment process. The potential for abuse is great."[137]

In a 1986 opinion, Judge Kozinski writes that "the danger of according legislative reports controlling weight" stems from the following facts: "Reports are usually written by staff or lobbyists, not legislators; few if any legislators read the reports; they are not voted on by the committee whose views they supposedly represent, much less by the full Senate or House of Representatives; they cannot be amended or modified on the floor by legislators who may disagree with the views expressed therein."[138]

Kozinski concludes that "[c]ommittee reports that . . . purport to explicate the meaning or applicability of particular statutory provisions can short-circuit the legislative process, leading to results never approved by Congress or the President. Of course, all this goes doubly for floor statements by individual legislators."[139]

To be sure, the Scalia-Kozinski strictures against legislative history are not new. Some years ago Justice Frankfurter objected to the use of remarks by a proponent to determine the meaning of the Fourteenth Amendment, asserting, "What was submitted for ratification was his proposal, not his speech."[140] At the same time, Justice Jackson complained that the "custom of remaking statutes to fit their histories" meant that statutory language "is no longer a safe basis on which a lawyer may advise his client."[141] But, Jackson argued, "it is only the words of the bill that have presidential approval. . . . It is not to be supposed that, in signing a bill, the President endorses the whole Congressional Record. For us to undertake to reconstruct an enactment from legislative history is merely to involve the Court in political controversies which are quite proper in the enactment of a bill but should have no place in its interpretation."[142] Jackson summed up his position in the pithy comment that the Court should "reach [its result] by analysis of the statute instead of by psychoanalysis of Congress."[143] A few years later, a leading lawyer characterized the types of things used as "legislative history" as "the ashcans of the legislative process."[144]

But these earlier critics of the use of legislative history did not go nearly as far as Justice Scalia and Judge Kozinski. Thus Justice Jackson was not opposed to proper use of committee reports, but only the tendency "to select casual statements from floor debates, not always distinguished for candor or accuracy, as a basis for making up our minds what law Congress intended to enact."[145]

Justice Scalia goes much further in his attitude toward legislative history. "Ironically but understandably enough," he asserts, "the more the courts have relied upon committee reports in recent years, the less reliable they have become."[146] Perhaps it was once not absurd to pretend that members of Congress had read and agreed with a committee report. Today, however, such an assumption is contrary to reality: "As anyone familiar with modern-day drafting of congressional committee reports is well aware, the references [in reports] were inserted, at best by a committee staff member on his or her own initiative, and at worst by a committee staff member at the suggestion of a lawyer-lobbyist; and the purpose of those references was not primarily to inform the Members of Congress what the bill meant . . . but rather to influence judicial construction."[147] Committee reports, Scalia goes on, "are increasingly unreliable evidence of what the voting Members of Congress actually had in mind."[148]

Indeed, Justice Scalia asserts, "If I were writing on a blank slate, I suppose I would call into question the *fundamental premise* upon which all use of legislative history is based—the generally accepted proposition . . . that 'interpretative doubts . . . are to be resolved by judicial resort to an intention entertained by the lawmaking body at the time of its enactment.'"[149] As Scalia sees it, "Judges interpret laws rather than reconstruct legislators' intentions."[150] Scalia would consequently replace the use of legislative history in statutory interpretation with a rule under which the meaning of a statute would be determined solely on the basis of the statutory language.[151]

Judge Kozinski is apparently also willing to support such an approach. According to him, if a legislator has doubts about a particular provision in a bill, he should try to change its language during the legislative process. "Courts should not allow individual legislators and their staffs to usurp the uniquely judicial function of statutory interpretation"[152] by relying upon statements made during the enactment process.

Under the Scalia-Kozinski approach, a statute "is to be interpreted . . . according to its most plausible objective import, [not] according to the unlegislated 'intent' of those who enacted it." This means, according to Justice Scalia, "that—once a statute is enacted—its meaning is to be determined on the basis of its text by the Executive officers charged with its enforcement and the Judicial officers charged with its application."[153]

The Scalia approach in practice may be seen from his concurring opinion in *INS v. Cardoza-Fonseca*.[154] At issue there was the decision by the Immigration and Naturalization Service that an alien was not eligible for asylum because she did not meet the statutory requirement that she show a "well founded fear" of persecution in her own country. Justice

Scalia argued that the Court's opinion expressed erroneous views on the meaning of the decision in the *Chevron* case,[155] the leading recent case on the scope of review of an administrative agency's interpretation of a statute. Under *Chevron,* "if the statute is silent or ambiguous with respect to the specific issue, the question for the court is whether the agency's answer is based on a permissible construction of the statute." This means that, in the absence of "unambiguously expressed intent by Congress, . . . a court may not substitute its own construction of a statutory provision for a reasonable interpretation made by the administrator of an agency."[156]

Justice Scalia tells us that *Chevron* has consistently been interpreted "as holding that courts must give effect to a reasonable agency interpretation of a statute unless that interpretation is inconsistent with a clearly expressed congressional intent." Scalia asserts that the *Cardoza-Fonseca* opinion is "flatly inconsistent" with this interpretation of *Chevron.* First, says Scalia, the Court "implies that courts may substitute their interpretation of a statute for that of an agency whenever, '[e]mploying traditional tools of statutory construction,' they are able to reach a conclusion as to the proper interpretation of the statute." To Scalia, this approach "is not an interpretation but an evisceration of *Chevron,*" since it "would make deference a doctrine of desperation, authorizing courts to defer only if they would otherwise be unable to construe the enactment at issue."[157]

The Scalia concurrence also takes issue with the implication in *Cardoza-Fonseca* "that courts may substitute their interpretation of a statute for that of an agency whenever they face 'a pure question of statutory construction for the courts to decide,' . . . rather than a 'question of interpretation [in which] the agency is required to apply [a legal standard] to a particular set of facts.'" There is no basis, according to Scalia, for the Court's distinction. In *Chevron* itself, Scalia notes, "the Court deferred to the Environmental Protection Agency's abstract interpretation of the phrase 'stationary source.'"[158] The rule of deference, in Scalia's view, should apply both to interpretations in the abstract and those applying the statutory standard to particular facts.

The Scalia *Cardoza-Fonseca* concurrence is wholly consistent with the justice's general posture on statutory interpretation. He criticizes the Court for making "excessive" use of legislative history in the case. "[W]here the language of the enactment at issue is clear, . . . there is simply no need for the lengthy effort to ascertain the import of the entire legislative history."[159] Where the statute is silent or ambiguous, the *Chevron* doctrine of deference should control.

Scalia's *Cardoza-Fonseca* approach bears out his view that the meaning of a statute "is to be determined on the basis of its text by the Executive officers charged with its enforcement"[160] and the courts. The result is that of deference to executive interpretation of statutes. Since, in Scalia's view, the courts should not resort to legislative history, what is left as an extrinsic aid is the interpretation of those charged with carrying out the statute. This, of course, agrees with the constitutional tilt toward executive power that has characterized many New Right jurists. The lion's share in the interpretation process, as in the carrying out of laws, is to rest with the executive, the legislative role being confined to the intent expressed in the bare words enacted.

9

DOES NEW RIGHT
JURISPRUDENCE MATTER?

I HAVE pointed out that despite Holmes's skeptical remark on the influence of jurisprudence, "I don't believe most judges knew or cared a sixpence for any school," few legal thinkers have had a greater influence on the law and the way judges think than the patrician from Boston. Holmes put his stamp on his own time as few men have done, and continues to set the parameters of legal debate to this day.

HOLMES AND JURISPRUDENCE

Holmes's influence on the law is usually stated in terms of his work on the Supreme Court, where his dissents were ultimately accepted as the prevailing jurisprudence. But Holmes was a legal theorist well before he was a judge.[1] While he was still a practicing lawyer and part-time Harvard lecturer, he received the invitation to deliver a series of lectures. He chose as his topic the common law, and the lectures were published in a book of that name in 1881. This was the book that was to change both Holmes's life and the course of American law.

The *London Spectator* called *The Common Law* "the most original work of legal speculation which has appeared in English since the publication of Sir Henry Maine's *Ancient Law*."[2] For the first time, an American jurist viewed the law as anthropologists might view it—as an organic part of the culture within which it grew.[3]

But *The Common Law* was anything but a dry antiquarian account of the historical minutiae so dear to a writer like Henry Spelman. As a state judge has written, "The book propounds an idea audacious and even revolutionary for the time."[4] The Holmes theme has become so settled in our thinking that we forget how radical it was when first announced a century ago. The very words Holmes used must have appeared strange within the context of legal scholarship: "experience," "expediency," "necessity," "life." Until then, books on American law resorted to an entirely different vocabulary: "rule," "precedent," "logic," "syllogism."[5] As Holmes's biographer tells us, "The time-honored way was to deduce the *corpus* from *a priori* postulates, fit part to part in beautiful, neat, logical cohesion."[6] Holmes rejected "the notion that a given [legal] system, ours, for instance, can be worked out like mathematics."[7] In his *Common Law*, he declared, "The law embodies the story of a nation's development through many centuries, and it cannot be dealt with as if it contained the axioms and corollaries of a book of mathematics."[8]

The great Holmes theme was stated at the very outset of *The Common Law*: "The life of the law has not been logic; it has been experience. The felt necessities of the time, the prevalent moral and political theories, intuitions of public policy, avowed or unconscious, even the prejudices which judges share with their fellow-men, have had a good deal more to do than the syllogism in determining the rules by which men should be governed."[9] Holmes was here pointing the way to a new era of jurisprudence. The courts, he urged, should recognize that they must perform a legislative function, in its deeper sense. The secret root from which the law draws its life is consideration of "what is expedient for the community." The "felt necessities of the time," intuitions of what best serve the public interest, "even the prejudices which judges share with their fellow-men," all have much more to do than logic in determining the legal rules that govern society. The analytical jurisprudence that judges profess to be applying is actually the result of their view of public policy, perhaps "the unconscious result of instinctive preferences and inarticulate convictions, but none the less traceable to views of public policy in the last analysis."[10]

In a lecture delivered in 1897, Holmes asserted "that the judges themselves have failed adequately to recognize their duty of weighing considerations of social advantage."[11] The judges of a century ago looked at the law as anything but the instrument of transformation it has since become. In law, as in nature, progress was then considered an evolution-ary movement that would only be impeded by outside intervention. As it was put by James C. Carter, the outstanding legal philosopher of the American Bar, "The popular estimate of the possibilities for good which may be realised through the enactment of law is, in my opinion, greatly exaggerated." In law, as in the economics of the day, laissez faire was the rule. "The Written Law," Carter affirmed, "is victorious upon paper and powerless elsewhere."[12]

A noted Holmes statement has it that "a general proposition is simply a string for the facts."[13] American law today differs sharply from that of a century ago, not only in general doctrines, but even more in its approach to facts. Not too long ago, the black-letter approach was the only one permitted in determining public-law issues. In 1911 a court stated in reply to an appeal based upon "the economic and sociological argu-ments" supporting a challenged regulatory law, "We have already admit-ted the strength of this appeal to a recognized and widely prevalent sentiment, but we think it is an appeal which must be made to the people and not to the courts."[14]

The judges at the turn of the century reached their restrictive conclu-sions deductively, from preconceived notions and precedents. To them, the legal system was a perfect but closed sphere; the least dent in it was an invalid subtraction from its essence.[15] During this century, the judi-cial method has become inductive, reasoning more and more from the changing facts of a relativist world.[16] The law has come to resemble a rubber ball: a dent pushed out of one side promptly reappears on the other.[17] The system has become fluid and inconstant, dependent upon the particular circumstances of time and place. As Holmes predicted in his 1897 lecture,[18] the black-letter judge has been replaced by the master of statistics, economics, and other disciplines.

Holmes was the leading prophet of the coming legal era. Although a member of the generation that sat at the feet of Charles Darwin and Herbert Spencer, he was able to temper his Darwinism with an innate skepticism that made it impossible for him to accept the dogmatic ap-proach of Spencer's legal disciples. As early as 1873, Holmes wrote, "It has always seemed to us a singular anomaly that believers in the theory of evolution and in the natural development of institutions by successive adaptations to the environment, should be found laying down a theory of government intended to establish its limits once and for all by a logical deduction from axioms."[19]

Above all, Holmes refused to confound intellectual dogma with the order of nature. "No concrete proposition," he stated in his 1897 speech, "is self-evident, no matter how ready we may be to accept it, not even Mr. Herbert Spencer's 'Every man has a right to do what he wills, provided he interferes not with a like right on the part of his neighbors.'"[20] Though Holmes was an eminent legal historian whose greatest work off the bench was a historical analysis of common-law doctrine, he rejected the negative attitude of Carter and the then-prevailing historical school of jurisprudence. To him, there was no inevitability in either history or law, except as men made it.[21]

When Holmes asserted in his *Common Law*, "The life of the law has not been logic: it has been experience," and that the law finds its philosophy in "considerations of what is expedient for the community concerned,"[22] he was stating the theme of twentieth-century jurisprudence. If the law reflected the "felt necessities of the time,"[23] then those needs, rather than any abstract reasoning, should determine what form the law should take. These were not, to be sure, the views subscribed to by American judges and lawyers at the turn of the century—or even by the majority of the Supreme Court during Holmes's tenure on that tribunal. But the good that men do also lives after them. If the nineteenth century was dominated by the passive jurisprudence of men like Carter, the twentieth was, ultimately, to be that of Mr. Justice Holmes.

ACADEMIC SCRIBBLERS AND THE LAW

What about the law of the next century? Will it be molded by the New Right jurisprudence? Or are the views of these allegedly conservative jurists destined to be relegated to legal limbo alongside Carter's conservative philosophy of a century ago?

Certainly no one among the New Right jurists today has the stature of a Holmes, or holds his potential to mold the jurisprudence of a century. Yet the law is not moved by its giants alone. In the law as elsewhere, the situation is aptly described in the words of John Maynard Keynes: "Practical men, who believe themselves to be quite exempt from any intellectual influences, are usually the slaves of some defunct economist.

[Those] in authority . . . are distilling their frenzy from some academic scribbler of a few years back."[24]

The Supreme Court itself may be unaware that in making a decision, it is following a view first advocated by some jurist who may be largely unknown outside the academic milieu. In the *Lopez-Mendoza* case, for example, the Court used cost-benefit analysis to determine whether the exclusionary rule should be applied in a given proceeding. The majority found that the costs involved in applying the rule outweighed the benefits and hence decided that the rule was not applicable in the case. As I showed in Chapter 6, *Lopez-Mendoza* directly followed the cost-benefit approach to the exclusionary rule that had been advocated a few years earlier by then-Professor Richard A. Posner. Since the *Lopez-Mendoza* opinion does not refer to Posner at all, it is probable that the justices did not even know that they were distilling their decision from the "academic scribbler" in Chicago. Yet it was the interest aroused by Posner's articles weighing the exclusionary rule in the cost-benefit scale and finding it wanting that set the stage for the Supreme Court decision a few years later. Without the "academic scribbling" on the matter, it is most unlikely that the justices would have even been aware of the cost-benefit approach, much less have elevated it to the top of the constitutional-law agenda.

In my 1984 Tagore Law Lectures at Calcutta, I sought "to give some account of the men whose work entitles them to be considered among the Makers of American Law."[25] All but one of the eleven men whose contribution to our legal history I reviewed were judges. Until this century, American legal development paralleled that of the English common law. Its growing point was case law; its primary contributors were judges. From this point of view, our law appears as a structure fashioned by generations of judges, each professing to be a pupil, yet each a builder who added his few bricks.[26]

The days when a Holmes could direct his bolts from Olympus at the law's inadequacies are, however, long gone. Today, the cutting edge of jurisprudence is in the academy rather than the forum. It is the "academic scribbler," more than the judge, who sets the themes for the developing law. "Tradition has it," Justice Brennan tells us, "that Jeremy Bentham once remarked that law is not made by judge alone but by Judge and Company. If, as is likely, his reference was to the lawyers in the case, surely today he would include the law professors in the 'Company.' Their contribution of analysis and criticism of the judge's work helps immeasurably to shape the law to keep it on course the better to serve society."[27]

NEW RIGHT JURISPRUDENCE DOES MATTER

The jurists discussed in this book have not limited themselves to efforts "to shape the law to keep it on course." Their views, if adopted, would work a veritable constitutional revolution placing the 1937 revolution in Supreme Court jurisprudence[28] well in the shade. Their leading academic theorist, Richard A. Epstein, has asked whether he is engaged in "only a quixotic effort to turn back the clock, to repeal the twentieth century."[29] Though intended as a jocular quip, there is more weight to the Epstein question than its author may have intended.

It could be said that New Right jurisprudence does not really matter, since the constitutional clock is obviously not going to be turned back by a century. The danger, however, is not that the Epstein or Siegan juristic corpus, or even the economic approach of Judge Posner, will suddenly be elevated to the level of accepted judicial doctrine. The peril is that, as Professor Epstein himself puts it, his "correct theory at the very least can lead to incremental changes in the proper direction."[30]

The Epstein hope in this respect has begun to be realized. As Epstein points out, "[T]he present structure of constitutional law does admit a high degree of play at the joints."[31] It is at the joints that Epstein's approach has begun to have its effect upon the courts themselves. At the least, for example, the Epstein assertion of the Takings Clause as the basis for a restricted view of public power has created a question about the correctness of the accepted law. The doubts he has implanted have begun to produce an incremental evolution in takings law.

The influence of Judge Posner's soi-disant economic analysis of law has been even greater. The Posner approach does not really subject law to economic analysis, but only to the criterion of a present-day revival of classical economics. With efficiency and wealth maximization as its end and the market as the instrument through which it is achieved, Posnerian jurisprudence leads to what he elsewhere deprecatingly terms the constitutionalization of laissez faire.[32]

255

Posner writes that it is scholars such as Epstein and Siegan who would interpret the Constitution as a guarantor of free markets.[33] Yet it is Posner himself who "was the first to suggest that the discredited 'liberty of contract' doctrine could be given a solid economic foundation and as good a jurisprudential basis as the Supreme Court's aggressive modern decisions protecting civil liberties."[34] Nevertheless, Posner denies advocating the Epstein-Siegan approach, declaring, "I have never believed, however, that such a restoration of the '*Lochner* era' . . . would be, on balance, sound constitutional law."[35] The denial is disingenuous. The Posner approach lends direct support to the Epstein-Siegan effort to take our public law back to the *Lochner* era. And there can be no doubt that this approach is increasingly reflected in the work of the courts. More and more judges are using Posnerian economic analysis as a tool. The result is to make the courts more receptive to attacks on economic regulation than they have been in half a century.

Illustrations of the changed judicial posture in this respect can be seen in the opinions by Justice Scalia and Judge Kozinski casting doubt upon the constitutionality of rent control.[36] A similar skepticism was expressed by Judge Posner in his opinion on the Chicago ordinance giving tenants certain legal rights against their landlords.[37] These opinions show that New Right jurisprudence does matter, since it is starting to be reflected in the case law itself.

Such reflection is, however, but a shadow of what it might be if judges like Posner were not bound by Supreme Court jurisprudence. The Posner opinion in the *Chicago Board of Realtors* case,[38] cast doubt upon both the Chicago ordinance at issue and upon the economic basis of rent control in general. Posner reached this opinion solely on the basis of his own economic theory, contrary though it was to court precedent in rent control cases. Judge Posner did not stop, however, with his skeptical attitude toward rent control. Plaintiffs in the case had claimed that the ordinance at issue violated both the Contract Clause and substantive due process. The Posner opinion concurred in the court's rejection of this claim, but only because it could not succeed under the settled Supreme Court case law.

According to the Posner opinion, "The Supreme Court . . . has rewritten the contract clause."[39] The judge was referring to the *Blaisdell* case[40]—the leading modern case on the Contract Clause. Posner stresses that *Blaisdell* was based on the emergency character of the legislation there. In *Chicago Board of Realtors*, on the other hand, there is "no emergency. . . . Chicago would not collapse if the ordinance weren't allowed to go into effect until existing leases, most of which are for only one year, expired. Chicago would be better off if the ordinance never went into effect."[41]

Subsequent Supreme Court decisions, have, however, virtually eliminated the "emergency" requirement and, according to Judge Posner, "defanged the contract clause." To Posner, on the contrary, "If the contract clause were taken seriously, the Chicago ordinance, to the extent it modifies existing leases as well as prescribing terms for future ones, would certainly violate the clause." Nevertheless, he writes, "[T]he clause isn't taken very seriously nowadays by those whose views matter the most (Justices of the Supreme Court)."[42] Consequently, the Contract Clause argument against the Chicago ordinance must be rejected.

The same is true of the substantive due process argument. With regard to it the Posner opinion states, "The plaintiffs have brought their case in the wrong era. Chicago's new ordinance indeed strikes at the heart of freedom of contract, but the Supreme Court's current conception of substantive due process does not embrace freedom of contract." Under the prevailing jurisprudence, "it is clear that the Chicago ordinance does not deny 'substantive due process,' though not because it is a reasonable ordinance, which it is not." That is the case because the "Court is not about to cut the welfare state down to size by invalidating unreasonable economic regulation such as the ordinance under attack in this case."[43]

The Posner economic analysis of law, with its lodestar of efficiency promoted by the market, takes a different approach. It would definitely "cut the welfare state down to size." The Chicago ordinance, in the Posner analysis, is, as the judge himself states, "not . . . a reasonable ordinance."[44] Hence, its restriction on the market would be ruled invalid but for the Supreme Court jurisprudence ruling the other way.

In addition, the Posner *Chicago Board of Realtors* opinion indicates agreement with the Epstein view on the Takings Clause. The opinion concludes by noting that the landlords had not raised on the appeal their "most promising" challenge—that is, "that the ordinance . . . violates the eminent domain clause of the Fifth Amendment . . . by taking away an important part of a landlord's property rights without compensation."[45] Of course, the same challenge could be raised against rent control in general, and it is hard to see why Judge Posner would not find it as "promising" there as Judge Kozinski did in the *Hall* case.[46]

CONSTITUTIONAL THEORY AND THE JUSTICES

Anyone who is familiar with the behind-the-scenes decision process in the Supreme Court will at first tend to agree with the Holmes remark about the influence of schools of jurisprudence upon the justices. I have had privileged access to the files of some of the justices—in particular to conference notes, correspondence, and memoranda on all the cases decided during the Warren and Burger tenures. One thing that stands out from examination of these materials over the years is the absence of discussions on juristic theory. The justices are concerned with deciding the cases before them and confine themselves to the issues involved, without seeking to place them in any broader jurisprudential perspective.

This does not mean that the justices do not approach cases with a definite point of view that determines their vote in most cases. This was particularly true of the Warren Court majority during the years after Justice Frankfurter retired. A few years ago, the present chief justice compared the Warren and Burger Courts in this respect. Justice Rehnquist stated that the impact of the Court had been diminished under Chief Justice Burger. "I don't think," he said, "that the Burger Court has as wide a sense of mission. Perhaps it doesn't have any sense of mission at all."[47]

Certainly the Warren Court did have Rehnquist's "sense of mission" when it virtually rewrote the corpus of our constitutional law. During Chief Justice Warren's tenure, concepts and principles that had appeared unduly radical not too long ago became accepted rules of law. The Warren Court led the movement to remake constitutional law in the image of an evolving society. In doing so, the justices had to perform the originative role that the jurist normally is not called upon to exercise in more stable times—a role usually considered more appropriate for the legislator than for the judge.

From this point of view, the Warren Court was the paradigm of the "result-oriented" court, using its power to secure the result it deemed right in the cases that came before it. Employing to the utmost the authority of the ermine, Warren and his colleagues never hesitated to do whatever they thought necessary to translate their own conceptions of fairness and justice into the law of the land.

This was plainly not true of the Burger Court. As Justice Rehnquist pointed out, that tribunal had no "sense of mission" comparable to that possessed by its predecessor. The lack of mission did not extend to the entire Court, however, only to the centrist majority that pointed the way during most of the Burger tenure.

Apropos of juristic motives, Justice Rehnquist has declared, "I don't know that a court should really have a sense of mission."[48] Yet Rehnquist himself was clearly a justice with a "sense of mission" and the same was true of some of his Burger Court colleagues as well. In this connection there is a 1986 analysis by Justice Blackmun of the tripartite division within the Burger Court. Blackmun said that he had always put "on the left" Justices Brennan and Marshall and "on the right" Chief Justice Burger and Justice Rehnquist. "Five of us," Blackmun concluded, were "in the middle"—namely, Justices Stewart, White, Powell, Stevens, and himself.[49]

There is no doubt that the two justices at each end of the Burger Court were judges with a definite "sense of mission." Stated broadly, Justices Brennan and Marshall saw it as their mission to preserve and, if possible, extend the Warren Court's liberal jurisprudence. To them the primary role of the courts was to serve as protectors of individual rights and they consistently voted to ensure the effectiveness of that role. At the other pole, Chief Justice Burger and Justice Rehnquist had the opposite judicial agenda. They sought what Rehnquist called "a halt to . . . the sweeping rules made in the days of the Warren Court"[50]—and not only a halt, but a rollback of much of the Warren jurisprudence. The Burger-Rehnquist conservative program included enlargement of government authority over individuals, a check to the expansion of criminal defendants' rights, and limitations on access to federal courts.

The actions of the opposed justices were based upon more or less fixed juristic views which served as the foundation for the jurisprudential edifices they sought to construct. They would generally adhere rigidly to those principles, which would enable Court-watchers to state with confidence how they would vote in almost all cases. Since their positions were normally fixed, it was rash to predict that they would vote differently in any important case. I was once told that the Brennan law clerks had confidently predicted that Justice Rehnquist would vote with Brennan in the *Bakke* case.[51] Anyone familiar with the Rehnquist record will find it hard to see the basis for their belief, given Rehnquist's reflex toward the right in cases involving racial classifications. At any rate, the Court community quickly saw where Rehnquist stood when he circulated a lengthy memorandum asserting that the special-admissions program at issue in *Bakke* was invalid.[52]

If the four opposing justices habitually cast their votes in accordance with their basic liberal or conservative principles, the same cannot be said of the justices "in the middle" of the Burger Court. They were essentially pragmatists considering cases on their individual facts and voting now with one end of the Court spectrum, now with the other. In certain fields, to be sure, the centrist justices would have a defined position. Thus Justices White and Powell would more often vote with the conservative bloc in criminal cases, while Justices Blackmun and Stevens were to be found with Justice Brennan in many cases involving infringements upon personal rights, particularly those growing out of the right of personal autonomy that Blackmun had enshrined in his *Roe v. Wade* opinion.[53]

Despite these tendencies, the center justices did not have anything like a defined juristic Weltanschauung. Nor did the Burger Court as a whole. As its decisions oscillated between the opposing blocs, the justices in the middle would hold the balance, tilting it at times in one direction, at times in the other. During most of the Burger tenure, it was the center justices who had the decisive votes and they prevented the Court from becoming a mere reflection of either faction. "I, with others," said Justice Blackmun, "have been trying to hold the center. I think we've been fairly lucky in how we've come out."[54]

From this point of view, the Supreme Court over the years has resembled the Burger Court more than the Warren Court. And the paradigmatic modern justice in this respect has been Justice Potter Stewart. While on the Court, Stewart never acted on the basis of any defined philosophy regarding the proper relationship between the state and its citizens. When asked if he was a liberal or a conservative, he answered, "I am a lawyer," adding, "I have some difficulty understanding what those terms mean even in the field of political life. . . . And I find it impossible to know what they mean when they are carried over to judicial work."[55]

What characterized Stewart was his pragmatic approach to issues that tended to polarize people. But pragmatism is generally the approach followed by those who sit on the highest bench. The thousands of conference notes I have examined show that the justices routinely operate case by case, reaching the result they deem justified by the individual facts and issues presented. Even those at the Court's polar extremes, such as Chief Justice Rehnquist or Justice Brennan, do not act on the basis of an overall juristic philosophy. They may have definite points of view, but these are hardly based upon an approach urged by any particular school of jurisprudence. It is in this sense that Holmes's comment quoted at the beginning of this chapter must be taken as valid.

It does not, however, follow from this conclusion that schools of legal philosophy do not matter in Supreme Court jurisprudence. On the contrary, as Keynes remarked with regard to economics, the justices who set new trends are all too often channeling the law into a mold formed by "some academic scribbler of a few years back." Justice O'Connor may have assumed that she was making new law when she applied cost-benefit analysis to test applicability of the exclusionary rule in administrative proceedings.[56] She was, however, only following the approach urged by then-Professor Posner in articles applying his economic approach to the constitutional issue. Similarly, Justice Scalia and the judges who have recently cast doubt upon the constitutionality of rent control have only been following the Siegan-Epstein-Posner approach to economic regulation.

JUNIOR SUPREME COURT

Mention should also be made of another factor in connection with the influence of constitutional theory on the courts. I have referred to Justice Brennan's use of the Bentham remark about the law being made "by Judge and Company."[57] Some years ago, Brennan used the Bentham observation in a different context. In a 1979 speech, the justice referred to his opinions as "opinions that came from the Brennan chambers over the past 23 years. I say from the 'Brennan chambers' because, as

Bentham said, the 'Law is not the work of judge alone but of judge and company.' The company in this case consisted of the 65 law clerks who have been associated with me on the Court."[58]

Justice Brennan was graciously acknowledging the role of what Justice Douglas once termed, in a letter to then-Justice Rehnquist, "the so-called Junior Supreme Court."[59] Douglas was making allusion to Rehnquist's earlier service as a law clerk to Justice Robert H. Jackson. At one time, the Douglas characterization of the clerk corps might have been taken as wholly in jest. By the time Douglas wrote, however, that was no longer the case.

At the outset of the Court's history, the Supreme Court law clerk would perform only the functions of an associate in a law firm, that is, research for senior members and assistance generally in the firm's work. It is doubtful that justices such as Holmes or Brandeis used their clerks as more than research assistants. More recently, however, justices have given their clerks an increasingly large share of responsibility, including the writing of opinions. "As the years passed," says Justice Douglas in his *Autobiography*, "it became more and more evident that the law clerks were drafting opinions."[60] Even the better justices have made more extensive use of their clerks in the drafting process than outside observers have realized. In the Court today, indeed, the routine procedure is for the clerks to draft virtually all opinions.

In one of his books, Judge Posner explains the present situation. "What," he asks, "are these able, intelligent, mostly young people doing? Surely not merely running citations in *Shepard's* and shelving the judge's law books. They are, in many situations, 'para-judges.' In some instances, it is to be feared, they are indeed invisible judges, for there are appellate judges whose literary style appears to change annually."[61]

The present chief justice has candidly described the opinion-writing process in his chambers. "In my case," Justice Rehnquist said, "the clerks do the first draft of almost all cases to which I have been assigned to write the Court's opinion." Only "when the case-load is heavy" does Rehnquist sometimes "help by doing the first draft of a case myself."[62] In his book on the Court, Rehnquist indicates that he has continued the practice of having his clerks prepare first drafts since his appointment as chief justice.[63]

To be sure, the justices themselves go over the drafts prepared by their clerks. "When a clerk writes the first draft," said Rehnquist, "I may revise it in toto." But that does not happen in many cases, where, states Rehnquist, "I may leave it [the clerk's draft] relatively unchanged."[64] Too many of the justices circulate drafts that are almost wholly the work of their clerks.

What makes the burgeoning role of the law clerks relevant to the present discussion is that they are fresh out of law school[65] and newly indoctrinated with the jurisprudence taught them there. After he had clerked for Justice Jackson, Rehnquist wrote a noted 1957 article in *U.S. News & World Report* entitled, "Who Writes Decisions of the Supreme Court?"[66] Rehnquist stated that the justices were delegating substantial responsibility to their clerks, who slanted materials to accord with their own views. The result, Rehnquist argued, was that the liberal point of view of the vast majority of the clerks had become the philosophy espoused by the Warren Court.

Today the situation is different. The judges tend to choose law clerks, so far as possible, in their own image. The judges appointed by President Reagan have, not unnaturally, selected clerks whose views are very different from those against which the Rehnquist animadversion was directed. The courts today are characterized by "the advent of generations of law students, who issue from the classrooms of conservative legal scholars to fill the chambers of conservative federal judges as their law clerks, and to proceed thereafter to the high ranks of federal government, to the offices of major law firms, and, to further the cycle, back to the classrooms of nationally recognized law schools"[67]—and then ultimately on to the bench themselves.

Law clerks could play a crucial part in elevating New Right jurisprudence to the level of accepted doctrine. Followers of the Posner economic approach have proliferated among the nation's law teachers. The many students who have been taught à la Posner leave the classroom as Posner disciples, eager to translate what they have learned into the law of the land. Those who become law clerks, fresh from exposure to New Right doctrine, have the opportunity to do so at the outset of their legal careers. For every academic critic of his work, a professor such as Richard Epstein has hundreds of avid acolytes, ready to mold the law in the Epstein model.

Thus New Right jurisprudence matters both because of its direct influence on law students and its consequent indirect influence on the judges themselves. At any rate, it is a mistake to assume that the views of most of the New Right theorists are so extreme that they will fall into obscurity of their own accord. On the contrary, valid or not, the jurisprudence of the "academic scribblers" such as Professors Posner and Epstein has begun to affect the way jurists think about law and even the way in which the courts decide cases. Their influence will only grow as increasing numbers of law clerks, and ultimately judges, issue from the classrooms of New Right academics.

A LIVING CONSTITUTION?

In the end, the underlying question in all public-law jurisprudence comes down to how we view the nation's Constitution.

During his confirmation hearings, Chief Justice Rehnquist was asked, "[H]ow can you not acknowledge that the Constitution is a living, breathing document . . . ?"[68] Some years earlier, then-Justice Rehnquist delivered a lecture entitled "The Notion of a Living Constitution."[69] In it he indicated that the question of "whether he believed in a living Constitution" was similar to asking whether he was in favor of any other desirable thing.

"At first blush," Rehnquist said, "it seems certain that a *living* Constitution is better than what must be its counterpart, a *dead* Constitution.[70] It would seem that only a necrophile could disagree." Indeed, the justice asserted, "If we could get one of the major public opinion research firms in the country to sample public opinion concerning whether the United States Constitution should be *living* or *dead*, the overwhelming majority of the responses doubtless would favor a *living* Constitution."[71]

Despite his flippancy on the matter, the question put to Chief Justice Rehnquist is a crucial one. Most of us today have no doubt about the proper answer. A basic document, drawn up in an age of knee-breeches and three-cornered hats, can serve the needs of an entirely different day only because our judges have recognized the truth of Marshall's celebrated reminder that it is a *constitution* they are expounding—an instrument that could hardly have been intended to endure through the ages if its provisions were fixed as irrevocably as the laws of the Medes and

Persians. The constantly evolving nature of constitutional doctrine has alone enabled our system to make the transition from the eighteenth to the twentieth century.

The outstanding feature of the Constitution is thus its plastic nature. Its key provisions are malleable and must be construed to meet the changing needs of different periods. Such provisions, Justice Frankfurter once pointed out, "do not carry contemporaneous fixity. By their very nature they imply a process of unfolding content."[72]

If, according to the Hughes saw, "the Constitution is what the judges say it is,"[73] then what judges say it is today will inevitably be different from what their predecessors asserted in days gone by. Our constitutional system is in a process of perpetual evolution: the Constitution is as much a *becoming* as it is a *being*. If the *ought* laid down in 1787 must run the gantlet of actual operation before it attains the practical status of an *is*, the *is* must also be given the characteristics of a *to be* for the system to remain viable.

The continuing viability of the system instituted by the framers has thus depended upon the recognition that our constitutional law has never been cast in a rigid mold. In our own day particularly, this has made for important changes in constitutional doctrine. Yet these changes have, in the main, been responses to the drastic transformation that American society has undergone. It is not so much the organic concepts that have been altered as the community that they serve. The contemporary unfolding of constitutional interpretation has mirrored the unfolding of the society itself.

If this seems obvious to most of us, it is because of Holmes's pioneering work. The seminal statement that the "felt necessities of the time" should determine legal rules means that as those necessities change, corresponding changes will occur in those rules as well. It was thus Holmes who articulated the concept of a "living Constitution" that is constantly being adapted to the evolving society in which it operates. How strange it would be if the Constitution alone among the institutions serving society were to remain unaffected by the transforming ferment that is continually altering and renovating societal institutions.

To paraphrase another Holmes metaphor, the Constitution is a magic mirror wherein we see reflected not only our own needs, but also the needs of those who went before us. Every important development in

American life has had its impact upon the living Constitution, from the founding of the republic to the stresses of the society two centuries later.

Now the New Right jurists, whom Judge Bork himself calls conservative constitutional revisionists,[74] seek to change all this. They would in effect undo the constitutional revolution brought about by acceptance of the Holmes jurisprudence in contemporary case law. Instead, they would roll back our constitutional law to that of over a century ago. In particular, they would substitute for the Holmes approach a doctrinaire jurisprudence that replaces the "felt necessities of the time" with "original intention," or one that would take the law back to the days when public power was weighed against the canons of classical economics.

It will be clear, I hope, that such a quantum leap backward in our law would have the most baneful consequences. If not for the Supreme Court jurisprudence which the New Right deplores, we would still be living in a society dominated by Jim Crow, child labor, the third degree, the rotten borough, and self-devouring individualism. Any jurisprudence supporting such a society scarcely deserves to be taken as seriously as it has been.

The New Right tocsin against the contemporary interpretation of the Constitution may begin on a note of tragedy, with warnings against the dire consequences of present-day jurisprudence. But it must inevitably end in farce. For it is farcical, toward the end of the twentieth century, to assert the need for a rollback of constitutional jurisprudence to that of a century ago. This is, however, the inevitable result of accepting the arguments of the jurists who constitute the legal New Right.

NOTES

NOTES TO THE INTRODUCTION

1. Kozinski, in Economic Liberties and the Judiciary xi (Dorne and Manne eds. 1987).
2. See Schwartz, The Supreme Court: Constitutional Revolution in Retrospect (1957); Corwin, Constitutional Revolution, Ltd. (1941).
3. The Words of Justice Brandeis 154 (Goldman ed. 1953).
4. West Coast Hotel Co. v. Parrish, 300 U.S. 379, 402 (1937).
5. Bork, The Tempting of America 223 (1989).
6. Children's Hospital v. Adkins, 284 Fed. 613, 622 (D.C. Cir. 1922).
7. Brown v. Board of Education, 347 U.S. 483 (1954).

NOTES TO CHAPTER 1

1. Meese, Address before American Bar Association, July 9, 1985, in The Great Debate: Interpreting Our Written Constitution 9 (1986).
2. Quoted in Pritchett, Civil Liberties and the Vinson Court 251 (1954).
3. 2 Holmes-Pollock Letters 115 (Howe ed., 2d ed. 1961).
4. Compare Hughes, The Supreme Court of the United States 68 (1928).
5. Holmes, The Common Law 1, 35 (1881).
6. Id. at 1.
7. Bork, in The Great Debate, supra note 1, at 43.
8. Brennan, id. at 14.
9. Id. at 10.
10. Meese, id. at 52.
11. Bork, The Tempting of America 143 (1989).
12. Published in Farrand, The Records of the Federal Convention of 1787, vols. 1 and 2 (1911).

13. Reprinted in 2 Schwartz, The Bill of Rights: A Documentary History 1016 (1971).
14. Macedo, The New Right v. The Constitution 9 (1986).
15. "As a practical matter, 'we know practically nothing about what went on in the state legislatures' during the process of ratifying the Bill of Rights." Brennan, J., dissenting, in Marsh v. Chambers, 463 U.S. 783, 815 (1983), citing Schwartz, op. cit. supra note 13, at 1171.
16. McCulloch v. Maryland, 4 Wheat. 316, 407 (U.S. 1819).
17. Ibid.
18. Bank of United States v. Deveaux, 5 Cranch 61, 87 (U.S. 1809).
19. McCulloch v. Maryland, 4 Wheat. 316, 407 (U.S. 1819).
20. Cardozo, The Nature of the Judicial Process 83 (1921).
21. United States v. Butler, 297 U.S. 1, 62 (1936).
22. Frankfurter, J., concurring, in Graves v. New York ex rel. O'Keefe, 306 U.S. 466, 491 (1939).
23. Article I, section 8, clause 5.
24. Galbraith, Money: Whence It Came, Where It Went 91 (1975).
25. See Schwartz, From Confederation to Nation: The American Constitution 1835–1877, 225 (1973).
26. 8 Wall. 603 (U.S. 1870).
27. Adams, The Education of Henry Adams 250 (1931 ed.).
28. 7 Am. L. Rev. 146 (1872).
29. Legal Tender Cases, 12 Wall. 457, 652–653, (U.S. 1871), per Field, J., dissenting.
30. Id. at 653.
31. Id. at 583–584, per Chase, C.J., dissenting.
32. Johnson, A Dictionary of the English Language (1755).
33. 2 Farrand, op. cit. supra note 12, at 168.
34. The debate extracts and Madison notes are in id. at 309–310.
35. 3 id. 172.
36. Legal Tender Cases, 12 Wall. 457, 529 (U.S. 1871).
37. Quoted in 3 Warren, The Supreme Court in United States History 236 (1922).
38. 14 Stat. 209 (1866).
39. 16 Stat. 44 (1869).
40. 12 Wall. 457 (U.S. 1870).
41. Supra note 5.
42. Loc. cit. supra note 10.
43. Schwartz, op. cit. supra note 13, at 1112.
44. 1 Stat. 73, 77 (1789).
45. What this punishment meant was graphically described in Blackstone: "The punishment of high treason in general is very solemn and terrible. 1. That the offender be drawn to the gallows, and not be carried or walk; though usually (by connivance at length ripened by humanity into law) a sledge or hurdle is allowed to preserve the offender from the extreme torment of being dragged on the ground or pavement. 2. That he be hanged by the neck, and then cut down alive. 3. That his entrails be taken out and burned, while he is yet alive. 4. That his head be cut off. 5. That his body be divided into four parts. 6. That his head and quarters be at the king's

disposal." Blackstone, Commentaries on the Laws of England 892 (Chase ed., 3d ed. 1890).

46. State v. Cannon, 190 A.2d 514, 517 (Del. 1963), from which these examples from the Delaware statute book are derived.

47. 5 The Founders' Constitution 374 (Kurland and Lerner eds. 1987).

48. James v. Commonwealth, 12 Serg. & R. 220, 225 (Pa. 1825).

49. Jackson v. Bishop, 404 F.2d 571, 579 (8th Cir. 1968). See Brian Schwartz, In the Name of Treatment: Autonomy, Civil Commitment, and the Right to Refuse Treatment, 50 Notre Dame Lawyer 808, 827 (1975).

50. Trop v. Dulles, 356 U.S. 86, 100–101 (1958).

51. Op. cit. supra note 1, at 23.

52. Rex v. Beardmore, 2 Burr. 792, 797 (1759).

53. Op. cit. supra note 47, at 372.

54. Dissenting in Federal Housing Administration v. Darlington, 358 U.S. 84, 92 (1958).

55. Frankfurter, J., concurring, in Graves v. New York ex. rel. O'Keefe, 306 U.S. 466, 491 (1939).

56. Loc. cit. supra note 10.

57. See Schwartz, The Great Rights of Mankind: A History of the American Bill of Rights 151–154 (1977).

58. Schwartz, op. cit. supra note 13, at 841.

59. 2 Session Laws of the State of New York 344 (1886).

60. 4 The Papers of Alexander Hamilton 35 (Syrett ed. 1962).

61. The Framing of India's Constitution: A Study 235 (1968).

62. Gopalan v. State of Madras (1950), 13 Supreme Court Journal 174. See Schwartz, A Comparative View of the Gopalan Case, 4 Indian Law Review 276 (1950).

63. Dissenting, in Poe v. Ullman, 367 U.S. 497, 541 (1961).

64. Hurtado v. California, 110 U.S. 516, 536 (1884).

65. Bork, op. cit. supra note 11, at 32.

66. Id. at 238.

67. Loc. cit. supra note 63.

68. Id. at 542.

69. Hurtado v. California, 110 U.S. 516, 532 (1884).

70. 347 U.S. 497 (1954).

71. 347 U.S. 483 (1954).

72. The Warren draft is reprinted in Schwartz, The Unpublished Opinions of the Warren Court 451 (1985).

73. 347 U.S. at 499.

74. Bork, op. cit. supra note 11, at 83.

75. 347 U.S. at 500.

76. Supra note 71.

77. 163 U.S. 537 (1896).

78. Op. cit. supra note 1, at 37–38.

79. Brown v. Board of Education, 345 U.S. 972 (1953).

80. See Schwartz, Super Chief: Earl Warren and His Supreme Court—A Judicial Biography 85 (1983).

81. 347 U.S. at 489.
82. The Jackson draft is in the *Brown* file, Robert H. Jackson Papers, Library of Congress.
83. The Vinson quotes are from the conference notes taken by Justices Burton and Jackson. See Schwartz, op. cit. supra note 80, at 74–75.
84. Carr v. Corning, 182 F.2d 14, 17 (D.C. Cir. 1950).
85. Supra note 82.
86. 472 U.S. 38 (1985).
87. Jaffree v. James, 544 F. Supp. 727, 732 (S.D. Ala. 1982).
88. Engel v. Vitale, 370 U.S. 421 (1962); Abington School District v. Schempp, 374 U.S. 203 (1963).
89. Jaffree v. Board of School Commissioners, 554 F. Supp. 1104, 1128 (S.D. Ala. 1983).
90. Id. at 1115.
91. Id. at 1119.
92. Ibid.
93. Id. at 1128.
94. 472 U.S. at 48.
95. Id. at 49.
96. Ibid.
97. Id. at 113.
98. Id. at 92.
99. Ibid.
100. Id. at 94.
101. Schwartz, op. cit. supra note 13, at 1061.
102. Id. at 1088.
103. 472 U.S. at 95.
104. Schwartz, op. cit. supra note 13, at 1088.
105. Ibid.
106. Ibid.
107. Id. at 1089.
108. Ibid.
109. 472 U.S. at 97.
110. Id. at 97–98.
111. Id. at 98.
112. Ibid.
113. Reprinted in op. cit. supra note 47, at 84.
114. 472 U.S. at 99.
115. Id. at 106.
116. See Kelly, Clio and the Court: An Illicit Love Affair, 1965 Sup. Ct. Rev. 119, 122. The term is defined, ibid. n. 13, as "the selection of data favorable to the position being advanced without regard to or concern for contradictory data or proper evaluation of the relevance of the data proffered."
117. 472 U.S. at 98.
118. Supra note 102.
119. Schwartz, op. cit. supra note 13, at 1089.
120. Id. at 1126.

121. Schwartz, op. cit. supra note 57, at 242.
122. Schwartz, op. cit. supra note 13, at 1162–1164.
123. Compare Kelly, supra note 116, at 140.
124. Brant, James Madison: Father of the Constitution 271 (1950).
125. On the other hand, according to 1 Works of Fisher Ames 690 (Allen ed. 1983), "The record of the debate reveals Ames' contribution." This statement is supported by the Ames motion introducing his substitute and his motion to have the amendments referred to the Select Committee and his statement in favor of the Bill of Rights. See also Bernhard, Fisher Ames: Federalist and Statesman 104–105 (1965), for Ames's support of the proposal for amendments to the Constitution.
126. Brant, loc. cit. supra note 124.
127. Ibid.
128. Justice Frankfurter, in McGowan v. Maryland, 366 U.S. 420, 465 (1961).
129. Lemon v. Kurtzman, 403 U.S. 602, 612 (1971).
130. Compare Kelly, supra note 116, at 140.
131. Concurring, in Adamson v. California, 332 U.S. 46, 64 (1947).
132. Brant, op. cit. supra note 124, at 272.
133. Op. cit. supra note 47, at 99.
134. Brant, op. cit. supra note 124, at 272.
135. Op. cit. supra note 47, at 103–104.
136. Marsh v. Chambers, 463 U.S. 783, 815 (1983). In this case the Court held that legislative chaplains do not violate the Establishment Clause.
137. Compare Kelly, supra note 116, at 156.
138. Id. at 142.
139. Concurring, in Abington School District v. Schempp, 374 U.S. 203, 240 (1963).
140. See id. at 236, n. 5.
141. Id. at 236.
142. Compare Lofgren, The Original Understanding of Original Intent? 5 Const. Commentary 77 (1988).
143. Powell, Some Aspects of Constitutionalism and Federalism, 14 North Carolina Law Review 1, 9 (1935).
144. Siegan, in Liberty, Property, and the Foundations of the American Constitution (Paul and Dickman eds. 1989).
145. Bork, op. cit. supra note 11, at 143.
146. Hammond, Sovereignty and an Empty Purse 23 (1970).

NOTES TO CHAPTER 2

1. Agatha Christie, Curtain 1 (1975).
2. McCulloch v. Maryland, 4 Wheat. 316, 407 (U.S. 1819).
3. Cohens v. Virginia, 6 Wheat. 264, 387 (U.S. 1821).
4. Compare Cabell v. Markham, 148 F.2d 737, 739 (2d Cir. 1945).
5. Kozinski, It Is a Constitution We Are Expounding: A Debate, 1987 Utah Law Review 977, 978.
6. Id. at 979, 980, 981.
7. Holmes, The Path of the Law, 10 Harvard Law Review 457, 469 (1897).

8. Dunne, Hugo Black and the Judicial Revolution 414 (1977).
9. See Schwartz, Swann's Way: The School Busing Case and the Supreme Court 35 (1986). The case in question was Swann v. Charlotte-Mecklenburg Board of Education, 402 U.S. 1 (1971).
10. 381 U.S. 479 (1965).
11. Id. at 484.
12. Schwartz, The Unpublished Opinions of the Warren Court 238 (1985). This statement does not appear in the final Griswold opinion.
13. 381 U.S. at 508.
14. Id. at 510.
15. In Time, Inc. v. Hill, 385 U.S. 374 (1967). The draft opinion is reprinted in Schwartz, op. cit. supra note 12, at 245.
16. The Black memo is reprinted, id. at 272. The quotes from the memo are from id. at 274–277, 285.
17. Adamson v. California, 332 U.S. 46, 69 (1947) (dissent).
18. Quoted in Schwartz, The Supreme Court: Constitutional Revolution in Retrospect 185 (1957).
19. Supra note 10.
20. Bork, Tradition and Morality in Constitutional Law 10 (1984).
21. Bork, The Tempting of America 147 (1989).
22. Bork, in The Great Debate: Interpreting Our Written Constitution 48, 49 (1986).
23. Bork, Neutral Principles and Some First Amendment Problems, 47 Indiana Law Journal 1, 10 (1971). See similarly Bork, op. cit. supra note 21, at 257.
24. Bork, supra note 22, at 11.
25. Dissenting, in Morrison v. Olson, 487 U.S. 654, 711 (1988).
26. Bork, op. cit. supra note 21, at 242.
27. Bork, supra note 22, at 9.
28. Id. at 10.
29. Ibid. See similarly Bork, op. cit. supra note 21, at 258–259.
30. Compare Barber, in Murphy and Pritchett, Courts, Judges, and Politics 643 (4th ed. 1986).
31. Compare 1 Pound, Jurisprudence 265 (1959).
32. Compare Delgado, Physical Control of the Mind 233 (1969).
33. Vonnegut, Slaughterhouse-Five.
34. Dennis v. United States, 341 U.S. 494, 508 (1951).
35. Pound, The Formative Era of American Law 26 (1950).
36. Wilkinson v. Leland, 2 Pet. 627, 646–647 (U.S. 1829).
37. Fletcher v. Peck, 6 Cranch 87, 135 (U.S. 1810).
38. White v. White, 5 Barb. 474, 484 (N.Y. 1849).
39. Pound, op. cit. supra note 35, at 17.
40. Compare Grey, Do We Have an Unwritten Constitution? 27 Stanford Law Review 703, 715 (1975).
41. Wood, The Creation of the American Republic 293 (1969). The Cannon quotes are from ibid.
42. Grey, supra note 40, at 716.
43. Calder v. Bull, 3 Dall. 386, 388 (U.S. 1798).
44. Dash v. Van Kleeck, 7 Johns. 477, 505 (N.Y. 1811).

45. See Patterson, The Forgotten Ninth Amendment (1955). Most of the literature on the amendment is reprinted in The Rights Retained by the People (Barnett ed. 1989).

46. 1 Blackstone's Commentaries 120.

47. 5 The Founders' Constitution 394 (Kurland and Lerner eds. 1987).

48. 1 Schwartz, The Bill of Rights: A Documentary History 200 (1971).

49. These include the guarantees of habeas corpus (the provision authorizing suspension of the writ has uniformly been interpreted as guaranteeing habeas corpus in the absence of suspension), trial by jury in criminal cases, the privileges and immunities of state citizens, and the prohibitions against bills of attainder, ex post facto laws, and religious tests. These guarantees would doubtless have been included in the Federal Bill of Rights, had they not already been contained in the text of the Constitution.

50. Schwartz, op. cit. supra note 48, at 438.

51. Ibid.

52. Id. at 439.

53. Mee, The Genius of the People 27 (1987).

54. The Federalist, No. 84.

55. Massachusetts, South Carolina, New Hampshire, Virginia, and New York. See Schwartz, The Great Rights of Mankind: A History of the American Bill of Rights 119 et seq. (1977).

56. 2 Schwartz, op. cit. supra note 48, at 1003.

57. 1 id. at 621.

58. 2 id. at 844.

59. Id. at 912, 970.

60. Schwartz, op. cit. supra note 55, at 233.

61. Except for a later change from "this Constitution" to "the Constitution," there was practically no congressional debate on the amendment. The only issue raised was in a statement by Gerry that "it ought to be 'deny or impair,' for the word 'disparage' was not of plain import." His motion to make the alteration was not seconded and the amendment then passed, apparently without further discussion. See 2 Schwartz, op. cit. supra note 48, at 1112.

62. Id. at 825.

63. Ibid.

64. Ibid.

65. Berger, The Ninth Amendment, 66 Cornell Law Review 1, 2–3 (1980).

66. 2 Schwartz, op. cit. supra note 48, at 1190.

67. Id. at 1031.

68. Richmond Newspapers v. Virginia, 448 U.S. 555, 579, n. 15 (1980).

69. Compare Dunbar, James Madison and the Ninth Amendment, 42 Virginia Law Review 627, 636–637 (1956).

70. Hardin Burnley to Madison, November 28, 1789, in 2 Schwartz, op. cit. supra note 48, at 1188.

71. Compare Dunbar, supra note 69, at 638.

72. Loc. cit. supra note 70.

73. Madison, supra note 67.

74. Loc. cit. supra note 70.

75. The Miscellaneous Writings of Joseph Story 519 (W. W. Story ed. 1852).
76. 1 Farrand, The Records of the Federal Convention of 1787, 541 (1911). See similarly, id. at 424, 533–534; 2 id. at 123.
77. Vanhorne's Lessee v. Dorrance, 2 Dall. 304, 310 (C. C. Pa. 1795).
78. Calder v. Bull, 3 Dall. 386, 388 (U.S. 1798).
79. Ibid.
80. Ibid.
81. 20 Wall. 655 (U.S. 1875).
82. Id. at 664.
83. Id. at 663.
84. Id. at 668–669.
85. Id. at 663.
86. Ibid.
87. Pound, Introduction, in Patterson, op. cit. supra note 45, at v.
88. The John Adams Papers 184 (Donovan ed. 1965).
89. See Schwartz, The Law in America: A History 150–151 (1974).
90. Prince v. Massachusetts, 321 U.S. 158, 166 (1944).
91. Tribe, American Constitutional Law 1414 (2d ed. 1988).
92. 262 U.S. 390 (1923).
93. 268 U.S. 510 (1925).
94. 347 U.S. 497 (1954).
95. 347 U.S. 483 (1954).
96. See Schwartz, Super Chief: Earl Warren and His Supreme Court—A Judicial Biography 99 (1983).
97. Ibid.
98. Dissenting, in Griswold v. Connecticut, 381 U.S. 479, 516 (1965).
99. 388 U.S. 1 (1967).
100. Schwartz, op. cit. supra note 96, at 668–669.
101. Id. at 669.
102. 388 U.S. at 12.
103. Supra note 10.
104. Supra p. 38.
105. Goldberg, J., concurring, 381 U.S. at 491.
106. See Schwartz, op. cit. supra note 96, at 577–578.
107. See Schwartz, op. cit. supra note 12, at 229.
108. Id. at 237.
109. Lamont v. Postmaster General, 381 U.S. 301, 308 (1965).
110. 381 U.S. at 484.
111. Id. at 486.
112. See Schwartz, op. cit. supra note 96, at 579–580.
113. Joined by Warren, C.J., and Brennan, J.
114. 381 U.S. at 484.
115. Id. at 491.
116. Compare Pound, Introduction, in Patterson, op. cit. supra note 45, at iii: "Nothing in the Constitution should be taken to be idle and of no moment."
117. 381 U.S. at 491.
118. Ibid.

119. Id. at 492.
120. Ibid.
121. Id. at 499.
122. Id. at 496.
123. Carey v. Population Services, 431 U.S. 678, 687 (1977).
124. Eisenstadt v. Baird, 405 U.S. 438, 453 (1973) (emphasis in original).
125. Schwartz, op. cit. supra note 12, at 243. The Fortas draft was the proposed opinion of the Court in Time, Inc. v. Hill, 385 U.S. 374 (1967). The last sentence quoted is contained in the ultimate Fortas dissent. Id. at 413.
126. Quilloin v. Walcott, 434 U.S. 246, 255 (1978).
127. Carey v. Population Services, 431 U.S. 678, 685 (1977).
128. 410 U.S. 113 (1973).
129. Id. at 210–211.
130. Schwartz, The Unpublished Opinions of the Burger Court 88 (1988).
131. 410 U.S. at 211–214.
132. Dissenting, in Olmstead v. United States, 277 U.S. 438, 478 (1928).
133. Strunsky, The Invasion of Privacy: The Modern Case of Mistaken Identity, 28 The American Scholar 219 (1959).
134. The phrase is from Browning's "Paracelsus."
135. Pavesich v. New England Life Ins. Co., 50 S.E. 68, 70 (Ga. 1905).
136. 410 U.S. at 213 (italics omitted).
137. McGowan v. Maryland, 366 U.S. 420 (1961).
138. Schwartz, op. cit. supra note 96, at 380.
139. Miller v. School District No. 167, 495 F.2d 658, 664, n.25 (7th Cir. 1974).
140. 381 U.S. at 496.
141. Id. at 497.
142. Ibid.
143. 425 U.S. 238 (1976).
144. Id. at 244.
145. Id. at 249.
146. Supra note 10.
147. 330 U.S. 75 (1947).
148. Id. at 94, 95. The law was nevertheless upheld because of the public interest in a nonpolitical civil service.
149. Harper v. Virginia Election Board, 383 U.S. 663, 667, 670 (1966).
150. Lansdale v. Tyler Junior College, 470 F.2d 659, 663 (11th Cir. 1987).
151. DeWeese v. Palm Beach, 812 F.2d 1365, 1367 (11th Cir. 1987).
152. Quoted in Miller v. School District No. 167, 495 F.2d 658, 665, n.26 (7th Cir. 1974).
153. 448 U.S. 555 (1980).
154. Schwartz, op. cit. supra note 130, at 485–486.
155. Id. at 486–487.
156. See Houchins v. KQED, 438 U.S. 1 (1978).
157. 448 U.S. at 579.
158. Id. at 579–580.
159. 357 U.S. 449 (1958).
160. Schwartz, op. cit. supra note 96, at 304.

161. Estelle v. Williams, 425 U.S. 501, 503 (1976).
162. 397 U.S. 358 (1970).
163. Black had voted with the majority at the conference.
164. 397 U.S. at 378 (dissent).
165. Crandall v. Nevada, 6 Wall. 35 (U.S. 1868).
166. Shapiro v. Thompson, 394 U.S. 618, 630–631 (1969).
167. 367 U.S. 497 (1961).
168. Supra note 10.
169. Schwartz, op. cit. supra note 96, at 379.
170. 367 U.S. at 540, 541, 542–543.
171. Id. at 543.
172. Supra note 162.
173. 397 U.S. at 372.
174. Poe v. Ullman, 367 U.S. at 542.
175. Harlan, J., id. at 541, quoting from Corfield v. Coryell, 6 Fed. Cas. 546 (C. C. Pa. 1823) (italics omitted).
176. Supra note 153.
177. 448 U.S. at 580.
178. Supra note 162.
179. 397 U.S. at 372, n. 5.
180. Id. at 377, 378.
181. Supra note 10.
182. Rochin v. California, 342 U.S. 165, 177 (1952).
183. LeRoy Fibre Co. v. Chicago, Mil. & St. P. Ry., 232 U.S. 340, 354 (1914).
184. Supra p. 42.
185. Goldberg, J., concurring, in Griswold v. Connecticut, 381 U.S. at 493.
186. 367 U.S. at 544.
187. Rochin v. California, 342 U.S. 165, 170 (1952).
188. Compare id. at 171.
189. 1 Bryce, The American Commonwealth 274 (1917).
190. Hobbes, in Hall, Readings in Jurisprudence 53 (1938).
191. Rochin v. California, 342 U.S. 165, 169 (1952).
192. Ibid.
193. Ibid.
194. Id. at 171–172.
195. Cahn, Authority and Responsibility, 51 Columbia Law Review 838, 850 (1951).

NOTES TO CHAPTER 3

1. Siegan, Economic Liberties and the Constitution (1980).
2. The Siegan nomination was rejected by the Senate Judiciary Committee. N.Y. Times, July 15, 1988, p. A12.
3. Siegan, op. cit. supra note 1, at 7.
4. Ibid.
5. Id. at 6–7.
6. 410 U.S. 113 (1973).

7. 198 U.S. 45 (1905).

8. 410 U.S. at 174.

9. Lincoln Union v. Northwestern Co., 335 U.S. 525, 537 (1949).

10. Siegan, op. cit. supra note 1, at 23.

11. 198 U.S. at 56.

12. Id. at 57.

13. Id. at 58.

14. Id. at 59.

15. Ibid.

16. Id. at 72.

17. Brandeis, J., dissenting, in Burns Baking Co. v. Bryan, 264 U.S. 504, 534 (1924).

18. Laski, The American Democracy 111 (1948).

19. Ferguson v. Skrupa, 372 U.S. 726, 729 (1963).

20. Ibid.

21. Id. at 730.

22. 198 U.S. at 75.

23. Ferguson v. Skrupa, 372 U.S. 726, 731–732 (1963).

24. Id. at 732.

25. Compare Kovacs v. Cooper, 336 U.S. 77, 95 (1949).

26. Siegan, The Supreme Court's Constitution 41 (1987).

27. Siegan, op. cit. supra note 1, at 318.

28. Paterson, J., in Vanhorne's Lessee v. Dorrance, 2 Dall. 304, 310 (C. C. Pa. 1795). Compare the similar statements made on the floor of the Framers' Convention. See 1 Farrand, The Records of the Federal Convention of 1787, 424, 533–4 (1911) ("property was the main object of Society"), 541 ("property was the primary object of Society"), 2 id. at 123.

29. 6 The Works of John Adams, 280 (C. F. Adams ed. 1851).

30. Dillon, Address of the President, 15 A.B.A. Reports 167, 210 (1892).

31. Brandeis, Business—A Profession liv (1914).

32. Children's Hospital v. Adkins, 284 Fed. 613, 622 (D.C. Cir. 1922).

33. Jhering, quoted in 1 Pound, Jurisprudence 429–430 (1959).

34. Siegan, op. cit. supra note 1, at 320.

35. Ibid.

36. Ibid.

37. Siegan, Rehabilitating *Lochner*, 22 San Diego Law Review 453 (1985).

38. Stevens, Judicial Restraint, 22 San Diego Law Review 437, 448 (1985).

39. Siegan, supra note 37, at 454.

40. Ferguson v. Skrupa, 372 U.S. 726, 731–732 (1963).

41. Supra p. 76.

42. Frankfurter, Of Law and Men 175 (1956).

43. The Words of Justice Brandeis, 54 (Goldman ed. 1953).

44. The term stems from the brief submitted by Brandeis in Muller v. Oregon, 208 U.S. 412 (1908).

45. 285 U.S. 262 (1932).

46. Id. at 282.

47. Id. at 291.

48. Id. at 292.

49. Id. at 300.
50. Loc. cit. supra note 43.
51. 285 U.S. at 304.
52. Id. at 286–287.
53. Posner, Economic Analysis of Law 590 (3d ed. 1986).
54. Id. at 592.
55. Id. at 593.
56. Fox and Sullivan, Antitrust—Retrospect and Prospective: Where Are We Coming? Where Are We Going? 62 New York University Law Review 936, 957 (1987).
57. See Cooley, A Treatise on the Constitutional Limitations which Rest upon the Legislative Power of the States of the American Union 356 (1868).
58. 157 U.S. 429 (1895).
59. Id. at 549, 39 Lawyers' Edition 807.
60. Id. at 607.
61. See Hume v. Moore-McCormack Lines, 121 F.2d 336, 339–340 (2d Cir. 1941).
62. Concurring, in American Federation of Labor v. American Sash Co., 335 U.S. 538, 543 (1949).
63. Jackson, The Struggle for Judicial Supremacy 48 (1941).
64. Budd v. New York, 143 U.S. 517, 551 (1892).
65. Douglas, J., dissenting, in Poe v. Ullman, 367 U.S. 497, 517 (1961).
66. Loc. cit. supra note 62.
67. 198 U.S. at 57.
68. Ibid.
69. Holmes, J., dissenting, in Adkins v. Children's Hospital, 261 U.S. 525, 568 (1923).
70. Venable, Growth or Evolution of Law, 23 A.B.A. Reports 278, 298 (1900).
71. See Hurst, Law and the Conditions of Freedom 10 (1956).
72. Written in 1891. See Pound, Liberty of Contract, 18 Yale Law Journal 454, 455 (1909).
73. Compare Pound, An Introduction to the Philosophy of Law 149 (1954).
74. Compare Pound, supra note 72, at 455–456.
75. Woolworth, Development of the Law of Contracts, 19 A.B.A. Reports 287, 318 (1896).
76. 2 Ely, Property and Contract in Their Relations to the Distribution of Wealth 555 (1914).
77. See Judson, Liberty of Contract under the Police Power, 14 A.B.A. Reports 231, 257 (1891).
78. West Coast Hotel Co. v. Parrish, 300 U.S. 379, 391 (1937).
79. Hand, Due Process of Law and the Eight-Hour Day, 21 Harvard Law Review 495, 495–496 (1908).
80. 165 U.S. 578 (1897).
81. Id. at 589.
82. Pound, op. cit. supra note 73, at 133.
83. See Hurst, op. cit. supra note 71, at 14.
84. Printing Co. v. Sampson, 19 Eq. 462, 465 (1875).
85. See Pound, op. cit. supra note 73, at 150.
86. Compare Pound, The Spirit of the Common Law 101 (1963 ed.). For cases following

the view stated, see Leep v. Railway Co., 58 Ark. 407 (1894); Ritchie v. People, 155 Ill. 98 (1895); Commonwealth v. Perry, 155 Mass. 117 (1891); State v. Loomis, 115 Mo. 307 (1893).

87. Maine, Popular Government 51 (1886).
88. So termed in M. Witmark & Sons v. Fred Fisher Music Co., 125 F.2d 949, 962, n. 17 (2d Cir. 1942).
89. Maine, Ancient Law 170 (9th ed. 1883).
90. See 1 Pound, Jurisprudence 207 (1959).
91. Farrington v. Tennessee, 95 U.S. 679, 682 (1878).
92. Compare 1 Pound, Jurisprudence 207–208.
93. In Centralization and the Law (Bigelow ed. 1906).
94. Pound, Interpretations of Legal History 60 (1923).
95. Woolworth, supra note 75, at 287.
96. 1 Pound, Jurisprudence 208.
97. Compare Pound, op. cit. supra note 94, at 63.
98. Addams, 13 American Journal of Sociology 772 (1908).
99. Compare 4 Pound, Jurisprudence 144–145.
100. Hitchcock, Address of the President, 13 A.B.A. Reports 164 (1890).
101. Hand, supra note 79, at 497.
102. Pound, supra note 72, at 481–482.
103. Spencer, Social Statics (abridged and revised) together with The Man Versus The State 277 (1892). The point made was noted in Twiss, Lawyers and the Constitution 130 (1942).
104. Spencer, op. cit. supra note 103, at 296–299.
105. "The power to pass usury laws exists by immemorial usage." State v. Goodwill, 10 S.E. 285, 287 (W. Va. 1889).
106. Frorer v. People, 31 N.E. 395, 399 (Ill. 1892).
107. Ely, op. cit. supra note 76, at 603.
108. Adair v. United States, 298 U.S. 161, 174–175 (1908).
109. State v. Haun, 59 Pac. 340, 346 (Kan. 1899).
110. Braceville Coal Co. v. People, 35 N.E. 62, 64 (Ill. 1893); State v. Haun, 59 Pac. 340, 346 (Kan. 1899).
111. Lochner v. New York, 198 U.S. 45, 57 (1905).
112. State v. Goodwill, 10 S.E. 285, 288 (W. Va. 1889).
113. Goodcharles v. Wigeman, 6 Atl. 354, 356 (Pa. 1886). See Pound, Jurisprudence 534.
114. Pound, supra note 72, at 454.
115. Compare 1 Pound, Jurisprudence, at 534.
116. Op. cit. supra note 43, at 79.
117. Higgins, A New Province for Law and Order, 29 Harvard Law Review 13, 29 (1915).
118. Vernon v. Bethell, 2 Eden 110, 113 (1762).
119. Stone, J., dissenting, in Morehead v. New York ex rel. Tipaldo, 298 U.S. 587, 632 (1936).
120. Quoted in Clark, Great Sayings by Great Lawyers 649 (1926).
121. 198 U.S. at 75.
122. People v. Budd, 117 N.Y. 1, 46–47 (1889) (dissenting opinion).

123. Compare Frankfurter, Mr. Justice Holmes and the Supreme Court 32 (1938).
124. Coauthored by C. D. Warner.
125. Garraty, The New Commonwealth 1 (1968).
126. Adams, The Education of Henry Adams 297−298 (1931 ed.).
127. Brown, The Distribution of Property, 16 A.B.A. Reports, 213, 227 (1893).
128. Nevins, America Through British Eyes 497 (1948).
129. Compare 1 The Collected Papers of Frederick William Maitland 267 (Fisher ed. 1911).
130. Spencer, op. cit. supra note 103, at 55, 117, 137.
131. Adams, op. cit. supra note 126, at 284.
132. Compare 1 Bryce, The American Commonwealth 401 (1917 ed.).
133. Spencer, op. cit. supra note 103, at 32.
134. See Garraty, op. cit. supra note 125, at 315.
135. Venable, Growth or Evolution of Law, 23 A.B.A. Reports 278, 302 (1900).
136. Choate, American Addresses 92 (1911).
137. Matter of Jacobs, 98 N.Y. 98, 104−105, 115 (1885).
138. People v. Gillson, 109 N.Y. 389, 398−399 (1888).
139. Holmes, J., dissenting, 198 U.S. at 75.
140. Id. at 63, 61.
141. Tiedeman, The Unwritten Constitution of the United States 76 (1890).
142. Id. at 76−79.
143. Woolworth, Address of the President, 20 A.B.A. Reports 203, 244 (1897).
144. Adams, op. cit. supra note 126, at 231.
145. Woolworth, The Development of the Law of Contracts, 19 A.B.A. Reports 287, 317 (1896).
146. Jackson, Indemnity the Essence of Insurance, 10 A.B.A. Reports, 261, 280−281 (1887).
147. Garraty, op. cit. supra note 125, at 315.
148. Parker, The Tyrannies of Free Government, 18 A.B.A. Reports 295, 302 (1895).
149. Op. cit. supra note 43, at 121.
150. Frank, J., dissenting, in M. Witmark & Sons v. Fred Fisher Music Co., 125 F.2d 949, 963 (2d Cir. 1942).
151. 3 Parrington, Main Currents in American Thought 17 (1930).
152. Frank, J., dissenting, in M. Witmark & Sons v. Fred Fisher Music Co., 125 F.2d 949, 967 (2d Cir. 1942).
153. Compare Dicey, Lectures on the Relation Between Law and Public Opinion in England During the Nineteenth Century 152 (2d ed. 1926).
154. Adams, in op. cit. supra note 93, at 64−65.
155. 2 Bryce, op. cit. supra note 132, at 591−594.
156. Bork, The Tempting of America 225 (1989).
157. Hume v. Moore-McCormack Lines, 121 F.2d 336, 340 (2d Cir. 194).
158. Ibid.

NOTES TO CHAPTER 4

1. Epstein's approach is contained in his Takings: Private Property and the Power of Eminent Domain (1985)—hereafter cited as "Epstein."

2. United States v. Carmack, 329 U.S. 230, 236 (1946).
3. Epstein 22, quoting 2 Blackstone's Commentaries 2.
4. Ibid.
5. Id. at 23.
6. Compare Merrill, Rent Seeking and the Compensation Principle, 80 Northwestern University Law Review 1561, 1566 (1986).
7. Grey, The Malthusian Constitution, 41 University of Miami Law Review 21, 23–24 (1986).
8. Charles River Bridge v. Warren Bridge, 11 Pet. 420, 642 (U.S. 1837).
9. See, e.g., United States v. Carmack, 329 U.S. 230 (1946).
10. Epstein 161, referring to Berman v. Parker, infra note 20.
11. 147 U.S. 282 (1893).
12. Id. at 297.
13. People v. La Fetra, 230 N.Y. 429, 450 (1921).
14. New York City Housing Authority v. Muller, 270 N.Y. 333, 341 (1936).
15. Gohld Realty Co. v. Hartford, 104 A.2d 365, 368–369 (Conn. 1954).
16. Barnidge v. United States, 101 F.2d 295, 298 (8th Cir. 1939).
17. Hawaii Housing Authority v. Midkiff, 467 U.S. 229, 240 (1984).
18. See Berman v. Parker, 348 U.S. 26, 33 (1954).
19. Epstein 162.
20. 348 U.S. 26 (1954).
21. Hawaii Housing Authority v. Midkiff, 467 U.S. 229, 240 (1984).
22. Epstein 178–179.
23. 348 U.S. at 33–34.
24. Schneider v. District of Columbia, 117 F. Supp. 705, 724 (D.C. 1953).
25. 348 U.S. at 32–33.
26. 2 Ely, Property and Contract in Their Relations to the Distribution of Wealth 783 (1914).
27. Passaic v. Paterson Bill Posting Co., 62 Atl. 267, 268 (N.J. 1905).
28. Loc. cit. supra note 26.
29. Note, 13 Law Quarterly Review 337, 338 (1897). This note is unsigned, but Pollock is stated as the author in 3 Pound, Jurisprudence 314 (1959).
30. See 1 Schwartz, The Bill of Rights: A Documentary History 85 (1971).
31. Id. at 73.
32. Id. at 322.
33. Id. at 323.
34. Id. at 342.
35. Id. at 400.
36. 2 id. at 1027.
37. Treanor, The Origins and Original Significance of the Just Compensation Clause of the Fifth Amendment, 94 Yale Law Journal 694, 711 (1985).
38. See Schwartz, The Great Rights of Mankind: A History of the American Bill of Rights 171 (1977).
39. Id. at 236.
40. Johnson, A Dictionary of the English Language (1755).
41. Epstein 101.
42. Tribe, American Constitutional Law 592–593 (2d ed. 1988).

43. 276 U.S. 272 (1928).
44. Keystone Bituminous Coal Ass'n v. DeBenedictis, 480 U.S. 470, 490 (1987).
45. Epstein 114–115.
46. Id. at 115.
47. 276 U.S. at 280.
48. Chicago B. & Q. R. Co. v. Chicago, 166 U.S. 226 (1897).
49. Goldblatt v. Hempstead, 369 U.S. 590, 594 (1962).
50. 1 Nichols, The Law of Eminent Domain 70 (3d ed. 1950).
51. Franco-Italian Packing Co. v. United States, 128 F. Supp. 408, 414 (Ct. Cl. 1955).
52. 369 U.S. 590 (1962).
53. Id. at 593.
54. United States v. Powelson, 319 U.S. 266, 284 (1943).
55. See Legal Tender Cases, 12 Wall. 457, 551 (U.S. 1871).
56. Supra p. 99.
57. Kaiser Aetna v. United States, 444 U.S. 164, 176 (1979).
58. Andrus v. Allard, 444 U.S. 51, 65–66 (1979).
59. Cheves v. Whitehead, 1 F. Supp. 321, 324 (S.D. Ga. 1932).
60. United States v. Dickinson, 331 U.S. 745, 748 (1947).
61. United States v. General Motors Corp., 323 U.S. 373, 378 (1945).
62. United States v. Kansas City Life Ins. Co., 339 U.S. 799, 809 (1950).
63. Compare United States v. Causby, 328 U.S. 256, 261 (1946).
64. United States v. Causby, 328 U.S. 256 (1946).
65. Griggs v. Allegheny County, 369 U.S. 84, 91 (1962).
66. United States v. Causby, 328 U.S. 256, 264–265 (1946).
67. 272 U.S. 365 (1926).
68. Id. at 386–387.
69. Epstein, 131–132.
70. Id. at 133.
71. 272 U.S. at 391.
72. 447 U.S. 255 (1980).
73. Id. at 261.
74. "The parties who benefit as of right from private covenants are well identified, while the persons who benefit from zoning normally are not." Epstein 104.
75. The quotes in this paragraph are from ibid.
76. Haas v. San Francisco, 605 F.2d 1117, 1121 (9th Cir. 1979).
77. Quoted in Williams, Planning Law and Democratic Living, 20 Law and Contemporary Problems 317, 333 (1955).
78. Ibid.
79. Compare id. at 318.
80. Gorieb v. Fox, 274 U.S. 603 (1927).
81. St. Louis Poster Advertising Co. v. St. Louis, 249 U.S. 269, 274 (1919).
82. As in State v. Wieland, 69 N.W.2d 217 (Wis. 1955). Compare the requirement that, after half of the buildings in a block are of a certain style, the remainder shall be of a "substantially similar" style. See Haar, Land-Use Planning, 312 (1959).
83. Compare Ordinance No. 21, 23–45 (1951), of Williamsburg, Virginia, which provides that any new building "shall have such design and character as not to

detract from the value and general harmony of buildings already existing in the surrounding area."

84. See State v. Wieland, 69 N.W.2d 217 (Wis. 1955); New Orleans v. Levy, 64 S.2d 798 (La. 1953); New Orleans v. Impastato, 3 S.2d 559 (La. 1941) (control over "appearance, color, texture of materials and architectural design" of buildings to be erected or altered in New Orleans); Opinion of the Justices, 128 N.E.2d 557 (Mass. 1955) (preservation of historic buildings and districts in Nantucket).

85. State v. Wieland, 69 N.W.2d 217, 222 (Wis. 1955).

86. 348 U.S. 26 (1954).

87. Supra p. 102.

88. 348 U.S. at 33.

89. Epstein 133.

90. Supra p. 104.

91. State v. New Orleans, 97 So. 440, 444 (La. 1923).

92. 260 U.S. 393 (1922).

93. Id. at 417.

94. Id. at 415.

95. Epstein 63–64.

96. 260 U.S. at 414.

97. Id. at 418–419.

98. Id. at 420.

99. 480 U.S. 470 (1987).

100. Id. at 484.

101. 260 U.S. at 413–414.

102. See Large, The Supreme Court and the Takings Clause: The Search for a Better Rule, 18 Environmental Law 3, 11–12 (1987).

103. Keystone Bituminous Coal Ass'n v. DeBenedictis, 480 U.S. at 509–510. See Large, supra note 102, at 36.

104. 480 U.S. at 496, 499.

105. 260 U.S. at 419.

106. 480 U.S. at 500.

107. Large, supra note 102, at 35.

108. 260 U.S. at 413.

109. Ibid.

110. Id. at 415.

111. Id. at 414.

112. First English Church v. Los Angeles County, 482 U.S. 304, 329 (1987).

113. San Diego Gas & Elec. Co. v. San Diego, 450 U.S. 621, 652 (1981).

114. Pumpelly v. Green Bay Co., 13 Wall. 166, 167–168 (U.S. 1872).

115. San Diego Gas & Elec. Co. v. San Diego, 450 U.S. 621, 653 (1981).

116. 444 U.S. 51 (1979).

117. Epstein 76.

118. 444 U.S. at 65–66.

119. Supra note 114.

120. Keystone Bituminous Coal Ass'n. v. DeBenedictis, 480 U.S. at 497.

121. Scalia, J., dissenting, in Pennell v. San Jose, U.S. 485 U.S. 1, 20 (1988).

122. Compare Stevens, J., dissenting, in First English Church v. Los Angeles County, 482 U.S. 304, 329 (1987).

123. Andrus v. Allard, 444 U.S. at 65.

124. The famous phrase of Stone, J., dissenting, in United States v. Butler, 297 U.S. 1, 85 (1936).

125. Posner, Economic Analysis of Law 52 (3d ed. 1986).

126. Id. at 52–53.

127. Railroad Retirement Board v. Alton R. Co., 295 U.S. 330, 374 (1935).

128. Helvering v. Davis, 301 U.S. 619 (1937); Steward Machine Co. v. Davis, 301 U.S. 548 (1937); Carmichael v. Southern Coal Co., 301 U.S. 495 (1937).

129. Compare Hughes, C.J., dissenting, in Railroad Retirement Board v. Alton R. Co., 295 U.S. 330, 384 (1935).

130. Supra note 128.

131. Reich, The New Property, 73 Yale Law Journal 733 (1964).

132. Helvering v. Davis, 301 U.S. 619, 640–641 (1937).

133. Epstein 100, 95.

134. Id. at 299.

135. Since Carmichael v. Southern Coal Co., 301 U.S. 495 (1937).

136. Epstein 310.

137. Carmichael v. Southern Coal Co., 301 U.S. 495, 528 (1937).

138. Id. at 521–522.

139. Epstein 314, 318, 324.

140. Id. at 322.

141. United States v. Carmack, 329 U.S. 230, 241–242 (1946).

142. Lochner v. New York, 198 U.S. 45 (1905).

143. Epstein, 324, 329.

144. Id. at 324.

145. Ross, Taking *Takings* Seriously, 80 Northwestern University Law Review 1591, 1604 (1986).

146. Epstein 329.

147. 447 U.S. 74 (1980).

148. 467 U.S. 229 (1984).

149. Epstein in Economic Liberties and the Judiciary 43 (Dorne and Manne eds. 1987).

150. Epstein 181.

151. 447 U.S. at 84.

152. 467 U.S. at 241.

153. 482 U.S. 304 (1987).

154. 483 U.S. 825 (1987).

155. 481 U.S. 704 (1987).

156. Id. at 719. Andrus v. Allard is discussed supra p. 122.

157. 485 U.S. 1 (1988).

158. Id. at 22.

159. Epstein, Rent Control and the Theory of Efficient Regulation, 54 Brooklyn Law Review 741, 755 (1988).

160. Chicago Board of Realtors v. Chicago, 819 F.2d 732, 745 (7th Cir. 1987).

161. 833 F.2d 1270 (9th Cir. 1986).

162. Id. at 1273.

163. Epstein, supra note 159, at 756.
164. 833 F.2d at 1275.
165. Id. at 1276–1277.
166. Id. at 1280.
167. Id. at 1278.
168. Compare id. at 1281–1284 (dissent from denial of en banc hearing).
169. Epstein, supra note 159, at 758.
170. 261 U.S. 525 (1923).
171. Id. at 557.
172. Supra note 142.
173. Bork, The Tempting of America 230 (1989).

NOTES TO CHAPTER 5

1. Graglia, Disaster by Decree: The Supreme Court Decisions on Race and the Schools (1976). The Reagan Administration had planned to appoint Professor Graglia to a federal appeals court, but did not make the nomination because of strong opposition. N.Y. Times, August 7, 1986, p. A25.
2. Brown v. Board of Education, 347 U.S. 483 (1954).
3. Graglia, When Honesty Is "Simply . . . Impractical" for the Supreme Court: How the Constitution Came to Require Busing for School Racial Balance, 85 Michigan Law Review 1153 (1987).
4. Swann v. Charlotte-Mecklenburg Board of Education, 402 U.S. 1 (1971); Schwartz, Swann's Way: The School Busing Case and the Supreme Court (1986).
5. Green v. County School Board, 391 U.S. 430, 438 (1968).
6. Dred Scott v. Sandford, 19 How. 393 (U.S. 1857).
7. Graglia, supra note 3, at 1154.
8. Lewis, Without Fear or Favor: A Biography of Chief Justice Roger Brooke Taney 470 (1965). This comment was about a pamphlet excoriating Chief Justice Taney after Dred Scott v. Sandford, 19 How. 393 (U.S. 1857).
9. Supra p. 24.
10. Siegan, The Supreme Court's Constitution: An Inquiry into Judicial Review and Its Impact on Society 93 (1987).
11. Berger, Government by Judiciary: The Transformation of the Fourteenth Amendment 125 (1977).
12. Supra p. 22.
13. 163 U.S. 537 (1896).
14. Graglia, op. cit. supra note 1, at 31–32.
15. Id. at 32.
16. Wilkinson, From Brown to Bakke: The Supreme Court and School Integration: 1954–1978, 35 (1979).
17. N.Y. Times, May 18, 1954, quoted in Kluger, Simple Justice 711 (1975).
18. 347 U.S. at 494, n.11.
19. Graglia, op. cit. supra note 1, at 27.
20. Ibid.

21. Schwartz, Super Chief: Earl Warren and His Supreme Court—A Judicial Biography 107 (1983).
22. Myrdal, An American Dilemma (1944).
23. Loc. cit. supra note 21.
24. Goldberg, Equality and Governmental Action, 39 New York University Law Review 205 (1964).
25. Brown v. Board of Education, 349 U.S. 294 (1955).
26. Id. at 301.
27. Schwartz, The Unpublished Opinions of the Warren Court 468 (1985).
28. See Schwartz, op. cit. supra note 21, at 93.
29. 349 U.S. at 301.
30. Id. at 299.
31. Id. at 300.
32. Siegan, op. cit. supra note 10, at 101. Section 5 gives Congress the power to enforce the amendment "by appropriate legislation."
33. Schwartz, op. cit. supra note 21, at 117–118.
34. Id. at 117.
35. See Schwartz, op. cit. supra note 4, at 114. The Burger draft is reprinted, id. at 208.
36. Id. at 117.
37. See id. at 117–184.
38. 402 U.S. at 15–16.
39. Id. at 17.
40. Compare 1 Pomeroy, Equity Jurisprudence § 423 (2d ed. 1892).
41. 402 U.S. at 15–16.
42. See Schwartz, op. cit. supra note 4, at 152–153.
43. Infra note 45.
44. Supra note 4.
45. 391 U.S. 430 (1968).
46. See Schwartz, op. cit. supra note 21, at 704.
47. Ibid. Compare Earl Warren–Justices, May 7, 1954, quoted id. at 97.
48. Id. at 704.
49. Id. at 704–705.
50. Id. at 705.
51. 391 U.S. at 435.
52. Id. at 437–438.
53. Id. at 439.
54. Ibid.
55. Schwartz, op. cit. supra note 21, at 116.
56. Id. at 706.
57. Graglia, op. cit. supra note 1, at 67.
58. Graglia, supra note 3, at 1157.
59. Siegan, op. cit. supra note 10, at 102.
60. Briggs v. Elliott, 132 F. Supp. 776, 777 (E.D.S.C. 1955). See Graglia, op. cit. supra note 1, at 38.
61. Compare Wilkinson, op. cit. supra note 16, at 82.
62. Brown v. Board of Education, 349 U.S. at 301.

63. Schwartz, op. cit. supra note 21, at 118.
64. Morison, The Oxford History of the American People 1086 (1965).
65. Supra note 53.
66. Schwartz, op. cit. supra note 4, at 148.
67. Id. at 152.
68. Graglia, op. cit. supra note 1, at 85.
69. Felix Frankfurter–Dear Brethren, January 15, 1954. Harold H. Burton Papers, Library of Congress.
70. United States v. Montgomery County Board of Education, 395 U.S. 225, 228 (1969).
71. Compare ibid.
72. Richmond Times-Dispatch, July 17, 1977, p. A–1.
73. Supra note 53.
74. 402 U.S. at 15–16.
75. Supra note 69.
76. Ibid.
77. Ibid.
78. Graglia, op. cit. supra note 1, at 257.
79. Siegan, op. cit. supra note 10, at 104.
80. Supra note 45.
81. 391 U.S. at 442, n. 6.
82. Compare Wilkinson, op. cit. supra note 16, at 117.
83. See Schwartz, op. cit. supra note 4, at 66.
84. United States v. Montgomery County Board of Education, 395 U.S. 225, 231 (1969).
85. Regents of the University of California v. Bakke, 438 U.S. 265 (1978).
86. Graglia, Racially Discriminatory Admission to Public Institutions of Higher Education, 9 Southwestern University Law Review 583 (1977).
87. Ibid.
88. Id. at 583–584.
89. DeFunis v. Odegaard, 507 P.2d 1169, 1199 (Wash. 1973) (dissent).
90. Loc. cit. supra note 86.
91. Quoted in Schwartz, Behind Bakke: Affirmative Action and the Supreme Court 13 (1988).
92. Id. at 13–14.
93. Id. at 14.
94. Graglia, supra note 86, at 586.
95. Keyes v. Denver School District, 413 U.S. 189 (1973).
96. Ibid.
97. Swann, 402 U.S. at 17–18.
98. Infra note 100.
99. Infra note 101.
100. Regents of the University of California v. Bakke, 438 U.S. 265 (1978).
101. 448 U.S. 448 (1980).
102. Quoted in Schwartz, op. cit. supra note 91, at 160.
103. Ibid.
104. Local 28, Sheet Metal Workers v. EEOC, 478 U.S. 421 (1986).

105. Lewis F. Powell–Chief Justice, March 6, 1986.
106. DeFunis v. Odegaard, 416 U.S. 312 (1974), discussed in Schwartz, op. cit. supra note 91, at 32.
107. Graglia, supra note 86, at 589.
108. 438 U.S. at 320.
109. Wygant v. Jackson Board of Education, 476 U.S. 267, 286 (1986).
110. Graglia, op. cit. supra note 1, at 31–32.
111. See Schwartz, op. cit. supra note 21, at 74.
112. Id. at 86.
113. Siegan, op. cit. supra note 10, at 101.
114. Supra p. 142.
115. Supra note 45.
116. Supra note 4.
117. Graglia, op. cit. supra note 1, at 67.
118. Compare Wilkinson, op. cit. supra note 16, at 100.
119. Griffin v. County School Board, 377 U.S. 218, 229 (1964).
120. Green, 391 U.S. at 442.
121. Swann, supra note 4.
122. Green, 391 U.S. at 439.
123. Swann, supra note 4.
124. Jones v. SEC, 298 U.S. 1, 33 (1936).

NOTES TO CHAPTER 6

1. Dissenting, in Lochner v. New York, 198 U.S. 45, 75 (1905).
2. Justice Harlan, joined by Justices White and Day, delivered a separate dissent.
3. Ferguson v. Skrupa, 372 U.S. 726, 729 (1963).
4. Id. at 731–732.
5. Id. at 732.
6. The famous remark of John L. O'Sullivan.
7. Lerner, The Mind and Faith of Justice Holmes 82 (1943).
8. Posner, The Jurisprudence of Skepticism, 86 Michigan Law Review 827, 852 (1988).
9. 10 The Works of Jeremy Bentham 142 (Bowring ed. 1962).
10. 3 Encyclopedia Brittanica 486 (1969 ed.).
11. 2 International Economic Papers 83 (1952) (translated from French, 1844).
12. Sassone and Schaffer, Cost-Benefit Analysis: A Handbook 3 (1978).
13. 33 U.S.C. §710a (1976).
14. American Textile Manufacturers Institute v. Donovan, 452 U.S. 490 (1981).
15. Weidenbaum, Business, Government and the Public 352 (2d ed. 1981).
16. Compare Kennedy, Cost-Benefit Analysis of Entitlement Problems: A Critique, 33 Stanford Law Review 387, 389 (1981).
17. 46 Fed. Reg. 13193 (1981).
18. Under section 1(b) of the Reagan order, "'Major rule' means any regulation that is likely to result in: (1) An annual effect on the economy of $100 million or more; (2)

A major increase in costs or prices for consumers, individual industries, Federal, State, or local government agencies, or geographic regions; or (3) Significant adverse effects on competition, employment, investment, productivity, innovation, or on the ability of United States-based enterprises to compete with foreign-based enterprises in domestic or export markets."

19. Supra note 12.
20. 15 U.S.C. §2056(a) (1976).
21. American Textile Manufacturers Institute v. Donovan, 452 U.S. 490, 511, n. 30 (1981).
22. American Petroleum Institute v. OSHA, 581 F.2d 493, 503 (5th Cir. 1978).
23. 15 U.S.C. §1912(b)(1).
24. Center for Auto Safety v. Peck, 751 F.2d 1336, 1339, 1351 (D.C. Cir. 1985).
25. Compare Viscusi, Regulatory Economics in the Courts: An Analysis of Judge Scalia's NHTSA Bumper Decision, 50 Law and Contemporary Problems 17 (1987).
26. 751 F.2d at 1351.
27. See Viscusi, supra note 25, at 27–28.
28. See 751 F.2d at 1344.
29. Id. at 1360.
30. Compare Viscusi, supra note 25.
31. 751 F.2d at 1342.
32. 42 U.S.C. §7409(b)(1).
33. 29 U.S.C. §651.
34. 452 U.S. 490 (1981).
35. Emphasis added.
36. 452 U.S. at 509.
37. Ibid.
38. Id. at 545, Rehnquist, J., dissenting.
39. Luke 14:28.
40. N.Y. Times, March 23, 1981, p. A16.
41. Executive Order 12,291, supra p. 166.
42. See Frohnmayer, Regulatory Reform: A Slogan in Search of Substance, 66 American Bar Association Journal 871, 873 (1980).
43. Infra p. 191.
44. See 49 U.S.C. §304.
45. See Schwartz, The Professor and the Commissions 115 et seq. (1959).
46. See Weidenbaum, op. cit. supra note 15, at 18–21.
47. See id. at 20.
48. Executive Order 12,291, section 3.
49. Supra note 34.
50. The evidence is analyzed in 43 Fed. Reg. at 27369 et seq.
51. Id. at 27370.
52. 452 U.S. at 542–543.
53. Chicago B. & Q. Ry. v. Babcock, 204 U.S. 585, 598 (1907).
54. Laski, The Limitations of the Expert, 162 Harper's 101 (1930).
55. 29 C.F.R. §§1910, 1043.
56. Compare National Law Journal, July 27, 1981, p. 29.
57. Posner, Rethinking the Fourth Amendment, 1981 Supreme Court Review 49;

Posner, Excessive Sanctions for Governmental Misconduct in Criminal Cases, 57 Washington Law Review 635 (1982).

58. Posner, Economic Analysis of Law 639–642 (3d ed. 1986).
59. Katz v. United States, 389 U.S. 347 (1967).
60. Posner, op. cit. supra note 58, at 639–640.
61. See id. at 148–150.
62. United States v. Carroll Towing Co., 159 F.2d 169, 173 (2d Cir. 1947).
63. United States Fidelity Co. v. Jadranska Slobodna Plovidba, 683 F.2d 1022, 1026 (7th Cir. 1982).
64. Posner, op. cit. supra note 58, at 640.
65. See Posner, Rethinking, supra note 57, at 71, 56, 74.
66. Posner, op. cit. supra note 58, at 641.
67. Ibid.
68. According to Posner, "This is not inconsistent with P having been very low at the time of the search. It may have been low because the police had no good reason to think the search would be productive—it was a shot in the dark—rather than because there were alternative methods, less invasive of privacy, of obtaining essential evidence." Ibid.
69. Ibid.
70. Posner, Excessive Sanctions, supra note 57, at 638.
71. Posner, Rethinking, supra note 57, at 74, citing Dunaway v. New York, 442 U.S. 200, 213 (1979).
72. 468 U.S. 897 (1984).
73. Id. at 906–907.
74. 468 U.S. 1032 (1984).
75. Though the Lopez-Mendoza opinion did not refer to Posner's articles on the subject.
76. The Brennan quotes are from a document headed, "I.N.S. v. LOPEZ-MENDOZA No. 83–491"—apparently the conference statement prepared by Brennan.
77. Frey argued the case for the Government.
78. 468 U.S. at 1046.
79. See Schwartz, Administrative Law §7.11 (2d ed. 1984).
80. 367 U.S. 643 (1961).
81. Supra note 72.
82. Supra note 10.
83. Supra note 9.
84. Compare Kennedy, supra note 16, at 388.
85. Brennan, J., dissenting in Leon, 468 U.S. at 929.
86. Tribe, Constitutional Choices viii (1985).
87. Ibid.
88. Posner, Excessive Sanctions, supra note 57, at 638.
89. Compare Morris, The Exclusionary Rule, Deterrence and Posner's Economic Analysis of Law, 57 Washington Law Review 647, 661 (1982).
90. N.Y. Times, August 31, 1988, p. A20.
91. Ibid.
92. Brennan, J., dissenting, in Leon, 468 U.S. at 929.

93. Compare Comment, A Federal Question: Does Priceless Mean Worthless? 14 St. Louis University Law Journal 268 (1969).

94. Posner, op. cit. supra note 58, at xix.

95. Supra note 17.

96. Supra notes 72, 74.

97. Hospital Corp. v. FTC, 807 F.2d 1381, 1392 (7th Cir. 1986).

98. Posner, Economic Analysis of Law xi (1973).

99. Id. at 1.

100. Posner, The Ethical and Political Basis of the Efficiency Norm in Common Law Adjudication, 8 Hofstra Law Review 487 (1980).

101. Posner, op. cit. supra note 58, at 9.

102. Leff, Economic Analysis of Law: Some Realism about Nominalism, 60 Virginia Law Review 451, 463 (1974).

103. Posner, op. cit. supra note 58, at 505.

104. Id. at 24–25.

105. 247 U.S. 251 (1918).

106. Supra note 1. Lochner is discussed more fully in Chapter 3.

107. Starting with NLRB v. Jones & Laughlin Steel Corp., 301 U.S. 1 (1937).

108. Epstein, The Proper Scope of the Commerce Power, 73 Virginia Law Review 1387, 1431 (1987).

109. Id. at 1429.

110. Id. at 1430.

111. Wilder, Farmer Boy (1933).

112. Epstein, supra note 108 at 1430–1431.

113. Id. at 1431.

114. 247 U.S. at 280.

115. Posner, op. cit. supra note 58, at 299, 311.

116. Id. at 589.

117. Id. at 590.

118. Id. at 590–592, supra p. 82.

119. Supra note 7.

120. Compare Ferguson v. Skrupa, 372 U.S. 726, 730 (1963).

121. Id. at 732.

122. 833 F.2d 1273 (9th Cir. 1986).

123. Supra p. 133.

124. 833 F.2d at 1280.

125. Id. at 1281.

126. Id. at 1281, n. 26.

127. 819 F.2d 732 (7th Cir. 1987).

128. Id. at 741.

129. Ibid.

130. Id. at 742.

131. Ibid.

132. Ibid.

133. Baldwin v. Missouri, 281 U.S. 586, 595 (1930).

134. Otis v. Parker, 187 U.S. 606, 609 (1903).

135. 1 Holmes-Pollock Letters 167 (2d ed. 1961).
136. Holmes, Collected Legal Papers 295 (1921).
137. Commonwealth v. Perry, 155 Mass. 117, 123 (1891).

NOTES TO CHAPTER 7

1. Compare Miller, Independent Agencies, 1986 Supreme Court Review 41.
2. Lewis, N.Y. Times, August 14, 1988, section 4, p. 23.
3. The Fettered Presidency: Legal Constraints on the Executive Branch 230 (Crovitz and Rabkin eds. 1989).
4. 1 de Tocqueville, Democracy in America, 72–73 (Bradley ed. 1945).
5. Adams, The Education of Henry Adams 294 (1931 ed.).
6. See Cushman, The Independent Regulatory Commissions 37 (1941).
7. Levy, The Law of the Commonwealth and Chief Justice Shaw 162 (1957).
8. 17 Congressional Record Appendix 457.
9. Id. at 444.
10. 94 U.S. 113 (1877).
11. Wabash, St. Louis & Pacific Railway Co. v. Illinois, 118 U.S. 57 (1886).
12. See Cushman, op. cit. supra note 6, at 38.
13. Landis, The Administrative Process 10 (1938).
14. Quoted in Cushman, op. cit. supra note 6, at 47.
15. Compare Landis, op. cit. supra note 13, at 186.
16. Chrysler Corp. v. Brown, 441 U.S. 281, 286, n. 4 (1979).
17. Miller, loc. cit. supra note 1.
18. 1 Schwartz, The Economic Regulation of Business and Industry 546 (1973). See also id. at 526–527.
19. See id. at 458.
20. Id. at 566.
21. Withrow v. Larkin, 421 U.S. 35 (1975).
22. Report of the President's Committee on Administrative Management 33 (1937).
23. Quoted in Cushman, op. cit. supra note 6, at 305.
24. Quoted in Schwartz, The Professor and the Commissions 46 (1959).
25. Humphrey's Executor v. United States, 295 U.S. 602, 629 (1935).
26. Ibid.
27. Wiener v. United States, 357 U.S. 349, 356 (1958).
28. 272 U.S. 52 (1926).
29. Id. at 117.
30. Id. at 164, 161.
31. Morrison v. Olson, 487 U.S. 654, 687–688 (1988).
32. Synar v. United States, 626 F. Supp. 1374, 1398 (D.C. 1986).
33. Ibid.
34. Ibid.
35. Washington Post, January 3, 1986, p. A17.
36. Hospital Corp. v. FTC, 807 F.2d 1381, 1392 (7th Cir. 1986).
37. Ibid.

38. James Miller, Director of the Office of Management and Budget, publicly supported the Meese position.
39. 131 Congressional Record S15178 (1985).
40. FTC v. American Nat'l Cellular, Inc., 810 F.2d 1511 (9th Cir. 1987).
41. Infra note 43.
42. FTC v. American Nat'l Cellular, 810 F.2d 1511, 1516–1517 (9th Cir. 1987).
43. 478 U.S. 714 (1986).
44. White, J., dissenting, id. at 760.
45. 54 U.S. Law Week 3710 (1986).
46. Supra notes 28, 25.
47. Synar v. United States, 626 F. Supp. 1374 (D.C. 1986). Though it is headed "per curiam," Justice Scalia undoubtedly wrote the opinion of the lower court in the case.
48. The Brennan quotes are from what is apparently a typed version of his conference statement, headed "*BOWSHER* v. *SYNAR* No. 85–1377,–1378,–1379."
49. N.Y. Times, March 8, 1986, p. 7.
50. See Schwartz, The Unpublished Opinions of the Burger Court Chapter 5 (1988).
51. For the Burger draft's text, see Schwartz, An Administrative Law "Might Have Been"—Chief Justice Burger's *Bowsher v. Synar* Draft, 42 Administrative Law Review 221, 223 (1990).
52. 295 U.S. at 630.
53. 478 U.S. at 725, n. 4.
54. Newsweek, July 23, 1979, p. 68.
55. Supra note 43.
56. 487 U.S. 654 (1988).
57. Supra note 25.
58. Supra note 28.
59. 487 U.S. at 686.
60. Id. at 706–707.
61. Id. at 689, 691.
62. Id. at 691, 692.
63. 272 U.S. at 164.
64. 487 U.S. at 691.
65. 46 Fed. Reg. 13193 (1981).
66. Supra notes 28, 25.
67. 295 U.S. at 629.
68. Wiener v. United States, 357 U.S. 349, 353 (1958).
69. Ibid.
70. See Schwartz, The Professor and the Commissions (1959).
71. The CAB went out of existence January 1, 1985. Its remaining regulatory functions were transferred to the Department of Transportation.
72. Chicago & Southern Airlines v. Waterman Steamship Corp., 333 U.S. 103, 109 (1948).
73. Ibid.
74. Now the Office of Management and Budget.
75. See Schwartz, op. cit. supra note 70, at 217.

76. 131 Congressional Record S15178 (1985).
77. Senator Proxmire, ibid.

NOTES TO CHAPTER 8

1. N.Y. Times, April 10, 1990, p. A19.
2. N.Y. Times Magazine, March 3, 1985, p. 83.
3. N.Y. Times, February 26, 1988, p. 8.
4. Lochner v. New York, 198 U.S. 45 (1905), supra
5. In Economic Liberties and the Judiciary 33–34 (Dorn and Manne eds. 1987).
6. Id. at 17.
7. The Economist, July 9, 1988, p. 21.
8. N.Y. Times, August 14, 1988, section 4, p. 23.
9. 485 U.S. 1 (1988), supra p. 132.
10. Posner, The Federal Courts: Crisis and Reform 319, 209 (1985).
11. Valley Forge Christian College v. Americans United, 454 U.S. 464, 471 (1982).
12. 485 U.S. at 19.
13. FCC v. Pottsville Broadcasting Co., 309 U.S. 134, 146 (1940).
14. Public Service Commission v. Wycoff Co., 344 U.S. 237, 243 (1952).
15. 485 U.S. at 22.
16. Adkins v. Children's Hospital, 261 U.S. 525, 557 (1923).
17. Ibid.
18. 626 F. Supp. 1374 (D.C. 1986).
19. 478 U.S. 714 (1986), supra p. 201.
20. 487 U.S. 654 (1988), supra p. 213.
21. 488 U.S. 361 (1989).
22. Supra p. 202.
23. 626 F. Supp. at 1395.
24. Humphrey's Executor v. United States, 295 U.S. 602 (1935), supra p.196.
25. 626 F. Supp. at 1398.
26. Supra p. 204.
27. Supra p. 205.
28. Supra p. 209.
29. See supra p. 212.
30. 487 U.S. 654 (1988).
31. 487 U.S. at 691, 706.
32. Id. at 708, 710.
33. Supra note 24.
34. 488 U.S. at ——.
35. 1 Schwartz, The Bill of Rights: A Documentary History 344 (197).
36. 2 id. at 1028.
37. Id. at 1150.
38. See his dissent in Morrison v. Olson, 487 U.S. at 697.
39. Mistretta v. United States, 488 U.S. at ——.
40. Dissenting, in Panama Refining Co. v. Ryan, 293 U.S. 388, 440 (1935).

41. Holmes, J., dissenting, in Springer v. Philippine Islands, 277 U.S. 189, 211 (1928).
42. 487 U.S. at 677.
43. Granfinanciera S.A. v. Nordberg, —— U.S. ——, —— (1989).
44. Id. at ——.
45. 285 U.S. 22 (1932).
46. Commodity Futures Trading Comm'n v. Schor, 478 U.S. 833, 856 (1986).
47. Quoted in Schwartz, Administrative Law: A Casebook 654 (3d ed. 1988).
48. See Culp, Judex Economicus, 50 Law and Contemporary Problems 95 (1987).
49. Kelman, On Democracy-Bashing: A Skeptical Look at the Theoretical and "Empirical" Practice of the Public Choice Movement, 74 Virginia Law Review 199 (1988).
50. Posner, Economic Analysis of Law (3d ed. 1986).
51. See supra p. 182.
52. Ibid. As seen there, Posner defines "efficiency" as "a technical term: it means exploiting economic resources in such a way that human satisfaction as measured by aggregate consumer willingness to pay for goods and services is maximized."
53. Posner, op. cit. supra note 10, at 198, 208.
54. Id. at 161.
55. Children's Habilitation Center v. NLRB, 887 F.2d 130 (7th Cir. 1989); NLRB v. Advertisers Mfg. Co., 823 F.2d 1086 (7th Cir. 1987); NLRB v. Acme Die Corp., 728 F.2d 959 (7th Cir. 1984); East Chicago Center v. NLRB, 710 F.2d 397 (7th Cir. 1983); NLRB v. RES-CARE, 705 F.2d 1461 (7th Cir. 1983); NLRB v. Coca-Cola Foods Div., 670 F.2d 84 (7th Cir. 1982).
56. NLRB v. Brooke Industries, 867 F.2d 834 (7th Cir. 1989); Nielsen Lithographing Co. v. NLRB, 854 F.2d 1063 (7th Cir. 1988); NLRB v. Certified Grocers, 806 F.2d 744 (7th Cir. 1986); International Union v. NLRB, 802 F.2d 969 (7th Cir. 1986); Continental Web Press v. NLRB, 742 F.2d 1087 (7th Cir. 1984); NLRB v. Village IX, 723 F.2d 1360 (7th Cir. 1983); NLRB v. American Medical Serv., Inc., 705 F.2d 1472 (7th Cir. 1983); Mosey Mfg. Co. v. NLRB, 701 F.2d 610 (7th Cir. 1983); NLRB v. Browning Ferris, 700 F.2d 385 (7th Cir. 1983); NLRB v. Loy Food Stores, 697 F.2d 698 (7th Cir. 1983); W.W. Grainger v. NLRB, 677 F.2d 557 (7th Cir. 1982). Most of the cases in this and the preceding note are taken from Shapiro, Richard Posner's Praxis, 48 Ohio State Law Journal 999, 1030–1032 (1987), an article which was of the greatest value to me in writing this section. For Judge Posner's reply to this article, see On Theory and Practice: Reply to "Richard Posner's Praxis," 49 Ohio State Law Journal 1077 (1989). Posner questions the inclusion of the Village IX case in this list on the ground that it involved a partial affirmance of the NLRB (id. at 1082). The portions of the Board order enforced, however, involved originally uncontested unfair labor practice findings, 723 F.2d at 1363. They were much less important than the findings reversed. This is particularly true of the finding that the employer's speech was a coercive threat, which presented what Posner termed the "most interesting and difficult question" in the case (id. at 1360).
57. Children's Habilitation Center v. NLRB, 887 F.2d 130, 132 (7th Cir. 1989).
58. Shapiro, supra note 56, at 1031–1032.

59. NLRB v. Certified Grocers, 806 F.2d 744, 749 (7th Cir. 1986).
60. Id. at 748.
61. Id. at 749.
62. Shapiro, supra note 56, at 1034.
63. 742 F.2d 1087 (7th Cir. 1984).
64. Id. at 1091, 1089, 1091.
65. Compare Shapiro, supra note 56, at 1034.
66. NLRB v. Village IX, 723 F.2d 1360, 1367 (7th Cir. 1983).
67. Id. at 1368, 1367.
68. That an administrative finding be found reasonable is all that is required for it to be upheld. Schwartz, Administrative Law § 10.8 (2d ed. 1984).
69. Shapiro, supra note 56, at 1035.
70. Posner, op. cit. supra note 10, at 299.
71. Ibid.
72. See Schwartz, The Law in America: A History 119–122 (1974).
73. Posner, op. cit. supra note 10, at 299.
74. Id. at 302.
75. Supra note 63.
76. Posner, op. cit. supra note 10, at 303–304.
77. 742 F.2d at 1090.
78. Posner, op. cit. supra note 10, at 305.
79. Compare Shapiro, supra note 56, at 1036.
80. See id. at 1040.
81. See Fox and Sullivan, Antitrust—Retrospective and Prospective: Where Are We Coming From? Where Are We Going? 62 New York University Law Review 936, 970 (1987).
82. Shapiro, supra note 56, at 1036, 1040. Plaintiffs, however, won partial victories in two more recent cases. State v. Panhandle Eastern Pipe Line, 852 F.2d 891 (7th Cir. 1988); Isaksen v. Vermont Castings, 825 F.2d 1158 (7th Cir. 1987).
83. Hospital Corp. v. FTC, 807 F.2d 1381 (7th Cir. 1980).
84. Compare Shapiro, supra note 56, at 1040.
85. See Schwartz, Administrative Law §15.12.
86. Reed v. Shorewood, 704 F.2d 943 (7th Cir. 1983).
87. Posner, op. cit. supra note 10, at 597. The rule was laid down in Board of Regents v. Roth, 408 U.S. 564 (1972).
88. Posner, op. cit. supra note 10, at 597.
89. Dauel v. Board of Trustees, 768 F.2d 128 (7th Cir. 1985). See, similarly, Parrett v. Connersville, 737 F.2d 690 (7th Cir. 1984). Compare Illinois Psychological Ass'n v. Falk, 818 F.2d 1337, 1344 (7th Cir. 1987).
90. See, e.g., Yatvin v. Madison School Dist., 840 F.2d 412 (7th Cir. 1988); Colaizzi v. Walker, 812 F.2d 304 (7th Cir. 1987); Brown v. Brienen, 722 F.2d 360 (7th Cir. 1983); Grimes v. Eastern Illinois University, 710 F.2d 386 (7th Cir. 1983); Lyznicki v. Board of Education, 707 F.2d 949 (7th Cir. 1983).
91. Brown v. Brienen, 722 F.2d 360, 365 (7th Cir. 1983).
92. Board of Regents v. Roth, 408 U.S. 564, 573 (1972).
93. Colaizzi v. Walker, 812 F.2d 304, 307 (7th Cir. 1987).
94. Ibid.

95. Ibid.

96. Colaizzi v. Walker, 812 F.2d 304 (7th Cir. 1987).

97. Board of Regents v. Roth, 408 U.S. 564 (1972).

98. Owen v. Independence, 445 U.S. 622 (1980).

99. Brunswick Corp. v. Riegel Textile, 752 F.2d 261 (7th Cir. 1984).

100. Jack Walters Corp. v. Morton Building, 737 F.2d 698 (7th Cir. 1984). See Shapiro, supra note 56, at 1039.

101. Jack Walters Corp. v. Morton Building, 737 F.2d 698, 713 (7th Cir. 1984). See also Isaksen v. Vermont Castings, 825 F.2d 1158, 1161–1162 (7th Cir. 1987), where Judge Posner went out of his way to indicate disagreement with "the Supreme Court . . . rule, now more than 75 years old, that makes resale price maintenance illegal per se"—indicating that, but for it, he would have ruled completely for defendant in this "rather sorry excuse for an anti-trust case."

102. Supra p. 187.

103. Illinois Psychological Ass'n v. Falk, 818 F.2d 1337, 1341 (7th Cir. 1987).

104. Ibid, citing Siegan, Economic Liberties and the Constitution (1980), discussed in Chapter 3.

105. Jack Walters Corp. v. Morton Building, 737 F.2d 698, 714 (7th Cir. 1984).

106. In op. cit. supra note 5, at xiii.

107. Id. at xviii.

108. In The Great Debate: Interpreting Our Written Constitution 20 (1986).

109. In op. cit. supra note 5, at xiii.

110. Id. at xvi, xvii–xviii.

111. 833 F.2d 1270 (9th Cir. 1986), supra pp. 133, 185.

112. Id. at 1281, n.26.

113. Supra p. 187.

114. Supra p. 239.

115. Supra p. 74.

116. Supra p. 225.

117. 857 F.2d 1245 (9th Cir. 1988).

118. Winberry v. Salisbury, 74 A.2d 406, 411 (N.J. 1950).

119. Id. at 412.

120. Ibid.

121. Hayburn's Case, 2 Dall. 411, 413–414 (U.S. 1792).

122. Winberry v. Salisbury, 74 A.2d 406, 413 (N.J. 1950).

123. 857 F.2d at 1252.

124. Sibbach v. Wilson & Co., 312 U.S. 1 (1941).

125. Under Union Pacific Railway v. Botsford, 141 U.S. 250 (1891).

126. Sibbach v. Wilson & Co., 312 U.S. 1, 17 (1941).

127. Id. at 14.

128. 488 U.S. 361 (1989).

129. Id. at ——.

130. Winberry v. Salisbury, 74 A.2d 406, 413 (N.J. 1950).

131. 857 F.2d at 1257.

132. 2A Singer, Statutes and Statutory Construction §48.01 (4th ed. 1984).

133. 777 F.2d 1 (D.C. Cir. 1985).

134. Id. at 7–8.

135. Quoted in Farber and Frickey, Legislative Intent and Public Choice, 74 Virginia Law Review 423, 442 (1988).
136. N.Y. Times, April 14, 1989, p. B5.
137. Wallace v. Christensen, 802 F.2d 1539, 1559 (9th Cir. 1986).
138. Id. at 1559–1560.
139. Id. at 1560.
140. Adamson v. California, 332 U.S. 46, 64 (1947).
141. Quoted in Curtis, It's Your Law 52 (1954).
142. Schwegmann Bros. v. Calvert Corp., 341 U.S. 384, 396 (1951).
143. United States v. Public Utilities Commission, 345 U.S. 295, 319 (1953).
144. Loc. cit. supra note 141.
145. Loc. cit. supra note 142.
146. Quoted in Farber and Frickey, supra note 135, at 443.
147. Blanchard v. Bergeron, 489 U.S. 87, —— (1989).
148. Ibid.
149. Id. at 454.
150. INS v. Cardoza-Fonseca, 480 U.S. 421, 452–453 (1987).
151. See Farber and Frickey, supra note 135, at 455.
152. Wallace v. Christensen, 802 F.2d 1539, 1560 (9th Cir. 1986).
153. Justice Scalia, quoted in Farber and Frickey, supra note 135, at 454.
154. 480 U.S. 421 (1987).
155. Chevron v. Natural Resources Defense Council, 467 U.S. 837 (1984).
156. Id. at 843–844.
157. 480 U.S. at 454.
158. Id. at 454–455.
159. Id. at 453.
160. Supra p. 247.

NOTES TO CHAPTER 9

1. Hurst, Justice Holmes on Legal History vii (1964).
2. Bowen, Yankee from Olympus: Justice Holmes and His Family 285 (1944).
3. Lerner, The Mind and Faith of Justice Holmes 46 (1954).
4. Kaplan, Encounters with O. W. Holmes, Jr., 96 Harvard Law Review 1828, 1829 (1983).
5. See Bowen, op. cit. supra note 2, at 285.
6. Ibid.
7. Holmes, The Path of the Law, in Collected Legal Papers 167, 180 (1921).
8. Holmes, The Common Law 1 (1881).
9. Ibid.
10. Id. at 1, 35–36.
11. Holmes, Collected Legal Papers 184.
12. Carter, Law: Its Origin, Growth and Function 221, 213 (1907).
13. 2 Holmes-Pollock Letters 13 (2d ed. 1961).
14. Ives v. South Buffalo Ry. Co., 201 N.Y. 271, 294 (1911).
15. Compare Cardozo, The Growth of the Law 72 (1924).

16. Compare ibid.
17. Compare Corwin, Constitutional Revolution, Ltd. 90 (1941).
18. Holmes, Collected Legal Papers 187.
19. Lerner, op. cit. supra note 3, at 50.
20. Holmes, Collected Legal Papers 181–182.
21. Frankfurter, Mr. Justice Holmes and the Supreme Court 9 (1938).
22. Holmes, The Common Law 1, 35.
23. Id. at 1.
24. Quoted, Harper's 8 (September 1988).
25. Schwartz, Some Makers of American Law 9 (1985).
26. Compare Hand, Mr. Justice Cardozo, 52 Harvard Law Review 361 (1939).
27. Brennan, 1988 Annual Survey of American Law xi (1989).
28. See Corwin, Constitutional Revolution, Ltd. (1941).
29. Epstein, Takings: Private Property and the Power of Eminent Domain 324 (1985).
30. Id. at 329.
31. Ibid.
32. Posner, The Constitution as an Economic Document, 56 George Washington Law Review 4, 20 (1987).
33. Ibid.
34. Ibid, n. 25.
35. Ibid.
36. Supra pp. 132, 133, 185.
37. Supra p. 186.
38. Chicago Board of Realtors v. Chicago, 819 F.2d 732 (7th Cir. 1987).
39. Id. at 743.
40. Home Building & Loan Ass'n v. Blaisdell, 290 U.S. 398 (1934).
41. 819 F.2d at 743.
42. Id. at 742–744.
43. Id. at 745.
44. Ibid.
45. Ibid.
46. Supra pp. 133, 185.
47. N.Y. Times Magazine, March 3, 1985, p. 35.
48. Ibid.
49. N.Y. Times, March 8, 1986, p. 7.
50. Loc. cit. supra note 47.
51. Regents of the University of California v. Bakke, 438 U.S. 265 (1978).
52. See Schwartz, Behind Bakke: Affirmative Action and the Supreme Court 71 (1988).
53. 410 U.S. 113 (1973).
54. N.Y. Times, March 8, 1986, p. 7.
55. Clayton, The Making of Justice: The Supreme Court in Action 217 (1964).
56. Supra p. 177.
57. Supra p. 254.
58. See Schwartz, Super Chief: Earl Warren and His Supreme Court—A Judicial Biography 59 (1983).
59. Quoted in Rehnquist, The Supreme Court: How It Was, How It Is 146 (1987).
60. Douglas, The Court Years 1939–1975, 173 (1980).

61. Posner, The Federal Courts: Crisis and Reform 106 (1985).
62. Harvard Law School Bulletin, Winter 1986, p. 28.
63. Rehnquist, op. cit. supra note 59, at 298.
64. Loc. cit. supra note 62.
65. Usually after a year with a lower court judge.
66. U.S. News & World Report, December 13, 1957, p. 74.
67. Collins and Skover, The Future of Liberal Legal Scholarship, 87 Michigan Law Review 189, 238 (1988).
68. Nomination of Justice William Hubbs Rehnquist, Hearings before Senate Judiciary Committee, 99th Cong., 2d Sess. 354 (1986).
69. 54 Texas Law Review 693 (1976).
70. Compare Bork, The Tempting of America 167 (1989).
71. Loc. cit. supra note 69.
72. Dissenting in Federal Housing Administration v. Darlington, Inc., 358 U.S. 84, 92 (1958).
73. Hughes, Addresses of Charles Evans Hughes 185 (2d ed. 1916).
74. Bork, op. cit. supra note 70, at 223.

INDEX OF CASES

INDEX OF CASES

INDEX